Another Bone-Swapping Event

ALSO BY BRAD FOX

Fiction

To Remain Nameless

Nonfiction

The Bathysphere Book: Effects of the Luminous Ocean Depths

Another Bone-Swapping Event

Brad Fox

Astra House
New York

For information about permission to reproduce selections from this book, please
contact permissions@astrahouse.com.

Lines from Chloe Garcia Roberts, ed., *Li Shangyin* and Alejo Carpentier,
The Lost Steps (Adrian Nathan West, tr.) used with permission.

Astra House
A Division of Astra Publishing House
astrahouse.com
Printed in the United States of America

Library of Congress Cataloging-in-Publication Data TK

ISBN: 978-1-6626-0316-7

First edition
10 9 8 7 6 5 4 3 2 1

Design by Alissa Theodor
The text is set in Bulmer MT Std Regular .
The titles are set in Bulmer MT Std Semibold .

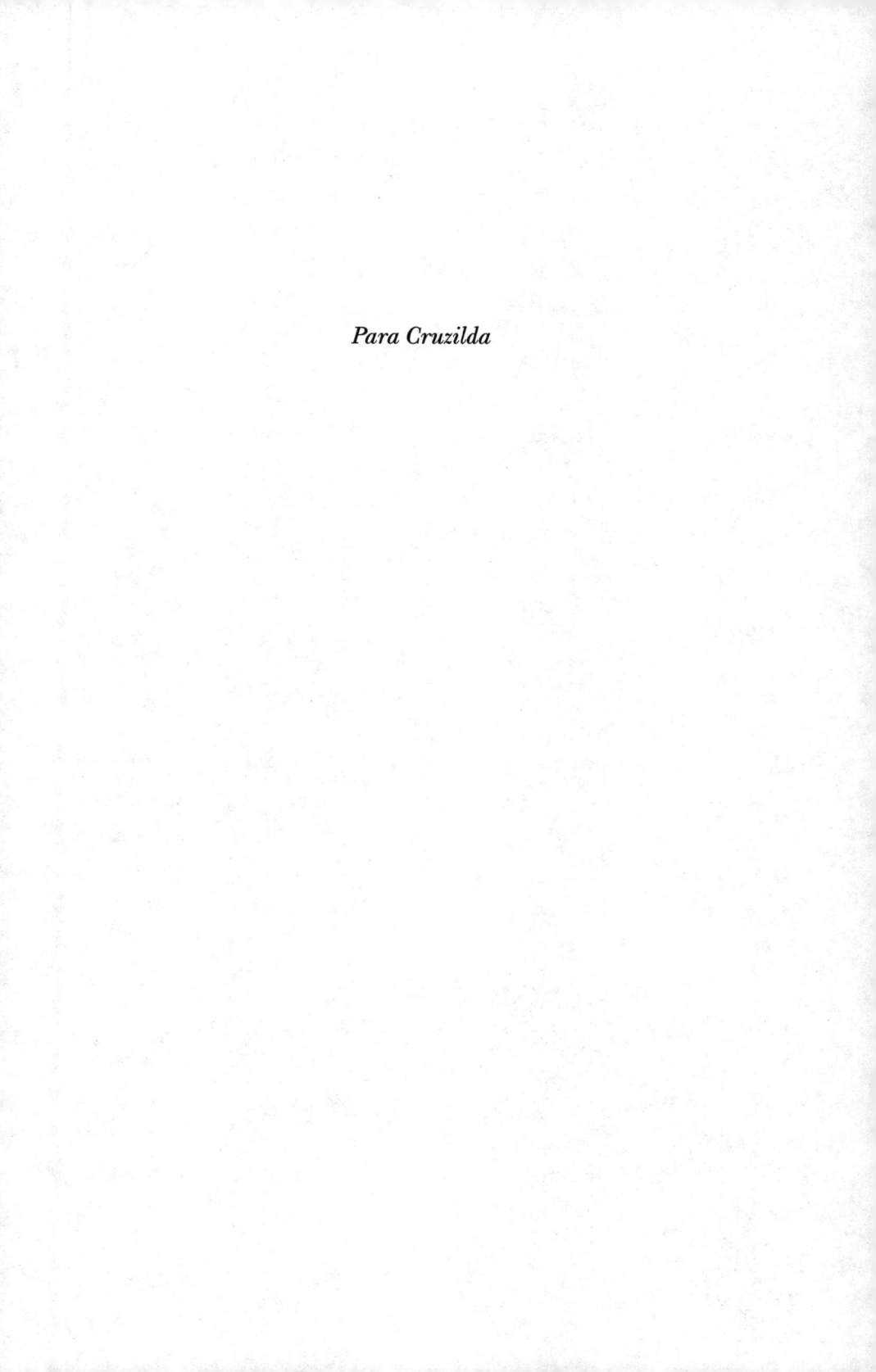

Para Cruzilda

Contents

Another Bone-Swapping Event

PLIGHT

I resolved to stand up from the stone where I sat looking off into the jungle. I put a hand on each knee and pressed, facing down as I straightened my legs. Halfway up I stopped myself. The forest floor had opened up beneath me and I was looking right through it. The dirt and soil and roots and insects were dense and pungent as ever, but also suddenly transparent. A veil fell away and solid ground showed itself weightless and conjectural, a membrane or lens. Beyond it or through it I could see shadows, movements, characters and landscapes, histories and possibilities.

I didn't seize up in surprise or fright. Rather, sensing this to be a revelatory moment, I remained where I was, tipped forward, peering through the forest floor into the flickerings and fragments. I felt my weight, my unsteady balance, soreness in my joints. It required composure and calm to maintain focus. But if I stayed still I could observe dimensions within dimensions, the finest details.

I saw an inverted image of the place where I stood, a replica of our collective plight: stuck in the high jungles of eastern Peru, four hours' walk from the nearest road, from the small city of Tarapoto with its markets and mototaxis. Trapped by curfew and closed borders, airliners grounded, an indeterminate state of emergency.

I gazed through transparent earth and saw the bustling planet at a standstill. Friends and family sheltering in place in Harlem and Brooklyn and Kansas City. The plazas of Mexico City deserted. I saw Belgrade and Istanbul without crowds or car horns, submerged in an uncanny quiet. There was no one on the Nile. Fish leapt above untroubled oceans while hospitals echoed with coughing and wheezing. Nearer to me I saw individuals along a forest path: kids hiding after an illegal crossing, then a loping gentleman with his pot-bellied sidekick, a wayfarer lost in the dark. They were close enough I could almost call to them, perhaps have a conversation.

I gave myself over, silently watching, until through the cityscapes and seascapes and details of life I sensed shades and shadows of something else, whatever lay beyond all that. Perhaps the land of the dead, or a zone of pure phantasms and confused delusions. But also—who knows—troubled destinies, trickery, forces that might cross over to affect us, that in our ignorance we'd attribute to ourselves, to luck or fate. If I looked long enough, I thought, I might discern or understand something, catch a glimpse of a hidden key.

Then through the pulse of frogs and insects I heard the crackle of dry leaves under a shoe. I turned and there was Miguel, his white shirt, sunglasses glinting beneath the brim of his cap.

¡Brak! he called. ¿Cómo estás?

He tipped his head back as he often did, peering out below his dark lenses. There was a hint of a smile on his face.

I rose to say hello, and we talked for a while about the day and the jungle. He asked if I'd heard any animals pass by. Then he went on with his rounds and I was alone again. I didn't go back over to where I'd been looking down at the forest floor to check if the reflected world was still there. I'd seen it once, and that was enough. When I stilled myself now it was all around me.

WE'RE ALL DEAD

News of a flu-like virus reached me in Mexico City in January. In February, back in New York, I ran into an old friend, an emergency room doctor, and as we walked through the East Village he told me he was waiting for a civilization-altering pandemic to back up patients at the door of his emergency room.

We'd been through SARS, swine flu; this seemed worse, maybe, but *civilization-altering?* One could only hope.

It was a week before we were scheduled to fly to Peru.

I was meant to stop in Dallas for a book fair, but someone from an infected cruise ship left quarantine, headed straight to the mall, then tested positive. Now the virus might be all over town and everyone pulled out of the fair. I pushed back my departure but still had to fly through Dallas, which meant Eszter and I would travel down separately. She asked if I planned to bring a laptop. What if our return flights are delayed? But I thought no, it's fine. I wouldn't mind not seeing my computer for a week or two.

I checked in behind a pair of Italians asking how long the Milan airport was supposed to stay closed. But I flew off just fine, made my connection, and woke up to the endless Pacific and the cliffs of Lima as I landed the next morning. Eszter flew straight from New York and landed a couple hours later. She'd been on the same plane as Nafis, who gave me a big hug when she introduced us. We flew over the Andes to Tarapoto, where Akos and Szilvia were already waiting for us. The sweltering, selvatic air enveloped us right off the plane.

Eszter with her big eyes and delightfully tangled hair, always a hint of humor around her mouth. When I met her she'd been working as a dancer and choreographer, and though she'd studied neuroscience and become a therapist, she still had that strength and balance. We'd been living together for fifteen years, and before we moved from Istanbul to New York in 2011, in the presence of a Turkish judge dressed in what looked like a boxing robe, we'd exchanged rings.

By 2019 she'd had several miscarriages. We went through years of miscarriages. Chinese herbs, dietary restrictions, a specialist on the Upper East Side who sent us home with a bag of loaded syringes. A world of advice and admonishments and contradictory clinicians. Nothing worked. It threw me into fits of depression, but Eszter's response was to get trained as a birth doula and start assisting women in labor.

Go right toward it, she thought, through the burning door.

We went to a clinic in Prague for IVF treatments, but no luck. We went back the next year to try once again, and when that didn't work Eszter decided no more needles and transfers and fertility clinics. After ten years of struggle she resolved to stop.

We loved each other, and there was no one I trusted more, but it was tearing us apart. The finality of her decision was disorienting to me, vertigo-inducing, but after so much time its finality brought a kind of relief.

But birth and motherhood were key to Eszter's sense of her own magic. To let all that go required a reimagining of who she was. In the recent years of loss and frustration both of us had gone to ayahuasca ceremonies downtown. The sudden popularization of psychedelics made me uncomfortable, but I'd been willing to try anything, and the medicine helped me, helped both of us, to jump out of our circuits.

After the last IVF transfer, when the pregnancy test came up negative, Eszter's mind went to a wayward Hasid serving medicine in Bushwick who'd invited her to visit his teacher in Peru.

I need to have my mind boggled, she said.

She came down and spent ten days with Miguel, drinking ayahuasca and dieting on a plant called bobinsana. When she got back she was ecstatic.

Whatever happens, she said, you need to experience this.

I'd first heard of ayahuasca twenty years before from someone who'd successfully slowed cancer with it. Though recently I'd heard of camps for foreigners, tech workers finding spirit animals. I was resistant to, even derisive about *shamanic tourism*. But I sensed the desolation lift from Eszter, and in subsequent months her enthusiasm didn't wane. She arranged this ten-day trip with Nafis, Akos, and Szilvia and suggested I join them.

I took stock of myself:

I'd spent my twenties as an itinerant journalist and NGO worker in the Balkans, and my adult life unrolled between contracts, grants, editing jobs, and books I was trying to write, always studying languages, struggling to understand and be understood, never being good enough to rest. I'd wandered to Berlin, Cairo, Mexico City, Istanbul, thinking I'd find a home. Instead I received a crash course in the ground-level effects of foreign policy, in neocolonialism and necrophilia. Now back in New York in my mid-forties, on the tail end of a graduate school fellowship as I finished my PhD, I was a mess of anxiety and insomnia and addictive tendencies. I had a book scheduled to come out in May and that meant the world to me, but I felt in terminal disarray.

Shamanic tourism be damned, I thought. Maybe I'd pull myself together. Maybe Eszter and I would see a way forward, whatever that might be.

A driver met us at the airport and we rolled through the small town in the back of a van. The reds and blues and oranges of the one-story buildings, the tight grid of streets thrumming with mototaxis, I'd never been to Peru before but I felt its kinship to Mexico, other places I'd been in Latin America. The van dropped us off in front of a hotel in the center of town, an overgrown patio surrounded by hammocks and bedrooms.

Szilvia and Akos were already checked in. They'd arrived early to catch their breath before we started. I'd met Szilvia once before but not her husband. Szilvia had been Eszter's client, and there was something odd about meeting in these circumstances.

Eszter had earned her license as a mental health practitioner two years before. She'd worked under supervision in a Queens clinic for a while, but now she had her own practice. Among her first private clients was Szilvia, a molecular biologist from northern Serbia. Eszter was from Budapest, and though Szilvia grew up across the border she was ethnically Hungarian. She'd lived in New York for years, working at a lab on the Upper East Side; she spoke perfect English, but she was happy to find a therapist she could talk to in her mother tongue, that complex agglutinating language no one else understood.

During a session Szilvia brought up a desire to come to Peru, and Eszter was surprised at the coincidence—she hadn't mentioned her recent experience. As a therapist she was conflicted. It might be improper to talk about, she thought, but she wanted to make sure Szilvia didn't end up with someone unreliable. So she told Szilvia about Miguel, and they began to discuss it. They came to a conclusion neither had expected:

they'd end their therapist-client relationship and travel to Peru together. Perhaps they'd discover new therapeutic possibilities.

We gathered for the first time in the hotel lobby with its rubber trees and ochre walls. Szilvia had clear pale skin and brown hair pulled straight back, a mole above her mouth. Her husband, Akos, was from Budapest— tall, tousled, with chiseled features and a calm but intense gaze. They'd recently married in a small civil ceremony and were scheduled to celebrate in Hungary in August. Szilvia wanted to make this trip together before they had kids, and Akos wanted that, too, but he had his own reasons. Having grown up in transition-era Hungary, now in his early thirties, he was among New York's top creative directors, currently freelancing at an ad agency on Canal St. But he'd never reconciled himself to advertising. It was meant to be a step toward something else, filmmaking perhaps, where he could use his creativity for more than money. Right now he was up for a new job, he was at a turning point. It would be good to step away for a bit.

Eszter introduced them to Nafis, who'd been here last time she came. A New York City firefighter, this was the third time he'd come to see Miguel. After his last visit he'd suffered a burn on the job. Recuperating in his basement apartment in Canarsie he got it in mind to change his life. He'd come again and start to learn to administer plant medicine. Perhaps he could be an access point for the Black community, a coach, serve in some way.

We sat in low chairs in the lobby and before long Miguel appeared in his baseball cap and jeans, buttoned up shirt, glint of a gold tooth, eyes behind dark glasses. Eszter had explained that he had an infection in his right eye. It was nearly swollen shut. So he always wore dark glasses to cover it. The light bothered him.

Miguel in his dark glasses and cap was sturdy-looking, around fifty, direct but a little remote. He was accompanied by his nephew Luis, a handsome twenty-two-year-old a head taller than his uncle, who was training to continue the family tradition.

Miguel said they'd come pick us up at eight the next morning.

And Abuelita? Eszter asked.

Already up the mountain, Miguel assured.

After they left, we walked through the crowded city to a little botanica where we bought wads of coca leaves, bottles of Agua de Florida, bricks of rough jungle cigarettes called mapachos.

The next morning before turning off my phone I checked the news for the last time. The stock market was crashing. The Mexican peso was collapsing. A standoff between the Saudis and Russians had sunk the price of oil. Milan was quarantined. All of Italy might follow. There were cases among Orthodox Jews just north of the Bronx.

We jumped in mototaxis and drove out of town, up and down muddy roads to the foot of a mountain. We marched into the forest and the online world began to fade. We were among rocks and rivulets, clambering through rapids. We scrambled over boulders and tree roots and up steep inclines, past vast high cliffs, bulging insect nests, crowded lanes of marching ants.

I walked behind Nafis. In his early forties, bearded and bald, he hopped across the wet stones with strength and agility.

As we made our way through the thickening vines and clouds of bugs, Nafis began telling me about serving in Kuwait as a US Marine. He was the only Muslim among the Marines, so the Kuwaitis adopted him and fed him, gave him platters of lamb and syrupy sweets.

I was the only Marine who gained weight, he said.

We'd been climbing an hour and now we got to a hilltop shelter where Nelson and Humberto—porters Miguel hired to take our stuff up the mountain—had dropped their loads to rest. They carried our bags along with pots and pans, beans and rice, big cabbage heads and bunches of carrots, all of it stuffed in plastic sacks yanked tight with cotton straps they wore around their foreheads. They carried these loads, as big as men, supported by their neck and core muscles, while we walked with nothing but our water bottles. But now they'd dropped their burdens and collapsed on a large stone.

Nafis stood looking at Humberto, his smooth cheeks.

You've got the face of a baby, he said in English.

Humberto looked at me to translate.

Dice que tienes cara de niño, I said.

Babyface, Nafis repeated with a grin.

Nelson elbowed Humberto and everyone laughed. Miguel said something and they laughed again, but he said it in Quechua and I couldn't understand. I'd never heard Quechua before and it was hard for me to even register its sound.

We passed around water bottles. Nafis and Eszter pulled out their bags of coca leaves and we all stuffed coca into our mouths with a dash of baking soda. The soda activated the bitter leaves, which I'd chewed a couple of times. The effect was mild but noticeable. The leaves gave us energy and lifted our spirits as we walked.

Nelson and Humberto placed the cotton straps back across their foreheads and got to their feet, bulging packs behind them.

We walked up the steep winding trail past termite mounds and swarms of ants. A wall of rock and mud oozed sparkling fresh water. We clutched knobs of wood on twisting trunks, all colors of moss. I felt the blanket of humidity as Nafis went on with his story.

There'd been one other Muslim Marine before me, he said, but that Marine went AWOL to visit Mecca. The other guys thought I was going to go AWOL, too. Then while I was deployed my father made the hajj. He was right there across the desert. I knew how much it meant to him and I thought about taking a Hummer and driving to Mecca to meet him. It's what the others expected of me anyway.

Some of the Marines questioned his loyalty, he told me. They suspected he might not be looking forward to crossing into Iraq and gunning down other Muslims.

I'm happy I never had to face that, Nafis said. I was lucky to be a technician, repairing gear, far from combat.

We came to another river crossing and Nelson dropped his burden to help people through the rapids. Large and sturdy and strong jawed, he stood directly in the current and steadied us while we stepped gingerly from one boulder to the next.

Now the path grew steeper, and we no longer talked as we zigzagged uphill. It was hard work just to make progress, and the slope was slippery enough that a false move could be dangerous.

At one of the switchbacks the foliage opened and I could see out over the mountains, treetops descending quickly into the ravine. I was drenched in sweat and could feel my mind quiet. The buoyancy of the coca tapered off and now it was one step after another.

Four hours and fourteen crossings, we rounded a final switchback and were spit out from under the canopy into a clearing. A butter-green hillside of clover cut through with a winding path of heavy stones. A structure of weathered boards with a corrugated iron roof, a few benches in front. All of it encircled by verdant, mist-covered peaks. Black and yellow birds swooped and cawed above us. We'd arrived.

When the Spanish entered this part of Peru in the seventeenth century, the big regional city was Lamas, built on a hilltop in the Andean foothills, the way down to the Amazon basin. The Spanish seized the town's upper areas, and everyone else was pushed down to a neighborhood called Wayku. Earthen houses with no windows, eventually wood and metal structures. A field for sport and festivals in the center. Close enough to walk up and trade with the Spanish but distinct, separate. Most of the families had a chacra, a place outside the city where they cultivated plantains and beans and hunted tapir and peccary. Miguel grew up in the center of Wayku. His grandfather's chacra was an hour away, and often his grandfather spent more time in the chacra than in town. He was known for his ability to cure people of disease and infestations of witchcraft, and often neighbors were waiting around for their time to see him. Miguel as a child remembers one visitor after another lined up for their turn with Grandfather Pedro.

Miguel's grandfather worked mostly as a tobaquero. He'd stuff a pipe or light a mapacho and submerge his visitors in smoke. He'd blow smoke on the crown of their heads, their palms and chest. He'd sing to them, and through the smoke and song he would cure them, disperse whatever miasma had encircled them. They came one after the other. Sometimes all day long. He also gave them macerations and infusions of different plants, but it was more smoke than anything else.

Abuelo Pedro's sons learned from him and from other men in the family. His son Antonio learned to suck out disease and foreign forces in the body and to serve the visionary mix of ayahuasca vine and chacruna leaf. Antonio's brother, also named Pedro, learned to work with tobacco like their father, but was interested in the whole range of plants. There were plants for strength—you couldn't win contests at the winter festival in Lamas without them—and there were plants for infection, for laziness. But it was not enough to determine which plant was which. You had to show people how to take them, cultivate a relationship with them. And that you did through restraint and song.

The second Pedro—Miguel's father—was not content to sit at the family chacra. This was the nineteen seventies. He strayed from Lamas looking for a wild place to hunt and accept visitors, a place to withdraw further from Wayku. Tarapoto was a much smaller town then, and Papá Pedro got to know a guy who lived in the valley of a swift river at the edge of town. He used to stay there when he was exploring, spending a few nights with his friend before roaming through the jungle. Walking farther and farther up, he eventually made it to the clearing atop the mountain where we were. It was known as Juliampampa after someone named Julián who'd long disappeared, who used to have his fields up there. There was a spring that provided fresh water, clean enough to cup with a leaf and drink without boiling. A perch where you felt lifted up, far from anyone else, a foothold in the world of mountains, animals, raw jungle.

Pedro brought his father up there and he took it in. It was a good spot. Miguel was a child but before long his father and grandfather brought him, too. A night in the valley outside Tarapoto then up, up, crossing the river fourteen times, zigzagging up the last steep stretch.

Over the years they cleared a few trees and built a shelter. Then cleared more trees and built a larger shelter. Papá Pedro and Abuelo Pedro, Miguel's older brother Pedro, eventually the whole Tapullima family, little by little, came to spend days up here hunting ocelot and jaguar, all kinds of monkeys and little hopping mammals called añujes. They cleared a couple of places to plant beans, potatoes, plantains, and medicinal plants.

When someone from the community was ill they might come up, too, to ask Miguel's father or grandfather for help. They put up a simple structure twenty minutes' walk from the main shelter. It was canvas on metal frames, not more than a tent isolated in the jungle. If you wanted to explore or cure something deeper, you needed to spend time out there, alone, days and even weeks at a time.

In the early 2000s the Peruvian government expanded the national park system, and the Cordillera Escalera—the mountain range surrounding Juliampampa—was included in the expansion, deemed an ecological reserve. Because the Tapullimas already had their chacra up there, their right to continue to use the land was written into the deed of the reserve. They can't develop it commercially, but they can use it, bring people, raise enough crops for the family. So four hours walk from town, up and down muddy slopes, you come to this clearing at the top of the mountain. You emerge from the mud and vines, the humid darkness beneath the canopy, into open sky and rushing wind, medicinal trees exploding into bloom. Clean water gushing from the spring. Macaws and monkeys calling in the distance. Hummingbirds everywhere.

I sat on the bench with Miguel surveying the area. He handed me a mapacho and we smoked in silence. Mountains off to the distance. Far below we could even see the city we'd left behind.

If it were closer to Tarapoto you'd have to deal with crooks and scroungers, Miguel said. Here it's good.

We smoked our mapachos and looked out at the mountains and the valley.

The main shelter had a couple of rooms where the family slept but was called the comedor because that's where everyone ate. There was a long table and place to hang hammocks in the open space. Shelves and some storage to one side, a simple kitchen to the other.

Humberto grabbed my bag and led me down a path. After five or ten minutes we came to a little hut beyond the main clearing where the jungle density began to encroach. A simple structure of wood and screen with an iron roof and an outhouse behind it. Inside I found a mosquito net over an old mattress on a wood-slat frame, a desk and a chair. There was a hammock strung in front.

When I strolled back to the comedor I found Eszter embracing an older woman, wiry with dark hair down to the small of her back.

Abuelita, Eszter said.

She turned her exquisitely lined face to meet me, her lively eyes, rapidly changing expression, constantly in a laugh. She grabbed my shoulders and I felt her sinewy strength.

I'd heard about Abuelita from Eszter. She was Shipiba from Pucallpa, several hours drive to the south, not Quechua-speaking like the Tapull-imas. She was a curandera skilled in natural medicine, but she worked differently than Miguel did. They were a complementary pair. And with her banter and her grin she was irresistible. I knew she'd taken care of Eszter during a difficult moment last year. You could see in Abuelita's smile and embrace that she loved Eszter.

Behind Abuelita, leaning over a wooden counter, was a young woman, perhaps a teenager, with sunny dimples and her hair in a braid, dressed in a soccer jersey and shorts: Luis's sister Karen. She was going to cook for us—simple meals of beans and rice and raw vegetables. The next day we'd go off even salt, but now we had a big meal to recharge after the climb. The rich scent of roast chicken billowed off the grill. Nafis was vegetarian and sliced an avocado over his rice, but the rest of us had soon sucked meat off the bones.

An hour later, while we were relaxing at the height of the afternoon, there was movement up the path. A wiry Peruvian guy followed by a larger blonde woman. They collapsed in the comedor. The Peruvian knew Miguel and they went off to talk, leaving the white woman at the long table with us.

She was Austrian, she told me, from Graz. She'd met *him* in Mexico.

She motioned with her head, indicating that *him* meant the wiry Peruvian who'd brought her, who'd gone off to talk to Miguel.

They soon reappeared. Miguel said something to Nelson, who disappeared down the stone steps. Miguel approached the Austrian woman and we listened, trying to figure out what was going on.

The wiry Peruvian was named Andrés, but Miguel called him Mashti. He was an old friend of the family, back after several months away. He and the Austrian were planning to stay two or three days.

She said her name was Herta. She'd been carrying her own bag and made it halfway up the mountain before she ran out of strength. Nelson had gone down to get her stuff.

I who hadn't carried my own stuff still found it in myself to look down on her.

Miguel and Mashti went off together. Eszter went with Abuelita somewhere, and Nafis, Akos, Szilvia, and I went to our huts, all scattered in different directions.

I lay in my hammock and smoked another mapacho, the thick black tobacco filling my throat and lungs. The pulse of the bugs receded as I thought of the fog of confusion I'd been living in, in New York, in Mexico City, struggling with writing, studying, teaching, struggling in my relationships, teetering at the edge of alcoholism. I wondered whether it had been the right decision to come here. Part of me found everything, including myself, ridiculous. Foreigners buying plane tickets, exchanging cash for indigenous cures, that legacy. I smoked again and slept fitfully, my body alert to the unfamiliar sounds, movement through the trees and vines.

We'd come for a ten-day diet. We'd stay alone in simple huts, meet only for meals of very basic food, and participate in several plant medicine ceremonies involving the vision-inducing brew of ayahuasca and chacruna. Also Miguel—in the style of his father and grandfather—would prescribe us plants to work with individually. He'd decide which plant that night, during the first ceremony, and tell us the next morning. For now, today, the diet started with a purge.

We met at the comedor but didn't eat breakfast. Instead we went over to another building, a twelve-sided structure called a maloca, where we'd conduct ceremonies. Behind it were a couple of benches surrounded by a drop-off shored up with stone walls. Luis lay a cloth over a small table and set out two bottles of murky, dark-colored liquid and wooden cups.

Buenos días con todos, Miguel said.

He explained that one bottle contained boiled tobacco and the other an herb called rosasisa. These plants would make us puke, which would clean out our bodies and prepare us for the diet.

Nafis and Akos would take tobacco, he said. Eszter, Szilvia, Herta, and I would take rosasisa.

I tried not to be insulted.

He lit a mapacho, uncapped the bottles, and began to sing in a high, sweet voice, blowing tobacco smoke into the bottles.

He beckoned to Nafis and poured out a shot. Nafis knocked it back, and Miguel motioned him down to the benches, the stone drop-off, where Luis handed him a liter-sized pitcher of water and a plastic bucket.

Miguel explained we were to drink several pitchers full of water. Up to five liters, he said, until we had puked everything up.

Nafis began to drink and soon he was puking heroically off the stone drop-off, retching sounds echoing over the valley.

The rosasisa was bitter and the water was tepid. I took down two liters and began to feel awful, sick and weak. I squatted over the plastic bucket and gagged, waiting for the puke to come up. Luis handed me more water and I struggled to drink it. I felt pressure in my eyeballs, helpless. Eventually yes— the water and rosasisa came back up, splattering into the bucket.

Miguel came over and began to beat my back and head with a fistful of dry leaves. The blows were gentle but the sound was sharp, and he sang over the beat in the same plaintive way he'd sung to the bottles. I puked again, Luis handed me more water, and Miguel moved on.

Szilvia was having trouble and Abuelita came over and soon a piercing voice emerged from Abuelita's chest, encircling us.

I was still squatting over my bucket, waiting for another pitcher of water to pour out of me. I wanted to puke out everything, all the junk of my being.

Abuelita was looking in my direction and saw the liquid splatter.

Dios te bendiga, she muttered, and left Szilvia to come near me.

She looked into my bucket then walked to Miguel, who came over.

How much water have you had?

Three or four liters, I said.

Okay, he said. That's enough. Go get some rest.

I collapsed on the bench, still feeling sick, and I saw them talking as if concerned.

Abuelita says there was something red, Miguel said. Have you had an ulcer?

No, I said.

Okay, he said. It's fine. Get some rest.

I staggered to the outhouse that was on the way to my hut, then made my way there and collapsed into the hammock.

What was wrong with me, I wondered. Was I beyond repair?

I lay there nauseous and aflood with self-pity, caught in webs of doubt. When I heard Luis blow into the conch shell—the indication we were to gather for lunch—I dragged myself down the path with effort. I sat with the others, who, it seemed to me, were happily exchanging war stories of their morning purge.

Eszter asked how I was doing.

If there's a problem, she said, you're in good hands here.

I was not comforted and after finishing a bland, saltless plate of food I returned to my hut, as if solitude might insulate me. I lay in the hammock, opened the notebook I'd brought, a gift from a friend in Mexico City who thought it was the stupidest thing in the world for me to come here.

You'll end up even more confused, she said. God, now I have to see you as one of those gringos who goes around like an idiot, so superficial, not learning anything.

She was right. I felt ruined. I wrote nothing.

We gathered in the maloca at sunset. Its twelve sides formed a circle, with a door on one side and the roof angled up to a point. There were ten mats arranged against the wall, each covered in blankets printed with cartoon animals—a lion, a panda, a teddy bear with a bow tie, a galloping horse. A traditional textile was set out in the middle of the space, a kind of altar with four candles at the corners and objects in the middle: Buddhist statuettes, a plastic unicorn, several matryoshka dolls.

Miguel assigned us places. He would be on the mat opposite the entrance. To his left, Abuelita and Luis, and to his right, Eszter. Couples were meant to be separate so we could concentrate internally. That meant after Eszter was Szilvia, then me, then Akos, then a space for a guard. Tonight it would be Nelson. The other way after Luis would be Mashti, Herta, then Nafis. We settled onto our mats. Nafis had brought various percussion instruments, an mbira, several stones. He spent a while setting himself up.

Miguel lay on his back, resting. A carved branch painted to look like a snake hung above his head. Also a drum and several more bunches of dry leaves—these were ceremonial percussion instruments called shakapas. Luis brought bottles of tinctures—Agua de Florida, which I recognized from neighborhood botanicas in Harlem and Washington Heights, and others I didn't know.

Miguel sat up.

Buenas noches con todos, he said.

He sat with his legs straight out in front of him and slightly apart, his plump belly slightly forward, hamstrings loose.

Tonight we'll have the first ceremony, he explained in his idiosyncratic Spanish. We learned from our parents and grandparents. It's a tradition in our family.

Here he gestured with his arms, showing turbulent forces moving around his chest and legs.

Ayahuasca means *death-vine*, he said. It connects us to the dead, to spirits. Sometimes it can be strong, but there's no reason to be scared.

We're here. Me, Abuelita, Luis. And if you need to get up, to go out to the bathroom, Nelson will help.

Nelson nodded. Eszter translated everything to Nafis, Akos, Szilvia, and Herta. I'd always loved Eszter's low, rich voice with its hint of a rasp.

Tonight we will drink ayahuasca-chacruna, Miguel said. We cooked it here in Juliampampa last week. It's good medicine. We take it to learn, but also to clean our bodies. It takes away what doesn't belong to us.

He picked up a 1.5-liter bottle that might have contained Coca-Cola but now contained something the same color but more viscous. He upended it a few times so the liquid sloshed around.

Any questions?

Mashti spoke now in Spanish:

I'd like to welcome everyone to Juliampampa, my spiritual home. I trained here, and Miguel's father Pedro gave me the nickname Mashti, which means *fulano*, as in *whoever*, which I wear proudly. And I'll say one thing—tonight is the last moment you can use your mind. After tonight, the spirits take over.

Eszter translated and we sat in silence for a moment. I thought about what Mashti said. What happened when we could no longer use our minds? Would we end up hypnotized like Herta?

Miguel lit a mapacho and asked permission from the spirits of the jungle, plants and animals, curanderos of the past. He opened the bottle of medicine, blew smoke into it, and began to sing. Again his high, plaintive voice. He screwed the cap back on and sloshed the bottle a few times, as if mixing smoke into the liquid, then opened it back up.

¡Esztercita!

She sat in front of him. Miguel filled a small wooden cup, which she held for a second, then knocked back.

Gracias, she said.

One by one we followed. The medicine was thick and bitter, but with an herbal flavor verging on sweetness. It reminded me of wormwood-infused booze from Hungary or the Balkans.

When everyone had been served, Luis went around with a mapacho and blew smoke on each of us, then Nelson doused the candles and we were in near perfect darkness.

It was hard to say how much time passed, but we were still in silence when the medicine started to take effect. I felt a tingling in my skin, carbonation all over. In the darkened maloca I saw colors, strings of lights, geometrical patterns—an Uzbek mosque patterned in iridescent thread. It was like a scrim between me and the world.

Miguel began to sing, and his plaintive voice now carried a stronger undercurrent. He kept a constant beat with one of the shakapas. The patterns responded to his voice and the sensations in my body grew. My afternoon of self-pity and ruination now resolved into grief.

I lay back on the mat and the voice changed. My mind adrift, it took a while to realize it was Luis singing now, the persistent beat of his shakapa gentler, like paper brushing a cheek. His tone was searching, a twisting melody echoing softly off the iron roof. Then from a momentary silence rose the piercing, almost intolerable tone of Abuelita. Why would anyone make that sound? She did not use a shakapa but sang out long high arhythmic lines without accompaniment. Finally a pattern formed and when the pulse entered her voice it was like a pressure drop. The air's ionization altered.

I drank from the stainless-steel water bottle I'd brought with me and the water softened and distributed the medicinal sensations. Miguel, Abuelita, and Luis took turns singing. Miguel asked Mashti to sing, too, and he sang in Spanish. Platitudes about curing and spirit and nature.

I guess you can sing whatever you want, I thought.

When Miguel took back the reins I felt secure and my wandering mind roamed freely through sounds and sensations. I knew the medicine can make you sick, but I didn't feel that. My body felt fine, and as the hours passed I felt better and better.

Eventually I got up to step outside. I switched on my headlamp with its red light. A little wobbly on my feet, I made my way to the door. Outside the scrim of lights was still there, now intermingling with the night sky and the stars, the swaying of branches. I stepped down the rocky path to the benches where we'd puked earlier. I lay down and watched the wind through the branches.

I'm fucked, I thought. I'm blind.

Blood coming out of my stomach. My failures and bad habits were as familiar to me as breathing. The medicine pulsed in my body but my mind was clear and sober.

The next morning we were back in the maloca. Plastic soda bottles labeled with masking tape and sharpie crowded together near the altar.

Miguel began speaking:

Eszter and Brad will take nina caspi, because they want to have a child.

I heard Eszter's warm voice speaking softly, and I wondered what she would say. She was across the room, but I could hear her saying that no, we weren't actually trying to have a child anymore. Her directness caused a painful churn in my intestines.

Miguel stopped to think.

Eszter will still take nina caspi, he said. It's good for the body. It heats you up, gives you force.

Luis grabbed one of the bottles from near the altar and placed it in front of her.

Szilvia will drink ajo sacha, Miguel said. Jungle garlic. Ajo sacha calms the mind.

I would drink nina caspi, too. It brings fire.

Akos would drink bobinsana, and so would Herta.

Bobinsana, Miguel said, is a beautiful plant.

Nafis would drink chuchuwasha, for strength.

Any questions?

I said I was concerned about drinking nina caspi if it brought fire.

I have a lot of fire, I said. So much it sometimes confuses me.

Miguel thought for a second.

In that case, Brad—from the beginning he pronounced it *Brak*—I'm going to give you bobinsana, too.

Nafis asked what happened and I translated.

Interesting, Nafis said.

Miguel sat in front of us one at a time, poured a cupful, blew smoke on it and sang to it before handing it to us.

Szilvia, immediately, grabbed a plastic bucket and puked.

You might feel dizzy, Miguel said. Just rest here, or you can go back to your hut. We'll have breakfast in an hour.

I drank down my cup of bobinsana—a bitter reddish liquid—and felt zonked. I'd hardly slept the night before and now lay in a blear on my mat.

This is bobinsana, Miguel said, pointing to several short trees in front of the comedor.

Broad, not as tall as me but twice as wide as my armspan, with dark, barky trunks as thick as a leg and main branches as thick as a forearm, then dividing into smaller branches with waxy, forest green leaves.

We brought these up and planted them, Miguel said. For medicine we use cuttings from trees along the Rio Mayo. They grow there wild, right along the river. Bobinsana is a water plant. She lives in the water. She can grow high even at the edge of the river, where the current is fast. It's about rooting. Bobinsana has good sensitive roots. Whoever drinks bobinsana has that power.

I walked over and looked at the tree. Its branches were covered with magenta globules that here and there exploded into fireworks of white and pink thread.

This is the first one we planted, Miguel said, pointing to a tree right in front of the kitchen. Fifteen years ago.

It was surrounded by mossy rocks and pecked by chickens, its trunk and branches dark except where covered with lichens.

We want the tree to be at least five years old, Miguel said. We peel the trunk and for each person we cook five or six kilos of bark in twenty liters of water. Dieting on bobinsana is like washing yourself from head to toe. Bobinsana cures you. Her emotion cures you. She has beautiful songs. Her mother is the mermaid, a siren. If bobinsana loves you—

He broke off in laughter.

And what about ayahuasca? I asked.

Ayahuasca is a base, he said. It's like a parent and ayahuasca is a child. Ayahuasca enters the body and sees everything with the help of bobinsana. Bobinsana opens the mind and sensitivities and brings visions. You can see the mermaid, love affairs that might come. Ayahuasca does the work.

It's female? I asked.

It can be male or female, he said, or it can be both. It can be whichever it chooses. Bobinsana is good for everyone. Whoever wants to cure their heart, their body.

As Karen prepared lunch, Abuelita spread out blankets and covered them with crafts. There were textiles, some embroidered with elaborate patterns, embroidered shirts and trousers and dresses.

Herta grabbed something and went off to try it on. Nafis was interested in an embroidered shirt.

That's ayahuasca, Abuelita said. Its icaro.

I knew the word *icaro* referred to curanderos' songs, but Abuelita said it also meant these patterns.

And looking again I could see the patterns were similar to what I'd seen when the medicine hit me, geometrical webs of filaments. I'd taken them for patterns off a mosque because that's what I was familiar with. But these patterns were not iterated from compass points like that. They were nodes and shapes repeated with subtle asymmetries that made the patterns start to swim. The traditional design around here, what Abuelita had rendered, was that scrim that lay over everything when the medicine hit.

I can make you one, she said. Bring me a shirt and I'll embroider it.

Herta appeared in a knee-length white dress covered in embroidered patterns. She did a spin in front of the comedor, very pleased.

Karen called us to eat. Herta changed back and sat across from me, squeezing in between Akos and Eszter.

Can I have olive oil? she asked Karen.

Karen said something to Luis, who came over to check on her.

The website mentioned olive oil, she said.

Luis apologized. There was no olive oil.

What website? I asked. Miguel has a website?

His, she indicated Mashti.

Mashti was on the phone with someone discussing a camera. Someone was supposed to bring a camera. Mashti had an intensity of focus I didn't understand. Herta, meanwhile, seemed to take up an inordinate amount of space. I wanted to talk to Nafis, to Szilvia, to Luis, but wherever I turned it was her, and she in turn kept one eye on Mashti.

You met in Mexico? I asked.

Yes, well, the last time.

What do you mean?

I mean I realized, she said, that we'd met many times before. In other lives.

It turned out she'd been in Tulum and gone to a ceremony that Mashti was officiating. He was a curandero in his own right, she said—*very powerful*—and during her vision she'd seen his face and understood they'd known each other for centuries. Afterward she'd spoken to him. She owns a piece of land in Paraguay—*It's very easy to get land there*—and she wanted him to come with her, to hold ceremonies in Paraguay. But first they were going to Europe. She would help. But before anything they had to come to Peru. He needed more medicine.

This is where he cooks his medicine, she said. We'll make a video here for publicity when we go to Europe. And when Miguel is away we will do ceremonies here, she said.

Miguel is going away?

Yes, she said. To Lima, for three months, for his eye.

Clearly she knew more than I did.

After lunch we went for a walk. Miguel wanted to show us around. We went up behind the comedor where the foliage thickened. He showed us an ajo sacha vine with its broad leaves growing two feet off the ground. He snapped a leaf and handed it around. It smelled distinctly of garlic. Nearby was a nina caspi tree, higher and narrower than bobinsana, with bright orange bean-like pods. There was another tree called uchu sanango.

Strong medicine, Miguel said. *Buenazo.*

And another tree, a shrub with white and lilac flowers on it.

Chiric sanango, Miguel said. Also very strong. Nafis dieted on it.

I was drunk the whole time, Nafis said, and imitated himself staggering, blind.

Eventually I would get to know all these plants. I'd be tranquilized by ajo sacha and flattened by chiric sanango. So many plants. But those first days, listening to Miguel, these were just sounds—*bobinsana, uchu sanango.* I followed in a daze, curious but very much at a distance.

We walked further up the hill and there was a tree wrapped in a vine the color of wet paper.

Ayahuasca, Miguel said. You can see its spiral.

Each of us reached out to touch the vine.

It looks like DNA, Szilvia said.

Miguel showed us the big plastic water tank where they gathered water from a spring further up the mountain. And we followed its pipe down past the comedor, along another stone path to the shower, where the pipe emptied onto a hollowed out palm trunk, the water running down its length like a gutter and splashing onto a small platform of stones.

We passed the shower and walked up a hill of mud and roots to a place where the path split in two.

Here it's virgin, Miguel said.

We followed a curving path, surrounded by thicknesses of trees and vines. Everything hummed with insects. There was a large and mossy boulder taller than me and twice as wide. Rounding the edge of the boulder we came into a small clearing dominated by an enormous, vine-covered tree.

Yanchamita! Miguel called to it, went up and lay his hand on the bark.

It looked ancient, extravagant, a universe of trunks and vines rising high above us creating a shaded clearing, protected by the canopy. Twenty feet back was another hut, just like the ones we were staying in. I walked to it and sat down on the step, looking up at the tree. I could hear Mashti talking to Herta:

This is where you come to be with the spirits high up in the trees.

She looked up at the spreading branches.

Really, she said, wide-eyed.

We continued down a dense path to an area where Miguel said they were trying to create a fish pond. Alongside the site of the future fishpond was another tall tree encircled in a thick, aged-looking vine.

Another ayahuasca vine, Miguel said.

Now I could see it was similar to the one we'd seen above the comedor, but larger, older.

This is the oldest one here, Miguel said.

He led us back into the thickness of the jungle and into another clearing. There was a small orchard of plantains up a hillside. We gathered at the summit, able to see distances here because the plantain trees didn't obscure everything like the wild trees of the virgin jungle. We took in the expanse of verdant mountains in all directions, snaking valleys, clouds gathering at the peaks, blue sky between them. Not a house or any sign of human activity except us.

I heard the conch shell call and appeared at the comedor as instructed. It was breakfast time, which meant another plate of saltless beans and rice or peas and bulgur, or soggy quinoa with a pile of shredded lettuce and carrots and a few slices of cucumber. Karen was still warming things up.

Amigo Brad!

She smiled and her dimples lit up the morning.

Mashti walked up from down the hill and for the first time we fell into conversation. His Spanish was clipped and rapid, but unlike Miguel he was easy to understand. He was a different generation—closer in age to Luis than Miguel, maybe thirty years old. There was a clarity in his expression, but his energy was distracted, agitated. He averted his gaze as he spoke to me, punctuating his talk with eye contact. He told me he was from Tarapoto. He'd worked for Miguel's dad.

You didn't meet Pedro? he asked.

I'd just arrived, I said.

A great curandero, I assisted him, then about a year ago, I grew wings.

He'd been to Mexico and before that he'd been giving ceremonies in Europe.

I use strong ayahuasca, Mashti said. Not like what they have here. I don't have time to take the Europeans through a ten-day diet. I have to hit them hard.

29

I asked about Tulum and he shrugged. He wasn't impressed with Tulum.

And now?

This is where I always cook my ayahuasca. But some of it spilled last night. I don't know how that happened. Half my ayahuasca is gone.

He threw up his hands in exasperation.

Szilvia and Akos appeared and sat at the long table. Karen began to serve our plates of saltless food. Miguel emerged from his room at the end of the comedor.

Wawki! Mashti called and went off to talk to him.

I'd had three cups of bobinsana by then, but that night we had another ceremony, so we wouldn't drink our assigned plants. No dinner either. After lunch we returned to our huts and only gathered again around sunset.

I sat by the benches where we'd puked. Luis came by and sat next to me, and we watched the sky change colors over Tarapoto. There was a huge tree in front of us, and a similar tree down the stone path toward the outhouse. Luis said they were *ojé* trees.

Ojés like to grow near the maloca, he said.

Darkness settled and we took our places inside and waited. Nafis set up his many percussion instruments and stones, Eszter took her place to the right of Miguel, who lay on his back under the carved snake. Herta wore the white embroidered dress she'd bought from Abuelita, and Mashti appeared in a shimmering, floor-length robe. He carried a camera and sat next to Herta, showing her how to operate it. Then he crouched by Miguel and spoke to him. Miguel handed him a headdress with a few feathers sticking up in front and Mashti returned to his place.

Miguel opened the ceremony and told us tonight we'd be drinking ayahuasca cielo, a different brew than we'd had last time.

It can be strong, he said.

He also pointed out we were on our second day of our plant diet, and those plants would be entering deeper into our bodies.

Any questions?

I remembered Mashti's comment about the spirits taking over, our minds no longer guiding us.

Miguel called us up one by one to sit in front of him. When it was Mashti's turn, he placed the feathered crown on his head and as Herta filmed, he made a small performance, holding his cup of medicine close to his chest before he drank it down.

Nelson blew out the candles and darkness was complete—sounds of the night, pulsing bugs and rising wind outside. Eventually I heard Miguel start to blow air through his lips, whistle, eventually shake his shakapa and sing. When Luis took over it seemed he sat for a long time just shaking his shakapa, and the touch of the leaves was like gentle fingertips.

It took longer for the tingling to begin. Anticipatory tension gave way slowly to other sensations, and when the visions came they were of tendons and organs, blood and phlegm and bile, synapses and nerve endings, cell walls and mitochondria. It was as if I'd zoomed in on the filamental patterns of the previous night, the asymmetries in Abuelita's embroidery, and now I could see up close that the filaments were living matter, pulsing and in flux.

I felt bobinsana wake up in me, or imagined I did: a young plant adrift in the swift river of my thoughts, vigilant for where to root down and withstand the shifting currents. The idea alarmed me. What if it attached to the first notion or person that came to mind? I'd be trapped, locked to whatever the plant had rooted into. But no, the effect might be to under-stand the impulse, to feel the need to root down. What's the most stable thing here? If you were to clutch onto something for dear life, what would it be?

Miguel seemed like a good choice, patriarch of the mountain, but that wasn't it either. Myself perhaps, my heart. Not my physical heart, my metaphorical heart, the heart's eye. For a moment I saw grasping plant tendrils encircle that imaginary place.

I laughed at these thoughts. So absurd. They floated above a continu-ing churn.

Abuelita sang and then Mashti. When Miguel sang again Mashti gathered his robe and left the maloca. In the ensuing quiet Miguel asked Nafis to sing, and Nafis now gathered one of his percussion instruments and began to shake it. Eventually he sang, and a big almost laughing tone filled the space—*Gra-ci-as!* He wasn't always on key but there was some-thing so direct and good-natured about Nafis's singing that I was won over. I felt a spark shoot out of my chest, white light.

That was it, I laughed to myself. That was bobinsana.

We sat in silence for a while. Szilvia started to cough and moan next to me. I needed to take a piss and grabbed my headlamp to make my way outside, emerging into the wind and stars.

The ojé roots snaked around the outhouse. It looked like they were moving. I stepped off the path to get a closer look and saw it was leaf-cutter ants in an endless march, steady and orderly. Each ant with a penny-sized shred of leaf in its pincher-like jaws, marching nonstop, carrying their burdens until they disappeared into a hole at the base of the ojé.

When I got back to the door of the maloca I found Eszter guiding Szilvia outside.

She's having a difficult time, Eszter said.

Eszter is always a good friend to her friends, I thought.

They walked off the way I'd come and I stepped back to the benches to sit in the night air for a moment. My mind went to Mashti and Herta and I could feel a swell of irritation, pressure in my head. It occurred to me that bobinsana had shown me the grasping vigilance for safe harbor, and that irritation with them was exactly such a harbor, shoring up a sense of superiority, as if I weren't just as foolish as they were. I wondered if bobinsana could show me the process in reverse, for those tendrils to slacken and let go and such stupidities might drift off and I could be there in the jungle with the ants and trees and wind.

I heard voices behind me. Eszter and Szilvia were at the door of the maloca. Eszter went inside and Szilvia walked down to where I was adrift in these thoughts.

Do you have a mapacho? she asked me.

I fished two out of my pocket and handed her one along with the lighter. We sat smoking, looking over the valley.

I felt strange—this was Eszter's client. Was I responsible for her?

Eszter kaže da pričaś Srpski, she said.

And I answered her in the same language. I did speak Serbian, I told her. I spent my twenties in the ex-Yugoslavia. Slovenia, Sarajevo, Skopje, Belgrade. I'd even been to Subotica, her hometown along the Hungarian border.

You actually speak pretty well, she said.

I miss it, I said. I miss speaking this language.

There's something specific about it, she said. It's true.

I asked how it felt for her to speak it, as opposed to Hungarian.

I'm like a completely different person, she said.

33

We both laughed and smoked and I felt the low tones of that language flow through me. I felt the gush of emotions I associated with those times. All the darkness and madness and joy and friendship, the war and post-war and the beauty of certain afternoons. With the swirl of medicinal visions fresh in my mind, the strangest thing to me was sitting on that bench speaking Serbian with Szilvia.

The medicine started to rise again. I could feel the effects intensify. For the first time I thought I might puke.

I need to get up, I told Szilvia, and I stepped away from her.

I found myself back atop the stone support wall I'd puked over the first morning. I thought I might have to piss, but the swell of medicine was powerful. Nausea and confusion. I fell to a squat. My head swirled like I was drunk. I couldn't stand and just rested where I was. Eventually Szilvia finished her mapacho and walked back up to the maloca and I was alone. The darkness oozed and vibrated. I have no idea how long I was there. Eventually I heard a voice.

Brak!

It was Miguel. Luis was with him.

Come inside, Miguel said. This is where the bad spirits wait.

I was unsteady on my feet and Luis escorted me back to the maloca.

When I got back to my mat I kicked over my stainless-steel water bottle, which clanged on the floor, breaking up the silence.

Luis left me and I was alone. I lay back and felt the wave course through me. I didn't know if I was drunk or sick or what. None of my thoughts completed.

Miguel sang again and Abuelita and Luis and their voices calmed me, kept my mind there in the room with the people I'd come with. The tendons and sinew and peristaltic visions subsided and eventually Miguel called us up one by one to sit in front of him for limpias—*cleanings*—when he beat us with a shakapa and sang to us, his voice rising and falling with the intensity of the blows, which because they were made with a clutch of dry leaves managed to be loud and sharp and soft at the same time. Then he stopped singing and blew tobacco smoke onto our heads and hands and chests.

When he'd cleaned us all like that with his shakapa and smoke, Nelson lit a candle. Mashti's place was empty. It seemed he hadn't come back after he sang the first time.

The ceremony is over, Miguel said.

I sought refuge in my hut lingering over that moment on the wall with the evil spirits. What evil spirits? I wondered. I felt something caught in my throat, like a half-finished sentence or a swallow of vomit. Was it something in my past, my marriage, something that needed to be uncovered? I lay down but there was no sleep to be had. Eventually the sun rose, Miguel stopped by to serve my morning cup of bobinsana, its red juice mixing with the acid I felt within me. I walked out to look over the valley, but the swirl of emotions continued. Every decision I'd ever made. I wanted to walk but where could I go?

I grabbed a towel and went to the shower, stood under the cold spring water that splashed out of the hollowed out palm trunk. Refreshed, I decided not to return to the comedor but walk the other direction, up the slope of mud and roots into the virgin forest. I walked back past the enormous moss-covered boulder and there was the yanchama tree. Its trunk appeared multiple, several trunks fused into one, cohabitating behind a skein of bark, rising high from the forest floor. Vines covered in other vines that sprouted leaves or were covered in grass or moss or lichens. It was impossible to see into its upper reaches.

I sat on the step of the hut, empty below the tree, and gazed up at it. A flash of color streaked through the leaves, an orange bird now perched on a branch, a kind of parrot with a black body and orange head with an orange crest. It bobbed for a moment then flew off, and when it spread its wings the orange was so bright it was like it erased my mind.

I walked back up to the comedor. Miguel had told us that the next day we were already scheduled to have another ceremony. It was hard for me to imagine going back into such intensities. And this one would be different. Instead of gathering at the maloca at night, we would remain in our huts alone, and he would come in the morning to give us medicine.

Eszter had told me what happened to her the year before. Drinking ayahuasca alone in the jungle she'd been wild and ecstatic. She thought she might go mad out there alone and never make it back to the life she'd left behind. She'd been unable to calm down until Abuelita came to sit with her, held her, massaged her while she ranted about healing and madness and solitude.

When I saw Miguel, I asked him if I could do the day ceremony down there where I'd been, beneath the yanchama tree.

You want to move in there?

It hadn't occurred to me, but yes, I did.

You have to be careful, he said. That's the real jungle. Animals pass by.

I nodded. He called to Nelson and Humberto, and soon I saw them carrying a mattress and bucket of filtered spring water to set up the hut.

I can help, I said, but Miguel brushed me off.

We'll take care of it.

I went to gather my things and drag my bag down.

Brak, Miguel stopped me. Remember to blow mapacho smoke when you move in. On the bed, on the floor.

Tobacco smoke—he called it *tabaquito*—clears out the spiders and scorpions.

If you see a scorpion, he said, kill it.

When I got there Nelson was hanging a hammock beneath the lip of the corrugated iron roof. When he left, I lit a mapacho and blew smoke everywhere, which quickly dissipated through the screen walls. I got down on all fours and blew smoke under the bed. Satisfied, I went outside and dropped into the hammock.

The change from one hut to another had refreshed my orientation. Here, I thought, something might happen.

Back in New York I'd wondered what books to bring. I'd gone to the bookstore with some ideas but instead grabbed whatever caught my eye, among them a collection by ninth-century Chinese poet Li Shangyin, notoriously difficult to translate.

I flipped through versions by Chloe Garcia Roberts, who'd edited the collection:

Twelve railings
Ring the emerald walls.

Rhinoceros horn protects against dust,
Jade protects against cold.

On Virgin's Bed Mountain,

No tree lacks a perched phoenix

The poems were of solitude and mortality, melancholy or lush with acceptance. Looking around at the jungle and the yanchama tree, I wondered at the effect of reading such lines here, brought across not only languages but continents and centuries. Perhaps, in a way, I was in the natural habitat of these poems. Swinging under the yanchama tree, feeling the hammock's fiber mesh around my shoulders, I looked up at the high branches.

We finished our evening meal, and Miguel called me over. He was standing with Herta and asked if I could translate.

I wanted to tell Miguel something, she said. I told him that during the three months he's in Lima I will assist at ceremonies here.

I translated.

Miguel blew air through his nose, half-laughed.

I could see his right eye behind his dark lenses. It was swollen almost completely shut. The swelling circled his eye. The skin around it was puffy, probably sensitive, painful.

Tell her, Miguel said, that what she thinks is going to happen is not going to happen. I sense a lot of confusion between the two of them.

I translated. Herta nodded.

If you want to be a part of what goes on here, Miguel continued, it takes preparation. You have to diet for at least a month. Until you do that you are welcome here as a guest, a student.

Herta listened and seemed to understand. She wanted to ask a question.

She said when she drinks the medicine she sees Mashti's face. It's like they've known each other before. She thought maybe it was because she was drinking medicine he'd prepared himself, but now she's here drinking Miguel's medicine, and still when the vision comes she sees his face.

I don't feel free, she said.

I translated.

I could say many things, Miguel said, but she's going to understand eventually.

She asked if it was normal that she sees Mashti's face, and Miguel laughed again and said:

If the intention is good it's okay, but if not—

And he shrugged.

But you're not giving me answers, Herta said.

She's going to understand, Miguel said.

She and Mashti were scheduled to leave the next morning. We'd have a few more days up here without them.

The walk to my new hut at night was longer and darker. Miguel told me to smoke a mapacho while I walked—that way the animals would know I was coming.

You'll hear animals pass at night, he said. If you get scared—mapacho.

He gestured smoking one of the rough cigarettes.

The yanchama tree waited just beyond the large boulder. The jungle canopy almost completely blocked out the moonlight, and only a few stars were visible between leaves and branches. A chorus of frogs resounded through the trees behind the hut.

Stepping inside the hut, I shone my light around. I relit my mapacho and blew smoke everywhere. On the floor, sure enough, I saw a small black scorpion.

In Mexico I'd learned to place scorpions gingerly outside, but I was in Miguel's territory. I grabbed a shoe, swatted it dead, and threw its remains into the darkness.

I was sorry to kill the scorpion, but I also felt a pang of pride at my competence. Tobacco smoke is said to be protective, I realized, because it alerts animals and drives away pests. The simplicity of it—I felt like I'd learned something.

I slept little that night, alert to the sounds outside.

In the morning I was back in the comedor. Miguel had asked me to go around and translate while he served everyone their morning medicine. I got up there to find Mashti and Herta with Nelson, ready to make the trek down the mountain.

Miguel watched them go, then turned to head toward Szilvia's hut.

He worked for my father for three years, Miguel said. He didn't train. He worked as a cook. He sat in ceremonies, sometimes assisted. But he never dieted, so he doesn't have power. He says my father called him Mashti, but it's not true. My father couldn't remember his name! Now he goes around the world: *El Curandero Fulanito*. He puts tobacco in his ayahuasca so it hits you very hard and makes you vomit, then an hour later there's nothing in your body. That's what he calls strong ayahuasca.

I told Miguel I was worried about his intentions for Juliampampa, but he just laughed.

He says he's going to come up here and do ceremonies, but that's not going to happen.

We passed by everyone's huts and at each place Miguel stopped, opened his bottle of ayahuasca and sang to it, poured out a cup, lit a mapacho and blew smoke onto the surface of the cup, then handed it over.

He did the same at my hut, blew mapacho smoke around the hut, my hammock, into the air under the tree, and left me.

I lay in the hammock, and after some time the effect of the plant started to kick in. The tingling. The jungle became more vivid. I needed to walk around the tree, to be close to it. I got down on the ground where a tangle of roots rose from the earth and submerged again. In the middle of the tangle was a single straight root coated in fine orange hairs. Among the natural twists and curves, its straightness captivated me. I thought of the Street Called Straight in Damascus, and the Straight Path of the Qur'an.

In my delirium I stripped off my shirt and pants and stood practically naked there by the yanchama tree. I laughed at myself like that, like I was learning something basic about what it meant to be human. When I was back at the comedor at the end, Akos and I talked about that feeling.

Exactly, Akos said. Like we might find our way back to our own humanity.

Mashti and Herta were gone and we all admitted we were relieved.

She took up so much space, Szilvia said.

The morning's delirium had left us in a wonderful mood. Happy to be back to our original group, we were at home in the jungle, with its colors and scents and sounds. We ate our saltless meal with relish.

The next ceremony was at night again. We gathered at sunset in the maloca. Miguel called us up one by one. The medicine he gave us was cielo, but a different batch.

This is Abuelita's recipe, Miguel said.

It was as thick as tar, horribly bitter, and when the visions came, it was not the swift currents of before. It was a raging flood, rapids and whirlpools breaking banks.

Eszter began to speak out loud, unable to control herself. She spoke as if possessed.

We're all dead, she said.

Everyone was dead. And we had to re-create everything, start the world from scratch.

We will start again, she said.

Miguel and Luis went close to her, blew tobacco on her and splashed her with Agua de Florida, but she continued to speak. I got to my feet and stumbled over, but Miguel stopped me.

We'll take care of her, he said.

Eszter lay behind them in the darkness, twisting on her mat, talking and murmuring as if unaware of where she was.

I watched as Miguel lit his mapacho again and squatted down next to her. She'd been here before. She trusted them. I went back to my place and listened, we all did.

All of us are dead, she said.

Eszter repeated this phrase in a hundred ways, her breath intensifying, and eventually I needed a moment to breathe. I walked out of the maloca, back to the benches where we puked, to smoke a mapacho with the evil spirits there. I wondered where I was, where I'd got to.

The wind rose and I could no longer hear Eszter's voice from the maloca.

At the end, when the forces calmed and Eszter quieted and Miguel called the ceremony to a close, he sat asking us:

Where do you think we go when we die?

No one had a good answer.

They say there's another world, Miguel said, but I think there's nothing.

No hay nada, he repeated.

Later we would think back on this ceremony—everyone dead—because it was the next morning, all of us still bleary from the turbulence of the night before, that a man came bearing news. He appeared wearing camp shorts and a khaki jacket, some kind of uniform. We watched him conference with Miguel at the top of the path. It was a park ranger announcing that the Cordillera Escalera Reserve, in which we were situated, was closed.

Peru has declared a state of emergency, Miguel said. There's going to be curfew. No one can travel. Borders are closed.

Did he say how long that was going to be? Nafis asked.

He doesn't know, Miguel said. We'll see.

We were supposed to fly home in three days.

A willowy Russian named Ivan arrived that same afternoon. Miguel guessed he must have been the last foreigner they let in the park.

I know him, Miguel said. He's been here before.

He appeared in a denim bucket-hat, tall and skinny as a broomstick. He dropped his things and pulled out a bag of fruit, sat silently peeling a granadilla.

We learned the state of emergency extended to March 30, more than a week after we were scheduled to fly home. Airlines were scrambling to know what to do.

I'd turned my phone off when we left Tarapoto—I wouldn't have any reception, anyway—but Nafis had bought a Peruvian SIM card, and Akos had some global roaming service. Luis and Miguel both tried to get news. Reception was bad, but if you stood in a certain place and held your phone in the air, you might be able to get a text or send an email.

The outside world came flooding in, but it was not the world we'd left behind. New York was completely closed, we heard. Eszter had been right. We'd need to start over. And we had to decide what to do.

Can we stay here? I asked Miguel. Can we extend our diet and keep drinking plants?

We'll cover expenses, Nafis said.

Akos and Szilvia nodded in agreement.

Miguel said he'd talk it over with the family.

I managed to get word of our situation to my sister. She'd once worked for the State Department, and said she'd see if she could get any information. She told me our mother had stopped by the Peruvian Connection at the strip mall near where we grew up and asked if they could help.

They're going to smuggle you out in a palette of alpaca sweaters, my sister said.

We learned the virus was already all over Peru. It arrived in Tarapoto with a curandero returning from Holland. He'd escaped quarantine in Lima and was trying to get to Iquitos. He'd flown to Tarapoto but started showing symptoms on the plane. Now he was quarantined in the local hospital.

Miguel called us together for a meeting.

We've talked it over with the family, he said. Nelson and Humberto will go down to Tarapoto. They're from the community so they can come and go from the park. They'll come back tomorrow night with food and supplies, and we can all stay another week.

We will see how long this state of emergency lasts, he said.

THE VIRUS IS YOU

Rain falls in torrents from the sky. A palm-sized spider disappears beneath the rock near where we swim. Not hairy like the tarantula in the wall but spindly and quick.

Day and night the river's rush blankets the garden, but now it's inaudible beneath the storm. It feels like the rains will destroy everything—batter the houses until they fall, uproot trees. Everything will slide down to be pulverized by boulders below. But then in an hour or two the rains let up and it's peaceful again. The sun comes out and the flowering bushes glisten.

Water drains from the tile roof, from the bamboo gutter, into the stone-lined ditch that surrounds the little house, issuing downhill toward the river now high in the storm's wake. Behind the flowering bushes erupts a spiky wall of yellow bamboo thirty feet high. The rain stops and the air quiets and the bamboo stalks clack against each other in the breeze.

The garden is all dragon fruit trees, coconut palms, branches ripe with avocados, cascades of red flowers. Big spiny blossoms called lion's tongues that look like penises, that sprout little yellow leaves at their tips like beads of dripping semen. The promiscuous blooms of the toé bush emit a dizzy-making fragrance in the evening.

Now in the calm after the storm, Jaru the cat hunts a tiny lizard on the shrub opposite here, rife with purple flowers. He stalks up flimsy branches, steps through thorns until he drops to the ground and leaps. But the lizard disappears into the bramble, so Jaru sits in the stone gutter licking his paws as if he's not the most elegant cat in the world.

Nelson and Humberto returned to Juliampampa with supplies, but soon the government said the state of emergency would extend for weeks. Now no one could say how long it would last. Holding our phones in the air to receive a text or load a webpage was not going to be sufficient. We'd need to check in with our families, our various jobs. Somehow we were going to have to go on with our lives.

Miguel told us about a lodge just outside the national park with electricity and wifi, closed now because of the situation, but he knew the owner, who said they'd make up a few beds for us when we were ready to come down. It was our best option. But we could hold off a bit longer. I who'd been the most reluctant to come here now adamant we extend our stay. Lockdown had somehow rendered irrelevant any resistance I might have felt to plant medicine. I was no longer concerned about shamanic tourism. Here we were trapped together. What else could I do but embrace my circumstances?

Miguel cooked up more chuchuwasha for Nafis, more bobinsana for Akos and ajo sacha for Szilvia, but switched the plants Eszter and I were drinking. Eszter went from nina caspi to renaquillo, a plant that was half-vine-half-tree. Miguel showed it to us growing down the path beyond the yanchama tree, a thick trunk with woody, crisscrossing tendrils grasping its host. It looked even more like DNA than ayahuasca.

Renaquillo is from earth, Miguel said. It's soft and loving. It can cure wounds. And it's attractive to other people.

46

He tapped it with his walking stick.

If a man comes asking about a woman, Miguel smiled, renaquillo can summon that woman and she will love him. Curanderos use it to call spirits. If you've dieted on renaquillo, you can call someone who isn't there. You can summon their spirit. If you want to talk to them you sing their icaro and they will come. But that requires longer diets.

Eszter stood admiring the unusual plant. I wondered what a week drinking renaquillo would do to her. She had recovered from her death-trance, and though we didn't know what was happening we were getting our bearings. It was good to talk through the situation with her, to know we could count on each other. But we still returned to our huts alone.

I switched from bobinsana to another water plant, a tree called yacushimbillo. Miguel led me down a more distant path and stopped at the edge of thick underbrush. He blew tobacco smoke on me and himself to protect us from snakes and swung his machete a few times to open a path. Once inside the brush he stopped at a moderately sized tree, its trunk hairy and leafy with moss and plants growing off its bark. Where its interior was exposed, the wood was lovely, dark and striated, brown and cream-colored. It had unmistakable webbed leaves growing in sets of eight.

This is yacushimbillo, he said. A good friend. It will bring strong dreams and visions.

My Mexican lit teacher used to gather students in the upstairs room of his apartment in the San Rafael. We'd read to each other and pick apart Revueltas or Rulfo. He told me Octavio Paz once assembled a group of friends to eat mushrooms. They'd traveled the inframundo together and had adventures and willed themselves to bring something back, something to show it had been more than a flickering figment. When they returned, my teacher told me, there was a sandal on the floor between them, a regular old leather sandal, as ordinary and solid as the floorboards.

What if I brought back an old shoe from my visions? Who would I be then?

Luis said I should ask the plants questions, and answers would come to me in dreams. I dreamt of brands of tobacco associated with famous pirates, of cigarettes that lit themselves, of a cash register of ice cream flavors.

Don't worry, Luis said, if I kept paying attention meanings would emerge.

I dreamt we landed in Turkey, which was an island in the Atlantic, not far from Philadelphia. I dreamt of a disease named Charles that made everyone talk like Sherlock Holmes. I dreamt of a religion called Hortobagyism devoted to a small, pale flower that blooms whenever a comedian dies.

The meaning could be found in Hortobagyism, I thought. In the little flower of comic death.

But in fact the change from bobinsana to yacushimbillo revealed that the plants Miguel gave us indeed had character and personality. During ceremonies on bobinsana I'd often experienced that spark in my heart, what I'd first felt when Nafis sang *Gra-ci-as* so forthright and off-key. Bobinsana was meant to be a water plant, too, but on yacushimbillo my nose ran, I drooled, tears streamed from my eyes. Whatever I thought about, I cried. I'd had trouble crying for years—ever since as a crybaby kid I'd learned to suppress my pain and sorrow—but now I cried nonstop. I found I could sit with my back against the wall of the maloca with tears streaming down my cheeks. With time it became ordinary as the floorboards, too.

And it was the second week of that first stint up the mountain that I began to take walks in the jungle alone. Miguel had led us down the path beyond my hut, past the renaquillo tree-vine and three huge, majestically buttressed sapoina trees, to a waterfall some half-hour walk away. Water cascaded from a high sheet of flat rock. Stacked boxes of sheer cliff-face, it brought to mind the houses above the Mtkvari River in the old city of Tbilisi.

I remembered sitting in a basement wine bar in that city with my friend Khaled and a bunch of art historians, passing around a centuries-old silver ladle. Each of us filled the ladle with amber-colored wine and stood to give a toast before drinking it down. Our toasts became more and more elaborate, euphoric and maudlin, into the early morning.

But from the high wall here, clean mountain water came crashing down into a small pool. When we went the first time Miguel told us a hedgehog had fallen and smashed to bits, so the pool was hazardous with quills. But over the next few days Nelson and Humberto put on rubber boots and cleaned out the animal remains. Then we came back and could stand under the crashing water, feeling renewed. Huge blue butterflies flapped in the mist. We wondered if we wanted to go down the mountain at all.

I spent hours in the hammock in front of the yanchama tree. I stared at its vines and lichens, the other trees it had enveloped as it grew. I walked past it into the jungle to visit the renaquillo, the sapoinas, and the waterfall.

On one of my solitary walks I heard a horrid sound, the snarl and snort of an animal of considerable size. I stepped quietly, imagining through the thick brush, just out of view, lurked a boar with sharp horns or an ape I'd never seen before. The snorting and growling continued, and I managed to record a bit of the sound before the animal disappeared without showing itself. When I brought my phone up to the comedor to play the sound for Miguel, he told me it was an *ispuitino*—the orange parrot I'd seen my first morning at the yanchama tree.

It was impossible for me to imagine such a sound coming from that beautiful crested bird.

Sometimes she fights with her rooster, Miguel said.

Soon I learned to spot the fat black woodpeckers with red heads and striped beaks. I learned the swooping black and yellow birds were called caciques, like pre-Columbian nobility.

Miguel told me his full name was Miguel Tapullima Cachique. He was one, too.

At the base of the yanchama, I found, there was a nest of enormous black ants. In Miguel's Quechua they were called isulas, but in Spanish they were called hormigas balas, because their bite felt like you'd been shot with a bullet. I learned to respect those inch-long creatures patrolling the tangled roots I stepped over every day. Their movements were robotic and menacing. So much larger than the other ants, it would be like me running into a giant taller than the yanchama tree, its jaws plump with venom, moving as if entranced.

On the door of my hut I found a walking stick that glowed scarlet. It seemed to strut by, on its way somewhere.

Insect mind, I thought. Insect body.

Akos and Szilvia went down before we did. Advertising might have been irreconcilable, but Akos had deadlines and was impatient to get back online. We gathered in the maloca for a ceremony before they cut their diets.

A ceremony, I was starting to suspect, contains the promise of a story that might express or reveal a lesson or clue, something to guide us or open some new possibility. Sometimes it was an incoherent mess, a flurry of disassociated imagery too rapid and various to make sense of. But then it settled, a scenario came into focus, a realization, sometimes the meaningful center of a thing we'd always known. Suspense was driven not by curiosity about what would happen next, but about what meaning might be revealed—a tiny perhaps necessary token to be redeemed upon encountering oblivion. Eventually the waves of intensity would subside and we'd have a chance to take stock of whatever we experienced or witnessed.

That night, soon after Miguel served us, Szilvia began to moan and cough and then start to vomit. Eszter and Miguel went to help her, and I could hear the piercing voice of Abuelita course through the darkness of the maloca.

Arkana wa no, she sang. *Limpia limpia wa no.*

High-pitched lines unfurled like razor wire through the air. Then, as before, her phrases became rhythmic. I hoped for the requisite mental restraint to absorb what was going on, but soon I was hanging on for dear life. The fabric of reality twisted and bent. The distinct scents of machine oil and bricks engulfed my head. Art nouveau patterns of old Budapest elevators scrambled my cognition.

I felt scolded: *Do it properly, show respect, learn to remain calm.*

But how to stay calm with Szilvia puking, Luis spitting Agua de Florida into the air, and these filamental webs spewing from Abuelita's throat?

An indigo light now lowered like a rifle scope aimed about my sternum, and *pwaaaaahhh!!!*—a searchlight lit up debris caught by gusts of wind, shreds of paper, wrought iron bars blown off fire escapes, glints and shards and glaring beams.

Brak, I heard a voice just beside me. ¿Cómo estás?

Miguel, somehow, had left Szilvia and crept up right next to me without me noticing.

Pure derangement of the senses, I thought.

Miguel was fifteen when his grandfather first invited him to a ceremony.

It was nice, he told me. You know, people vomiting.

His grandfather turned to him and said: *Hey grandson, how about a diet? Maybe you're interested?*

Miguel said fine, and his grandfather gave him ajo sacha to diet on. In the weeks after the diet, he could feel his energy lift. He realized he'd been a lazy teenager, but now he was on his feet and ready to work.

It felt good, so he went back to his grandfather to diet on another plant. He took chuchuwasha, bobinsana, bachuja, acerohuasca.

Dieting, dieting, dieting, he said.

Then he got called up for military service and after that he drifted. He lived outside Lima for a while. He went to Yurimaguas to work construction. He came back to Tarapoto and Lamas sometimes, but if he came up to Juliampampa it was because he was looking for an out-of-the-way place to spend a weekend with a girlfriend. He wasn't interested in following in his father's and grandfather's footsteps.

Instead of bobinsana or ajo sacha, he and his brother planted coca plants beyond the plantain orchard. Coca is medicinal, sure, but that's not why they planted it. They harvested it to sell it to the dealers in town. Someone eventually informed on them. One of Miguel's brothers spent six months in jail and the government came and fumigated their coca trees.

Miguel was walking round the jungle at one point when *bang!* he went down—shot. Blood everywhere, his knee was shattered.

A trap, he realized. He'd sprung a tripwire connected to a rifle some poachers had set up. He crawled back to the comedor, crying for help.

Somehow he got down the mountain, and was laid up in the hospital for three months. The doctors doubted he'd be able to walk again. His aunt was visiting when the doctors said they were going to have to amputate. His aunt told Miguel's uncle, who was also a curandero, and he came to talk to the doctors.

Don't cut his leg off, he said. Let's see if we can cure him. We'll give him plants.

Miguel's uncle wrapped his leg in bandages soaked in plant macerations. They drank ayahuasca together. He gave Miguel a mixture of twenty-four plants, vines and trees and everything.

I dieted on that mixture for six weeks, Miguel said. No salt, no meat, just beans, peas, quinoa, rice, and that mix of plants.

He stayed in a hut up in the mountains for six weeks, then kept post-dietary restrictions for six months. Later he did a three-month diet on chiric sanango—a strong plant good for bones.

In a dream, he heard: *You had strayed from the plants, and you were punished, but we are healing you.*

They sent the injury so he would come back and learn.

I was cured, Miguel said. I could walk. Look at me now. In that way I understood the power of the plants, and I started taking more plants, and by now I am with the plants.

Szilvia coughed and moaned through most of the night. At the end of the ceremony Miguel called her and Akos in front of him and beat them with his shakapa as she sang.

Chucha, Miguel said. Seems like Szilvia has *susto*.

The word meant fright, but Miguel used it like the name of an ailment.

Tomorrow, he said, Abuelita will massage her.

The next day I heard Luis blow the conch for lunch and walked from my hut up to the comedor. When I arrived, no one was there. Just Ivan, last foreigner let in the park, who lay silent in a hammock with a book.

The women are in the maloca with Abuelita, Luis said. She's giving sobadas.

Sobadas—*rubbings*—were the names for traditional massages. I would eventually get one, too. Abuelita came to my hut, unfolded a heavy wool blanket on the floorboards and had me lay face up. She pressed her strong fingers into my guts. In certain places a sharp pain flared up and I winced.

Sí, she said. Tienes susto.

For Abuelita, I learned, fright was something that lodged in the guts and had to be worked out. If you didn't massage out echoes of fright, all kinds of ailments might develop.

It was the same language of trauma used by Eszter's psychotherapist colleagues and my grad school classmates. Shocks to the fight-flight response that remained embedded in our bodies, radiating through our experience in unseen ways.

As Abuelita massaged me she talked about her daughter back home in Pucallpa, who she'd heard from finally.

A big group of Americans were trapped, Abuelita's daughter said. They heard about the state of emergency and went to the airport, but all the flights were canceled. They camped out in the airport, sleeping on the floor. Abuelita's daughter brought fruit from the market for them. Later she went to buy bread and biscuits, but by the time she got back to the airport the Americans were gone. They'd been loaded on an emergency flight to Lima.

As Abuelita spoke she continued to prod into the depths of my intestines.

I asked her where she'd learned this kind of massage, and she said all the women in her family knew how to rub out fright.

My grandfather was a *chitanero*, she said.

I didn't know the word.

He mixes plants together. If he gives it to someone, they die.

A poisoner, I thought.

Abuelita now slapped me on the belly and asked me to sit up. I faced her and she placed her palms on either side of my head, just above my ears. She began to press and press with all her strength. I thought my skull would crack and my brains would mush out onto the floorboards of the hut. Abuelita with her hands full of brains would cackle like the ispuitino fighting with her man.

But then she slid her hands up and off my head. It was like my flattened head now bounced back into shape. I was done. I felt great.

Szilvia and Eszter emerged from their sobadas and we all sat for lunch. The mosquitos were out in force. Eszter slapped one on her arm so a splat of blood appeared.

I don't want to kill anyone, she said, but as my father used to say: *Off to the light you go!*

Abuelita told us her son is trapped in Lima and needs money to get home, Szilvia said. Perhaps we can collect enough between us to help her.

Sure, I said.

I thought of Abuelita's rhythmic singing, how it pierced the air in the maloca. Akos told me he imagined the world would eventually explode and time would come to an end, but Abuelita's singing would continue to ring out through the emptiness.

With her beautiful face and her laugh, her strong fingers and her piercing voice, we all adored Abuelita. And Eszter and Szilvia—who were both in their different ways working to heal people—began to see her as a true teacher.

When I described Miguel to a friend later, he was taken by the image of his eye.

A blind seer, my friend said.

It was true that with my senses deranged by the medicine, if I stepped out into the moonlight to smoke a mapacho with Miguel, the swelling around his eye seemed to pulse grotesquely.

How could this master of plant medicine allow such a condition to go untreated?

He told me he'd been seated around the fire cooking ayahuasca—just in the shelter down from the comedor where they cooked our plants a few days ago. He was sitting on a log, watching the fire, when a spark shot out from the flame and flew into his eye. He flushed it out and thought he'd cleaned it, but it became irritated and began to swell.

After some months it was swollen completely shut. Nothing helped. Someone who'd come out for a diet recommended a specialist in Lima, but that would cost money. Eventually another student offered to pay for it, so Miguel traveled to Lima to see the specialist. He had minor surgery, but when they removed the bandages, he realized the specialist hadn't treated the cause of the swelling, but had only altered the shape of his eyelid, trying to create some space so he could see. The irritation increased and his situation was even worse.

Another group of students from Spain went so far as to fly Miguel to Barcelona. He had some tests done and was awaiting surgery. But the surgery was postponed and postponed again. Finally he ran out of money and had to fly back to Peru.

Médicos, Miguel said, just want money.

But can't the plant medicine help?

I'm going to try uchu sanango, Miguel said. When I have time I'm going to do a good diet on uchu sanango.

An inconspicuous tree when he pointed it out, I'd already heard Miguel discuss its medicinal properties with much respect.

Muy poderoso, he said. Buena medicina.

Twelve days into that first stint in Juliampampa, with Akos and Szilvia already down the hill, Miguel arrived at 8 a.m. to serve me a morning cup of medicine—another day ceremony. He blew tobacco smoke around the hut, on my chest and head and hands, then we sat to chat before he left.

I'm starting to feel like you all are part of the family, he said.

I told him it was an honor to go through this period of uncertainty together.

He said there was a small wildlife conservation center at the base of the mountain, and one of the staff members had been diagnosed with the virus.

It's getting closer, he said.

He left me alone, and I picked up the book of Li Shangyin. At the back of the collection the editor had included poems by earlier translators. I flipped to one by Lucas Klein called "Twist of the Drugs":

North of Turmeric Hall, but east from the painted towers,
where the medicine's bone-swapping magic works.

I wondered again what it meant to read such lines here, detached in time and across languages. *Bone-swapping.* I thought of games of dominoes on the corners of Washington Heights. I imagined an exchange of hard tissue—what could be learned from that?

I spent the day contemplating the trees and vines, insects and birds. Big woody roots aswirl in different sizes and shapes, chipped and slashed in a complicated embrace. It was impossible to tell where the roots came from, which tree they belonged to. Were they, perhaps, beings unto themselves? Were there woody plants that were not trees or vines in the air but only roots in the ground, rising and falling like wooden sea serpents of the earth?

When the medicine came on, space began to shift, as if the jungle expanded and deepened. I thought about the veil of frustration that had troubled me, whatever it was that had kept the forces within me swirling in confusion, so much work and so little fruition. I wondered if the medicine would help.

The promise of help is so seductive, I thought. We're all so acutely aware of our failings. What if something could make us better?

I saw my father as a child. As an adult he was six foot four. He went to college on a football scholarship and played defensive end. He was a big and loving guy. I saw how he was cast as an athlete in a family of scientists and engineers. He'd grown up with undiagnosed dyslexia, and it was as if I could inhabit his body as letters sometimes shifted and swam across the page. I felt the disorientation it had caused him, that had affected his self-definition, his life choices.

Standing beneath the yanchama tree, alone in the jungle, I felt my vigilance circulate. It was like the urge to care for something, to watch a child. My attention began to circle counterclockwise like a spotlight. I could feel it light up my left side, the visual field but also my shoulder and arm, the jungle nearby, and then circle behind me to reconnect on my right side. This vigilant field circled continuously, and the tingling I often felt now took on this motion, until it stabilized into a constant brightness, left-arm-right-arm, from above and below. I found if I stood still the circling remained constant and complete. My senses felt completely alive. My nose and ears and eyes brightened, the palms of my hands and soles of my feet, but also my lungs and heart. I thought of the intimate exchange happening at every breath, the chemical reactions in my chest, and my heart marking time and managing dynamics, speeding up or slowing down according to my environment or feelings or thoughts.

Hearts and lungs are sense organs like eyes and ears, I realized—mirrors of the jungle within.

What else could I sense? I wondered. Could I pick up on things now that would have been too subtle for my unmedicated body to register? Could I sense the movement of the virus in the valley below?

America, I thought. This southern continent. Infections from elsewhere were inscribed in its history. This was nothing new.

I stood with my feet on the ground, wondering if an echo remained of the first European footstep on this side of the world, when Gerónimo de Aguilar shipwrecked in the Yucatán in 1511. Did that event resonate through the soil? Surely continents were as sensitive as my lungs.

I knew there must have been others, lost sailors who'd washed ashore here, from Africa, from Arabia. But they hadn't been in the service of a royal court, never came back. We never heard their stories, but the continent, I could only assume, remembered.

Miguel stopped by to check on me and I told him I thought I'd understood something. He, as always, took it with a laugh. He sat down on the steps of my hut.

Yacushimbillo can teach you a lot of things, he said, but it can also take you underwater. Its owner is yakuruna.

Miguel often talked about plants having *owners*.

Yakuruna, he said, is a big snake like a boa that lives in the deep river. If yakuruna loves you, it's like the siren, she can take you down to live with her.

But it's good for me?

It can be. I think it will be.

I asked how he knows what plant to give people.

I learned from my father and grandfather, he said. But also from the plants. I get messages during ceremonies; I see what each person needs. The messages come: *Give Brad bobinsana*. It comes to your mind.

I wondered what that might feel like.

Sometimes I see my grandfather, he went on, or my father. My father helped me a lot before he died. He would advise me, tell me what plant to serve. Sometimes he comes to me in a vision and he says *Give Szilvia ajo sacha.*

Before we went down we had a last ceremony in the maloca. It was a clear night with a bright moon, and I spent half of it outside. I watched the moonlight penetrate the branches of the ojé tree above the outhouse. It looked like a coral fan under the sea, its neural branches glimmering in the cool light. The filamental strands of the icaros shot through everything I looked at, like forcefields, energy exchanges, echoes of some Samarkand mosque. At one point mist rolled in from the mountains, enswathing peaks, slicing the moon, coating us with tiny droplets. I was under the spell of Li Shangyin and saw phoenixes perched everywhere. But no—these were fireflies and they were really there, their lights connecting to the filamental webs. It was as if we were given a chance to see the layer of connectivity that undergirds our existence, as real as or realer than we are.

O moon, I thought, bright and shiny moon.

When I went inside and sat on my mat in the darkness, the brilliance of the moon and stars shone under my eyelids. I closed and opened and closed them but the luminosity did not alter.

Brak, Miguel said. Do you want to sing?

I had no idea. To sing? I didn't know how to sing. But yes, I thought. Why not. I opened my mouth and from the depths of my chest some sound came out, something between a moan and a growl and an attempt to hit a pitch. I had no idea what I was doing but it felt good to make sounds. It was like I could move the luminosity by humming and moaning. The tip of my nose and lips still tingled with yacushimbillo. Likely to drool, I must have sounded insane. I could hear Nafis cracking up across the maloca. I didn't blame him for laughing. I'd be laughing, too. But for me it was as if my inner life was now in the room and I could stir it with the sound coming from my chest and throat. If my voice lowered the points of light thickened, and if I were very quiet the motion nearly halted. Some kind of heightened sensitivity. It was like the sounds had to be dragged out of the basement and beaten like rugs. God knows what dust and murk were released into the night air.

What was going on?

Szilvia wasn't around to understand my Serbian-Bosnian language, and maybe because I didn't have a witness I found those were the words that came to me:

O kako sam sretan bio, I sang—*O how happy I was.*

Youth slipping away, the sweetness of doom.

Outside, under the moonlight, the leaf-cutter ants continued their endless march. Each carrying a piece of leaf they'd razored with their jaws, carrying it down into the hole below. It could only be that down there below they were reassembling the trees piece by piece, as if they were turning the whole world inside out.

Miguel called the ceremony to a close and Nelson lit a candle. I was calm but still wide awake. Miguel said we could sleep in the maloca, but I wanted to get back to the yanchama tree. I grabbed my headlight, lit a mapacho, and made my way through the darkened jungle.

As I walked through the dark, alert for snakes on the path, I imagined rounding the large boulder to find some creature seated in the chair in my hut, human-sized but covered in scales or leaves, an elderly being stopped for a brief rest, waiting to talk to me. I thought: we assume the world is known, and only precedented things can happen, but now with everything upside down, we might discover something completely new.

Instead of a leafy senior citizen, I opened the door to my hut, shined my headlamp around, and found a rat on a beam beneath the roof, just above eye level. It was not like the fat sewer rats I watched on subway platforms. It was fist-sized, tawny, with a puff of hair at the end of its long tail. More gerbil than rat, really. But I grabbed the broom and chased it around until I managed to scoot the beast out the door. I relit my mapacho and blew smoke everywhere. Gerbil or not, I did not want to share my house with a rat.

I slept like a stone in a burlap sack and woke up to the sun through the canopy striking me in the face. Clouds rolled in and the air cooled. The rustle of leaves threatened to become a roar, perhaps a storm, but no, it calmed.

Luis blew the conch and we gathered at the comedor. Karen was cutting up papaya and apples and scooping out the luscious flesh of granadillas, but first Miguel set out small bowls of diced tomato, onions, salt, and lime—just a few spoonfuls for Nafis, Eszter and I. He blew smoke on each little bowl and handed them to us. Sour and salty, the first salt we'd had in seventeen days, the sensation was so strong it was like chewing aluminum. The fruit, then a bowl of oatmeal with honey, sweet and luscious. Waves of sensation swept over, as mind-bending as the starry night.

After cutting the diet, Miguel said there were complicated restrictions we'd have to observe the next six weeks.

I'll lay it out for you tonight after dinner, he said.

But today, if we wanted, they would roast another chicken. And there was one last avocado for Nafis. Ivan the late-coming Russian had spent the afternoons since he came in the comedor hammock, recording voice messages, reading *The Power of Now* in Russian. He hadn't said a word to any of us, but now he began to talk. He said he didn't want any of our food. He'd brought his own fruit. He'd eaten nothing but fruit since he arrived.

Eventually, he said, I will stop eating entirely and turn into—he paused, as if wondering whether to tell us—*into light.*

As Ivan turned into light, Karen killed, plucked, and roasted a rooster. We dug a hole under the ojé tree and poured out the dregs from our bottles of bobinsana, yacushimbillo, nina caspi, renaquillo, and chuchuwasha. We tossed in a few lentils, split peas, quinoa, and rice. We all said thanks. Luis blew the conch in the four directions, and that closed the diet.

The next morning we would head down the mountain. I returned to my hut to find the gerbil-rat again taking refuge below my roof. The reality of what we were heading back to started to sink in: New York in lockdown, everything closed. No idea how long we'd be in this lodge at the edge of Tarapoto. Universities closed. People physically apart, further into virtual life with its incipient logistics. What would happen to small businesses with loans and overhead? How many shops would disappear forever? What will the city be like a year from now? Writing? Traveling? Where will it all lead? I took some satisfaction in all that had happened since we'd arrived seventeen days before, but felt a gathering darkness, my personal confusion was laughable in the face of it. I let the gerbil-rat stay.

Nelson and Humberto had gathered everything into enormous packs and loaded them onto their foreheads. They carried not only our bags, but

Miguel's, Abuelita's, also some kitchenware and other things. Karen had four chickens tied by their ankles hanging head-down off a wooden frame slung over her shoulder:

We don't know when we'll be back up in Juliampampa, amigo Brad.

Luis gave us each a walking stick to steady ourselves during the descent. We wore rubber boots to aid us when scrambling over boulders and to provide minimal protection from snakes. Karen with her chickens wore flip-flops. Abuelita, with a smile, walked barefoot.

I found myself again walking with Nafis, listening to his stories.

His father had been an early follower of Elijah Muhammad. He knew and respected Malcolm X but didn't follow him after Malcolm's transformative pilgrimage to Mecca. Nafis's father stayed with the Nation until some time in the nineteen seventies when, before Nafis was born, the whole family, like Malcolm, left the Nation and converted to straight Sunni Islam.

He laughed, remembering his older brother's reaction: *Wait, so white people aren't the devil anymore?*

By the time Nafis was out of diapers he was attending Friday prayers at a mosque in Atlanta, mostly among similar families.

Our post-dietary restrictions forbid many things, but coca was okay, so we were buoyant and chatty with the bitter leaves in our mouths.

Nafis kept on with the description of the community he grew up in:

I came up in a very special brand of Islam, he said. A lot of converts, a lot of people who came from First Resurrection, Nation of Islam. They're converting out of Black churches, where they didn't separate men and women. They grafted their social environment to their religion, so they were Muslim but it was still backyard fundraisers, fish fries.

I'd first encountered Islam in Bosnia, and I was less familiar with American versions of the religion. But Nafis said it wasn't until he joined the marines and deployed to Kuwait that he met other kinds of Muslims. It was there that he'd first encountered Shi'ites. He'd just recently started to find out about Sufism.

I asked if he knew Michael Muhammad Knight's book *Tripping with Allah.*

A white American convert trying to reconcile Islam with his interest in ayahuasca, I described.

Interesting, he said.

Nafis told me his interest in plants had begun taking mushrooms a few years before. He didn't know anyone who was into that kind of thing, but he bought some mushrooms and lay in his bed feeling his body vibrating like a tuning fork, and he began to wonder about what the Qur'an says about the natural and supernatural.

There's the story about Muhammad and the spider, he said. The prophet is on the run from Mecca to Medina and ducks into a cave. Some assassins are searching for him, and they arrive at the cave's mouth right after he's gone in. About to enter, they find a spider has spun its web over the entrance and conclude Muhammad isn't in there, so they move on.

What's the meaning of that spider? Nafis turned back to ask.

Patron saint of narrow escapes, I thought, as we made our way through the trees and vines, down the slippery switchbacks.

Then there's the Night of Power, Nafis went on, when Muhammad was transported to meet all the prophets of the past. And there are stories about djinn—beings of smokeless fire. But what did I know about djinn? You know—I always remember Allah is first, that everything is an aspect of the divine. But I looked around my room. I was a Muslim who kept the fast during Ramadan, but I had Ganesh posters on my wall, a statue of a Buddha with a dragon. I thought: I'm getting far removed.

I could feel Nafis's alarm, remembering this moment.

I got up and took everything down, put those statues away. I needed to clear my mind, clean up my house. That's when I decided not to eat meat.

We stopped at a stream beneath soaring cliffs, where Miguel showed us the water was clean enough to drink.

Cristalín, he called it, bending down to scoop some up in a leaf.

We followed his example and drank from the cool stream, then stepped through the vines and the brush and Nafis went on with his story:

After my divorce, right before I was about to come see Don Miguel the second time, I was in my apartment at night chewing on mushrooms and wondering about things.

He stopped to hold a hand to his chin, in imitation of himself wondering about things.

I know there's an order to the universe, he said. It's like me versus an ant. An ant is one of God's creatures and has every right to be respected and treated as such, but what I do within the world is totally different from what the ant does, even as he does things that are beyond my capability. The truth is just *true*—the source of it is for us to discern. The first word of the Qur'an is *read,* like seek knowledge. Seeking is a good thing—it helps us grow. I thought of a family friend who we saw as kind of clairvoyant. She said she'd received a message for me in specific words. The message was *Forget what you've been taught.*

I saw then that it was in relation to Islam, Nafis said. It meant I might go in directions my parents didn't go. And since then I haven't carried the same burden in my heart.

My resistance to plant medicine had been aesthetic and political, but Nafis had to find peace with the prohibitions of his religion. I wondered what was the difference, and what it said about us. Eszter, walking ahead with Szilvia and Luis, seemed to have no discomfort at all.

The path fell, then rose again, and we stopped for a second to catch our breath. We were at the bank of the river, about to make our way across the boulders, trying not to fall into the rapids. Another huge blue butterfly flitted by, rising up toward the blue of the sky.

And now we're here, Nafis laughed.

Another place where traditions were grafting onto each other, I came to see, contingent on switchbacks of history already acting on us.

We came to the gates of the park. By order of the state of emergency, once we exited we would not be allowed back in. Only members of the community like Nelson and Humberto had permission to come and go. We walked out—it was just the end of March—believing our exit was final.

Luis's father—Miguel's younger brother Liborio—and Miguel's son Jonathan met us at the exit to the park with a couple of mototaxis. We piled in and bumped down the dirt road along the Shilcayo river—the same river we'd been crossing all day, which had now slowed and broadened into a continuous flow—until we got to this wall of yellow bamboo with its wooden gate.

The place was called Las Coconas, after a fat yellow berry that grew in the garden. Miguel opened the gate himself before disappearing.

We've got to get home before curfew, he said.

He told us he'd come check on us the next day. Abuelita went with the Tapullimas. Forbidden by the state of emergency from returning to Pucallpa, she would stay with Miguel and his wife in their house in Tarapoto.

Las Coconas was a cluster of screened-in bungalows spanning both sides of the dirt road and encircling a pair of open kitchens and a reception area. It was meant to house around sixty people. We thought it would be just us, but the woman who led us to our places—a sunny, brown-haired woman named Teodora—told us another group of guests had arrived the night before.

Kicked out of Sachawasi, she said.

Teodora explained that Sachawasi was a famous retreat center just next door, where people undergo months-long treatments for serious addiction.

People come for nine months, she said. But it just closed down overnight and everyone had to leave, so we let a group of them come here.

She told us the people let out of Sachawasi would use one kitchen, and we would share the other with her and her boyfriend Jorge, the owner's son.

Is that Miguel's friend? I asked.

We're all friends with Miguelito, Teodora smiled. As far as I'm concerned, he saved my life.

Her Spanish was very natural, with an accent I wasn't familiar with. It turned out she was Romanian, from Constanza, the old Black Sea port south of the Danube Delta. She'd been living in Madrid, working as a physical therapist, when she started to have an awful weakness in her arms. Doctors diagnosed her with a rare condition. Oxygen wasn't penetrating her bones, so her marrow was turning black and dying. The doctors said she faced the possibility of regular bone marrow transplants—a risky and invasive procedure. More likely, they told her, she faced amputation.

She got us settled in, showed us the police registration documents, led us to the kitchen, and went on with her story.

She'd been to Peru once before but had a terrible experience. She'd wanted to try ayahuasca but had ended up with some charlatans who'd driven her out somewhere, dropped her off with a cup of medicine and a bluetooth speaker playing recorded icaros. They said they'd come back for her the next day, but by the time they arrived she was nauseous, dehydrated, terrorized.

They dropped her off in Tarapoto and she somehow found her way to Las Coconas. She'd told the whole story to Jorge's father as he repaired the roof of her bungalow. She left Peru swearing never to come back, but once she was back in Madrid she received a note from Jorge—who she hadn't even met.

He was very sorry to hear about her experience, he said. He knew a good curandero who uses the medicine to cure disease. If she ever comes back, he'll connect her.

Now, desperate, faced with bone marrow transplants and amputations, she wrote to him about her situation, asked if his curandero friend might help her.

Jorge consulted with Miguel and told her to come.

She arrived and Miguel took her up to Juliampampa. He prepared compresses for her—raw cotton soaked in plant infusions. He gave her renaquillo, another plant called uña de gato, eventually chiric sanango.

Chiric sanango is what really cured me, she said.

She went back to Madrid, to her doctors there, who were dumbfounded.

This is impossible! they said. How did this happen?

By then, Teodora and Jorge had grown close, and she longed to be back in the jungle, near these people who'd cured her. When we met her she'd been here four years. She was practicing acrobatics. Her arms were strong. It was the best advertisement for Miguel I could think of.

Las Coconas—a walled garden of cats and birds. Most mornings a crew of squirrel-sized tamarin monkeys scampered through, hanging from roof-beams, checking for fruit left carelessly out on the kitchen table. Jaru the cat stalked the garden chasing lizards. A family of toucans nested at the garden's far end. I'd never seen their huge colorful beaks in the wild or heard toucans cry—a sound like the mewing of kittens. I learned they're intelligent as crows, and their spectacular but awkward-looking beaks are lightweight and razor sharp.

Miguel explained that the first days after cutting the diet were very important. Our bodies were sensitive and the plants were still working in us. We needed to be careful what we took in.

Your diet is like a newborn baby, Miguel said, and you have to protect it.

For every day we'd lived saltless, on beans and rice and our plant infusions, we needed to live for three times as many days under restriction. That meant, most importantly, no alcohol, spice, pork, or sex—all powerful forces that would disrupt our requisite placidity. But the restrictions went far beyond that, especially on these first days: no sugar, coffee, black pepper, dairy, nothing fermented. Nuts that were too oily would make us sick. The acid in citrus or other sour fruits would halt the medicinal effects. That meant avoiding the deliciously gloppy maracuyás that were in season. These additional restrictions would taper off over the next month and a half.

Our group being dominated by Hungarians, we decided that first night to cook a huge chicken soup. We went down the block and came back with everything we needed. Soon we put that Cocona kitchen to work.

All foreigners in Peru were supposed to be accounted for, but we'd been up in Juliampampa when the order went out, so were unregistered. Jorge was supposed to alert the police of our presence but instead backdated our check-in and when the inspector came by he said we must have been gone last time he passed. That made it official. By order of the state of emergency we were to be back in the lodge every day by 6:00 p.m. No one—Peruvian or foreigner—was allowed to move house or travel to other cities.

There were international flights from Lima, but in order to get there we'd have to hire a private car and driver, request government permission, and make the twenty-hour drive over the Andes. In Lima, we heard, we would struggle to get a room—everything was closed down. If we did find somewhere to stay we'd exist in lockdown conditions until we could get on one of the US government's so-called *humanitarian flights*. But unlike other countries, the US expected its citizens to pay for their humanitarianism. The State Department did not announce the cost of the flights, so rumors circulated on social media—a group quickly formed called Americans Stuck in Peru. We heard that before boarding we'd have to sign documents pledging to pay for the flight when the bill came. It would be in the next six months, and we'd have another six months to pay. If we didn't pay, a hold would be put on our passports. People claimed the tickets cost fifteen hundred dollars a head, maybe two grand.

If we managed to find a car and driver, the trip to Lima alone would cost two thousand dollars. A hotel in Lima—for how long?—surviving under lockdown, then the flights; Eszter and I calculated that for the two of us, in the best scenario, it would cost six thousand dollars to get back to New York.

And for what?—to be locked down in our one-bedroom apartment. Friends told us about sirens day and night, shortages of basic goods, prices escalating. Who knew how long this would last. With its vile government and well-armed citizenry, America sounded like the worst place in the world to await a dystopian meltdown.

Better stay where we were, we thought, with the rain and the river and Jaru the cat. There was a fruit stand down the block, a family that sold chickens and eggs. The market was still open in town about a half hour's walk away, even the supermarket, though at the entrance to each there were uniformed guards aiming gun-like instruments at your chest or forehead to check for fever.

We found a box store at the edge of town that was open, and Akos bought a hundred-and-fifty-dollar laptop. He installed Zoom and began having meetings, sending emails.

I can do whatever I need to do from here, he realized.

For Szilvia it was more difficult. She'd spent the last years working in an Upper East Side lab studying the neurodegenerative condition known as Huntington's disease. She worked long hours with her arms in sleeves dropping genetic material into a petri dish and monitoring results. Huntington's disease usually shows in middle age or after, but Szilvia and her team had experimented on stem cells just a few days old that carried the genetic marker. Though symptoms manifest later in life, the condition could already be identified in the womb. They were finalizing work on their experiment, preparing to publish it as a paper in a scientific journal. It would be a major milestone in Szilvia's career. No minor discovery, it might revolutionize the way the disease was treated and lead to other discoveries as well. But in order to finish the work, she needed to put all her data in order, and that was not easy to do on a cheap laptop from the Tarapoto box store, over the spotty connectivity at Las Coconas.

But Szilvia was not complaining. She was very happy to be working as best she could from the hammock, strolling to the fruit stand down the way, living with the animals and birds. She said life in the lab had closed her heart, and she felt renewed here, alive. Like Akos and I after the first day ceremony, she'd been given back her humanity.

What had the plant medicine done to her scientific mind? I wondered whether she would see something different in her results, glimpsing them through this window in the jungle.

Eszter, meanwhile, was swamped in logistics. When we left she'd been working out of two different offices in New York, which meant now she'd be paying Manhattan rent for two offices that were not only closed but a continent away. So as it became clear we weren't going back she made pleading calls and managed to get herself taken off one lease, then the other. Her clients wrote and were happy to meet online and so she found a sheltered corner of the garden and began seeing clients. A friend of ours needed a workspace and asked to use our apartment as an office, which would help minimize our expenses.

Once the panic of the first days of lockdown passed, we came to feel very lucky. We had a garden to loll in and river to swim in, with the jungle all around us and only the mountains behind.

Vultures circled above the Shilcayo. What appeared at first to be a corpse lying athwart shallow rapids was a large red stone with a coconut resting in its crevice. A yelp like a dog in pain was another voice of the toucan. It had hardly rained all week and the river was low and clear.

Despite the state of emergency with its strict shelter-at-home order, a family had come to wash. Children splashed, their father washing some colorful plastic sheeting while their mother watched in front of a small speaker playing pop music with lyrics in English. Up the hill from the river, a bikini top dried on a plastic chair.

On a boulder nearby, seven feet above the riverbed, Nafis had taken a seat as he'd done every day since we came down. Cross-legged, shirtless, burn scars on his right shoulder, his name tattooed in Arabic letters across his back, he lowered his chin, stretched out his arms, and began to chant:

HAR—har-AY—har-EE

He chanted for an hour or more, those repetitive syllables echoing through the yellow bamboo as it bent and clacked in the wind. It was a chant he'd learned in New Mexico when he was visiting his girlfriend right before he came. He committed to doing those chants for forty days, and we got used to the sound, learned to connect it with the afternoon.

We'd been here a couple of weeks, making twice-weekly trips to town for supplies, but otherwise lolling in our hammocks or dunking ourselves in the water. Eszter and I shared her computer. As long as connectivity held she saw clients online, and between her sessions I worked at my various jobs—writing a book about ocean exploration which doubled as my dissertation, researching traces of Mae West in Harlem for a Scottish filmmaker, and using my terminally inadequate Arabic to interpret a ninth-century Iraqi thieves ode called "Song of the Banu Sasan":

We're the best of the best on land or at sea
Our stallions pound the earth worldwide

We summer where it's cool and winter under date palms

We respect no authority so no one doubts our supremacy

Within a few days of our arrival at Las Coconas, the patients let out of Sachawasi managed to get on flights back to Europe, and Teodora and Jorge moved us across the road to the rooms they'd vacated. There was just one patient remaining—a well-built Frenchman with golden curls who paced the garden making phone calls.

He'd been in the center for several months, he told us, but was only halfway through his treatment. Now he had to get home, but what was he going home to?

Impossible, he repeated. Impossible.

I never learned what he'd gone in for—a serious addiction? He looked physically healthy but frantic. His nervous system was like a frayed shirt. But with the pandemic, everything upside down, who could blame him? As he gestured nervously amid the flowering bushes, I buried myself in Arabic dictionaries, looking up obscure words and struggling to form legible phrases. With everything so uncertain, the struggle to make sense of those poetic boasts served as ballast for my mind, seeming to echo or invert the desperation of the moment:

We're every madman and madwoman with charms at their throats

with dangling earrings and leather-brass cuffs

all the scammers and hucksters and ranters passing hats

all the plate-lickers and scrap-scroungers crying *Help me I'm cold!*

Our neighbor eventually got on a flight home—it seemed the French weren't asking their citizens to sign away their passports. He packed his bag, spat out his goodbyes, and was gone. Now it was just the five of us—Szilvia, Akos, Eszter, Nafis, and I—along with Teodora and Jorge and two staff members who lived across the street: Teresa who cooked and cleaned and her husband Viviano, the gardener. They were born and bred Tarapoteños—Jorge had grown up in Lima—so it was with Teresa and Viviano that we accustomized ourselves to the swooping melodies and Quechua-infused vocabularies of Tarapoteño Spanish.

We checked in with our families, moved our lives online, and adjusted to the simplicity of daily life between Tarapoto and the jungle.

Eszter and I had been through so much together over the years—adrift in Mexico and Istanbul, hustling in New York. We'd been consistent and we'd been passionate, but with her stunned by childlessness and me feeling frustrated with writing and struggling with my depressive, anxiety-ridden tendencies, we'd both begun to roam in our own worlds. We'd always traveled separately—easy independence was one of the virtues of our relationship—but recently that independence had acquired a new flavor.

I'd been fatalistic about children and childlessness. I didn't know I'd be happy to have a kid until we lost our first pregnancy. For Eszter I felt the decision to definitively give up the dream of motherhood made her weightless. Who would she be now that her sense of purpose had been scrambled? She'd been despondent but also in a way thrilled, open to the new. She'd always been open to the new, it was her character, but now that openness might lead to flailing or flourishing, something new to devote herself to. It was impossible not to ask who we would be to each other now that all the parameters were different. Before we'd come I'd wondered if our time here might reveal a reason to go on or to separate.

But lockdown asserted itself and Eszter and I had to make quick decisions, digest our circumstances, deal with practicalities and stomach how strange it all was. If not already by the time Nelson and Humberto were pulling hedgehog quills out of the cascade pool, definitely by the time we were installed in Las Coconas, we were firmly in cahoots. Playing it by ear, adapting to the unforeseen—it was what we were best at. Eszter approached challenges with a light heart and boundless optimism. She was the best of companions.

Up in Juliampampa Eszter and I had sat on opposite sides of the maloca and stayed in huts fifteen minutes walk from each other. Now in Las Coconas though we shared a room we slept in separate beds. It was key to the post-dietary restrictions, which we intended to take seriously. So with physical contact between us restricted and our circumstances so unusual, it was easy to put aside questions of who we were to each other. What remained was the warm, trusting, joyful friendship we'd always shared.

There was a shortage of medical staff in Tarapoto, and Teodora told us an organization dispatching doctors from other parts of the country had called. They wanted to rent the entire lodge. Twenty doctors for two months. They'd work shifts at the hospital and rest here. We lived with that possibility, that our idyll at the jungle's edge might become a medical encampment, but it didn't happen. They never appeared.

A relief, we had to admit.

On May 1, a novel I'd written was set to be published. It was my first book to come out in the US, after many years of struggle and rejection. I'd planned a launch at a bookstore downtown with a beloved writer-mentor, and there was to be an afterparty in a basement bar on Bleeker St. After that I had a few other launch events lined up in Boston, Princeton, Philadelphia. Now I was here and all that was canceled. Instead I set up

Eszter's computer in a corner of Las Coconas and talked into the camera, as friends and family tuned in from Kansas City, from New York, from Berlin, from Istanbul. I'd never experienced anything like it. I talked and listened for an hour or so, overwhelmed by this rare concatenation of close people scattered everywhere, then shut the laptop and I was back in the jungle. Night had fallen and I went to the kitchen where the others were finishing prep for our evening meal.

Akos woke up in the morning feeling sick to his stomach—no symptoms of COVID, we concluded. We called Miguel to see if perhaps he'd inadvertently broken the rules of the diet. Miguel was always warning us to take it very seriously.

Your stomach might swell up, he'd say.

Now he asked no questions but showed up right away. He had Akos smoke a mapacho and hold the tobacco smoke in his lungs—three deep inhalations. Then he prepared him an infusion of ginger, lemon, oregano, and a medicinal cinnamon that grew wild in the mountain. He sang to the cup and handed it to Akos, who drank it down and felt better right away.

Eszter felt similar symptoms the next day, and he came again.

Who knows what this is!

He boiled cinnamon and tobacco in a bit of water for five minutes, sang to it, and had her drink it. Like Akos, she felt better immediately, and whatever it was, that was the end of it. No one else had symptoms, and it was heartening to feel cared for by Miguel.

Teresa came by and told us the police had raided a curfew-violating party in Lima. Such a huge party, she said, that in the chaos of the raid thirteen people were stampeded to death running for exits.

People here love to party, she shrugged.

And we are every beggar with a bent spine
and every beggar who pretends to be deaf
and all the mutilated beggars with their hacked off hands
and the roadside gangs—those lords of dust
and all those Bible-reading zealots who pretend to convert
and whoever passes out water claiming descent from Muhammad
or flubs their tongue like a Bedu or tricks pilgrims or fakes blindness
or babbles all through afternoon prayers

Unable to travel back to her hometown, with nothing to do, Abuelita often came by to visit us in the afternoon. She sat in the garden embroidering or taught Eszter and Szilvia how to give sobadas. A month into lockdown, Miguel came by and said that he, Abuelita, Luis, his son Jonathan, and Jorge were going to go up to Juliampampa to diet. Miguel was supposed to have a group, but by now all his groups had canceled through the end of the year.

What are we going to do? he wondered.

We heard that six people had died in Tarapoto the previous Saturday.

How many died today? we wondered.

Miguel would take advantage of the opportunity to see if he could cure the swelling in his eye. He and Luis would diet on uchu sanango. Jorge and Jonathan would take ajo sacha. Abuelita would take renaquillo. They would stay for two weeks.

At the beginning of *Locus Solus*, Raymond Roussel recounts a story he attributes to Ibn Battuta. He describes a young, just, and benevolent queen ruling Timbuktu who's beset by mental illness. When the symptoms take over, her benevolence disappears and instead she raves and orders executions and crop burnings. Out of respect for her the citizenry obey these orders and suffer the consequences. Desperate for help, the queen's subjects gather around a sculpture of a child made of soil gathered by all the surrounding communities. Representing their collective earth, they implore the idol to heal their queen. A storm passes and gales batter the city. A few days after the storm, a small flowering plant begins to grow from the sculpture—a seed implanted by the wind. People gather its flowers and prepare a tea for the queen, who is healed.

Now, in the uncertainty unleashed by a global pandemic, the world turned upside down, Miguel would take this small group up the mountain, and with the help of what he knew from his father and grandfather, try to heal himself. I imagined some Amazonian *Decameron* with them entertaining each other through the jungle afternoons with stories of sex and magic and betrayal, Miguel and Abuelita with their characteristic laughs.

¡Chucha!

I walked into Tarapoto and found a bookstore and bought a book of stories by Róger Rumrrill. A regional author, his stories depicted life along the Ucayali and Huallaga rivers. The collection was called *El viborero*, and the title story described a man with the power to hypnotize poisonous snakes with his gaze. He travels along the river and into the jungle and eventually gains fame for his talent. People call him to rid them of infestations.

The viborero is called to a house where a beautiful young woman is being threatened by a snake. He asks where her husband is, and she says he's in the jungle working. The viborero tracks the husband, hypnotizes a snake and orders it to kill the man. Then he explains to the wife: I'm very sorry I wasn't able to save your husband but let me stay and protect you. He and the beautiful woman start a life together, have a child, and the viborero is happy. But then he meets a snake he's unable to hypnotize. The snake sneaks by him and kills his wife and child. The viborero is driven mad by grief. He lives for many year alone in the jungle, studying the plants and preparing rejuvenating potions for himself. He becomes like a young man, flooded with libido, seducing young girls claiming to protect them from snakes. Until a man comes across the viborero with his ten-year-old daughter and calls the police, who arrest him and imprison him. The man spends his last years in prison with the lust of a twenty year-old coursing through his eighty-year-old body.

The Banu Sasan, no doubt, would have recognized him as one of their own.

We are the beggar boys—those beardless youths
dressed in white and acting like idiots
and we're the lech who leads one of them off
so hungry he'll eat drug-spiked stew

Miguel, Abuelita, and the rest came down after two weeks in Juliam-pampa. Miguel's eye was improved but not healed.

I received a message, he said, that I will need at some point to diet on uchu sanango for one month. That's what I need to heal.

Luis said the medicine had caused him to faint. Miguel had served him a cup of uchu sanango one morning, and he felt his consciousness slip away. In the dream-state that followed, the plant's spirit appeared to him.

See, the plant said, this is what can happen. When you start to serve uchu sanango, give no more than this.

Luis came out of his reverie and felt edified.

Coming down the mountain they found Tarapoto in turmoil. This was an area where most households didn't have a refrigerator. Families needed to go to the market every day to get what they needed, also to sell what they had. That's how life functioned. But the government would hardly let people out of their houses. No one was allowed down to the river—we could only go because we stayed right next to it—but that's where people washed and did their laundry. And still, with the strictest measures in place, the virus spread. Numbers in Tarapoto were worse than across the border in Brazil, where there were no measures at all. People were getting sick, people were dying. And those who weren't dying were hungry, poor, unwashed, getting sick from other things.

At first local travel was forbidden to keep the virus out. But now with numbers so high, local travel was forbidden to keep the virus in. Which meant Abuelita still wasn't allowed to go home. So she was back at Miguel's house, driving Miguel's wife crazy.

She's always out around town, Miguel's wife said. She'll bring the virus here.

But Abuelita needed to survive, too. The only thing she had was her embroidery. So she was wandering around, hoping to avoid the police and find someone to buy her embroidery. We all bought pieces from her. Too many.

The dirt road that ran past Las Coconas swerved through the jungle and dead-ended at the entrance to the National Park, now closed by order of the state of emergency. If I laced up running shoes and jogged up there, I reached the gate in twenty minutes. The road was called Prolongación Alerta, and it ran past a closed down orchid greenhouse and the animal reserve called Urku, where the first case of COVID in the area had been reported. It ran past a luxury retreat center called Serpentina—no doubt named after the twisting curves of the Shilcayo River. The retreat center was closed, too, of course, but Miguel knew the owner of that place, so he arranged to hold a ceremony there.

We gathered in Serpentina's maloca, which was beautifully constructed of tropical hardwood, with its pitched roof not of corrugated iron but expertly assembled palm thatch. The floorboards shone with lacquer and to each side were bathrooms of shining marble. I thought of Eszter and me laughing as we scrolled through Istanbul apartment ads, where such facilities were inevitably called *Hilton bathrooms*. It was bizarre to remember that here. The maloca sat atop a hill, surrounded on three sides by jungle, but with a sloping garden in front of it, a path lined with solar lamps leading through rustic bungalows similar to what we stayed in but elevated to exquisite comfort. It was empty except for a guard who sat near the wall by the road.

We gathered there—Miguel, Abuelita, Luis, Eszter, Szilvia, Akos, Nafis and me. It felt like a family reunion. Miguel served us medicine and turned out the lights and we sat in the darkness like in Juliampampa. Abuelita collapsed in a heap early on. She didn't sing and hardly moved the entire night.

Nafis tried to sing but his usual gleeful sounds dissolved into incoherence. At some point he let out a wail of grief. Miguel's singing alone carried us, and I found myself sitting up on my mat, eventually with a growing need to get up for a piss. My thoughts would circulate from the grieving sounds of Nafis, the state of the world, Miguel's singing, my need to piss. The pleasant cycling I'd felt during the day ceremony now felt like a kind of madness. I wondered when need would outweigh entropy and I'd have to make my way to one of the Hilton bathrooms. The cycling of thoughts felt like a doom-loop—a lost soul seeking escape through end-less lifetimes, relentless through rising intensity, virus spreading outside, the darkness, the sounds of the insects, my body with its needs and pres-sures. Virus-darkness-piss-virus-darkness-piss.

Bing!

Someone tapped on my back.

Bing!

It happened again.

I knew no one was actually there, but whatever it was had roused me from my trance. My cycling thoughts scattered, the chain that linked one to the other broke and opened up. Helium filled my brain and I let out a gleeful laugh, a laugh buried inside a sob erupting from the doom-loop's release. I could feel laughter wrack my body, shaking my spine, a tone of sorrow and mourning inseparable from laughter.

I still did not get up to piss.

When Miguel called the ceremony to an end, Abuelita managed to pull herself up from the floor. Everyone was quiet.

What's this virus? Miguel asked. Is it a plague from God? What's its message?

Later I stood outside on the deck in front of the maloca with Miguel and Luis.

Do you smell that? Miguel asked.

The palms? I asked. The scent of thatch was nostalgic to me. It reminded me of Mexico.

No, Miguel said. Not the palms, something else, something rotten, burning, growing, trying to kill us. Do you smell it?

I don't think so, I said.

Luis was silent.

This virus makes me want to laugh, Miguel said, but I also have to stop to realize what's going on.

I heard in China, Luis said, normality has returned.

It's not true, I said. Normality is finished.

We all laughed, but the sorrow and mourning was in this laughter, too, because we knew it was true.

It was like with strong psychedelics—in the middle of the experience you ask yourself when this will end. When will I be normal again? Then you realize it may shift, relinquish its intensity, but you will never be normal again. That way of being is over.

Miguel said it seemed to him like a kind of war.

They say it comes from the war in Iraq, he said. When the Americans bombed the Iranian general last January.

This made sense to me. A miasma off the invasion of Iraq. All the ignorance and ordnance of that war wafted through the world like poison gas.

What do you think? Miguel asked.

I told him I thought it was a product of the interconnectedness of the world.

When the Spanish came to the Americas people died by the millions of the flu and other diseases. But the flu had been developing in Europe and Asia over tens of thousands years. Now someone gets sick in Wuhan and a few weeks later a person dies just down the street on Prolongación Alerta.

Szilvia said we have better remedies: anti-viral medications, respirators, and we understand better how diseases spread. But the problem is we have to stop business and make decisions on some logic other than money, distribute food and resources so people can survive.

Miguel said people were robbing oxygen from the hospitals in Tarapoto, stealing money meant to distribute food and medicines.

That's what it comes down to, we all agreed. Short-term thinking, valuing money over life.

Chucha, Miguel said.

Luis now began to talk about his vision. He said he couldn't sing throughout the ceremony.

I was battling death, he said. I was being interrogated. They were asking me: *Where is the virus? Where is the virus?* And the answer eventually came: *The virus is you.*

He was the virus, Luis told us, so instead of singing, he imagined himself going out into space to some faraway planet and burying the virus there and cleaning himself and cleaning himself until it was safe for him to come back.

It's like a poker game, Nafis said. If you don't know who the virus is, the virus is you.

And we're the astrologers with their omens and signs
who read astrolabes and furnace flames and shout *The end is nigh!*

EARTHQUAKE SEASON

Here beneath the yanchama tree nights are dark and loud. Frogs and insects, animal calls and animal movements. Rocks tumbling in the gorge, winds rising, spatterings of rain. Asleep, awake, on the mattress, in the hammock. Poking around near the hut by flashlight, attentive to nocturnal snakes. Sometimes aiming the flashlight into the canopy or off into the surrounding density.

Are those eyes?

Inside the hut with the flashlight off and the candles blown out, beneath the croaks and buzzes, falling rocks and rising winds, there emerges a wakeful cocoon, an insistent pulse.

Night settles, frog croaks darken, footsteps recede.

An enveloping fog of sound, a wavering mist. The resonant tensions of the planet, tectonic plates about to strike and slip.

May through June, we've heard, is earthquake season.

Is that the grinding in my jaw and brain?

Clouds collapse and fragment, motion within motion. Momentum and gravity drawing arcs and spirals, particles accrete into disks and balls, planetesimals in motion. Clumps of earth, stone, heavy materials concentrating, densifying, settling together, sucked or packed or pulled or falling toward the spinning center.

Even now in the loud darkness, the tension and the spinning are not abstractions but some radiant effect of the beginning of things, the ongoing life of things. Body and tissue, soil and stone and forces of matter, pressure and pleasure. Submerged, inseparable, a grinding crucible, one, now, always. It becomes solid enough to lie down in.

May into June the state of emergency showed no sign of lifting, so we packed our bags and cleared our schedules. Miguel assured us it would be no problem to enter the closed down park, and sure enough they waved us through as we headed back up to Juliampampa.

We know everyone, he said.

We'd watched the murder of George Floyd with horror if not surprise, that intolerable snuff that drove everyone onto the street. Soon the Minneapolis police station was in flames, patrol vans upended in Ft. Greene. In my home town of Kansas City, the name of a racist real estate developer my great-grandfather had worked for was finally stripped from street signs and city memorials.

Nafis and I talked about it every day. We all did. But us, the only two Americans there, and spanning the color line, it was a pedal point between us. We returned to it through that season in Las Coconas, along with the rains and animals, me translating at the table, his afternoons on the boulder.

I try not to see footage of those killings, Nafis said. I don't want to feel all that rage.

I didn't want to watch the Godawful snuff either, but through that desperate season, the stasis of lockdown, the protests brought a strange optimism. The pressure so great, injustice so undeniable, maybe something would happen.

We'd been sucked into our screens, made calls to check in, but now it was time to disconnect for a while.

I'd heard from my old friend Khaled, who'd passed me the silver wine ladle in the Tbilisi basement. He and his wife and young son lived above a funeral parlor in Harlem. Khaled said now there were lines out the door day and night, one funeral after another. And the sirens, my God.

I imagined him trying to shield little Walid from the sound. Answering questions about what it all meant.

They'd all got sick right away, he said, before they even knew what was going on. In the flush of fever he dreamed of the jasmine bushes that grew by his childhood home in Damascus.

For us, the morning after another four-hour climb into the high jungle, we stood puking over the stone wall. I drank rosasisa and imagined letting everything go, barfing all the sorrow and confusion, all the implicatedness out of my body.

We sat with Miguel in the maloca at night. He opened a ceremony by taking stock of our situation.

He told us seventy people died in Tarapoto that week. Hospital overcrowded, farmers unable to bring crops to market. So they can't sell, can't buy, a chain of dependent clauses.

Families have hoisted the white flag, Miguel said.

The great cumbia bandleader Tulio Trigoso, a Tarapoto celebrity since the 1980s, died of COVID the day we walked up. He was seventy-four. All the respirator tanks had been sold on the black market and doctors couldn't scrounge one fast enough.

Miguel also took a moment to remember his neighbor Don Pancho:

I saw him working in the garden—*¡Hola Don Pancho!* A week later he's dead.

Then he asked permission to hold a ceremony from the animals and spirits of the mountain and jungle, from the curanderos of the past, and from Nuestro Señor Jesucristo.

Miguel sang. Luis sang in his free and searching style. We listened to Abuelita pierce the atmosphere for a while. Miguel's son Jonathan was with us for the first time. He'd been on a tear down in Tarapoto, driving a moto-taxi, drinking and smoking too much, who knows what else. He was in his early twenties, about Luis's age, but hadn't shown any interest in following the family tradition. With lockdown he'd come up with his father and dieted for the first time. Now here he was with us. He strummed a couple of chords on an old guitar and sang in a high voice, sweet but with a mischievous edge.

I stepped outside into the starry night and found Miguel zipping up after a piss, now looking at the sky above the comedor.

See, he pointed, those two bright stars.

I followed his gaze.

They like to appear when we have ceremonies.

Then he motioned to the thick jungle up the slope from us. He said he'd seen an animal in there, some kind of tigrillo, during their diet in May.

Right now there were lights blinking between the trees.

Diablitos, Miguel said with a laugh. Sometimes they come close.

He went back inside and I was alone. The mountains sloped down to the valley below, where the lights of Tarapoto twinkled, where the pandemic was wreaking havoc. Corpses laid out on concrete. Sacrifices of lockdown for nothing. The rest of the world with its precincts in flames.

Here in Juliampampa the maloca's high-pointed roof silhouetted against the glowing sky. Behind it the ojé tree with its neural circuitry reached up into the night. And beyond that the slope toward the peaks, the surrounding density of the high jungle. The clover-covered field gave way to thick vines and trees, everything covered in hojarasca—that layer of dead leaves and branches and fallen vines that constantly decayed, home to all kinds of insects breaking things down so the soil was constantly renewed, overflowing with fertility, shoots of new trees, new vines, new densities.

Looking further into the darkness I could see flickerings among the trees. I knew somewhere in there more ayahuasca vines grew, and ajo sacha vines, chacruna bushes, an uchu sanango tree, sprouting clusters of hierba luisa we drank all day in our tea. Beyond that the wild jungle grew as it always had.

I thought of Khidr, *the green one,* the riddler-saint of Muslim legend who appears in times of need. I remembered the ceremony in Serpentina, when excruciating mental cycles encircled my need to piss, which I could observe but couldn't control. I remembered the *ping*—that tap on the back that had broken the circuit—how grateful I was for it.

Alone outside the maloca gazing at Tarapoto and the ojé tree, my attention settled on the blackness of the jungle with its flickering that might have been fireflies or effects of chacruna, and my mind was an open palm palpating the world around me for some order, some reason to connect one thing to another.

Was that ping, I wondered, a visit from Khidr?

In the morning I heard pounding from the comedor—Nelson macerating plants. Or perhaps their cousin Ermojines who'd taken Humberto's place on the way up.

Miguel had discussed the plants he'd give us back in Las Coconas. For Nafis, he would prepare uchu sanango—the same plant he'd given himself and Luis during their diet in May. A powerful plant, Miguel said he only offered it to experienced students, and Nafis was the most experienced among us.

Eszter was gaining experience, too, and Miguel would give her chiric sanango. Szilvia would take nina caspi.

Eszter and I had spent the long afternoons in Las Coconas talking about what the plants we'd dieted on had done to us.

When I met Eszter she'd been in rehearsals for a dance performance, at the same time she was deep in postgraduate work in neuroscience. She stayed in an apartment overlooking the Danube with no furniture except a thin mattress on the floor. She managed to come off as composed and bright while living on whiskey, Marlboro lights, and dry Hungarian rolls. We'd stay out all night, and she'd wake up late for call time at the theater. From there she'd rush off to gather data or meet faculty somewhere, discuss how her findings could help design rehabilitation regimes for stroke victims. She gave people little beanbags to throw at a target, then certain participants only imagined doing so. Marking the varying outcomes, she was able to quantify the imagination's effect on the body.

What did all that was flooding our imaginations here do to us? And what of the subtle effects of the plants we were drinking?

Eszter felt nina caspi's fire had thawed her nervous system. It gave her healthy aggression, sharpened her ability to act. Raised in a conflict-avoidant family, now she felt she would brook no bullshit. What would happen to Szilvia?

Akos and I would take ajo sacha, the jungle garlic that Szilvia had taken on the March diet.

A very delicious, odoriferous plant, Miguel said.

He'd pointed out ajo sacha to us a few times already, its skinny stem sometimes rising up five feet or so, sometimes curling up close to the ground. The stems were hairy with moss at the base and splotchy with lichens above—a yellowish color like bee pollen—here and there sprouting leaves in groups of four. If you snap them they smell strongly of garlic.

We'd drink an infusion of the pulped roots of a five-year-old plant.

My father and grandfather took ajo sacha to cure the body, Miguel said. If you have pains here or there, it gets rid of pains.

Miguel patted his body to show places you might feel pain.

But then after taking it, he went on, we looked to see what else ajo sacha could be used for. When you can't relax, when your mind is too unsettled, ajo sacha can help calm the mind. We saw it can help people get off cocaine.

I told him I was smoking too many mapachos, and he said while I drank ajo sacha I should smoke one every night before I slept and no more.

It helps with addiction, Miguel said, because it reduces your mental activity. Ajo sacha calms you when you don't know what to do, when you're exhausted. But if you don't respect it, it can have bad effects.

We'd heard these speeches before. And we'd shown we could respect the diet. We'd meticulously observed the tapering off of restrictions after the last round of plants.

I don't give it to people I don't think will respect it, Miguel said. I might see in advance—*don't give it to that person. They may be affected by sorcery.* It's not easy to get rid of a problem like that. But if you use ajo sacha properly you can take those things out, too—if someone has a bad spirit stuck in their body and can't get it out. You have to know what you're doing. It's important to keep your mind tranquil when you diet on ajo sacha. Don't think too much.

Miguel would repeat these warnings:

When it's over, if you eat chili and drink alcohol, or eat too much meat, there can be problems. There's a small bird called an urfa that makes its nest with lots of sticks, no leaves at all. They like to eat them in Lamas. If you're dieting on ajo sacha and you eat an urfa it's certain you'll get hexed.

Miguel poured Akos and me a shot of the puce liquid, which tasted strongly of garlic. We promised not to eat any small birds.

Now we've dieted together, he said, so we're connected. If you're not respecting the restrictions I can feel it. It comes as a message during a ceremony. I might ask the plant how things are going. When you were dieting on bobinsana I could sing her icaro and ask how you're doing. Are you respecting the diet? She told me you're doing very well. It comes as a message. Then I know.

In the evening by the yanchama Miguel arrived to serve me my evening cup of ajo sacha, then blew mapacho smoke around the hut. He walked out to the enormous tree—*el arbolito*, he calls it—and blew smoke up its trunk, then tossed the mapacho butt into the leaves at its base. He looked up at the tree for a moment then gave a short laugh:

Está bien.

Miguel had known the tree all his life, since his father and grandfather began bringing him here. I asked if he knew how old it was.

You remember the last end of the world?

What?

The last end of the world, he said. That's how old.

I cased the hut at night before sleeping, fumigating it with tobacco, including the bed and covers. Another small black scorpion crawled out from under the bed, and I crushed it with a copy of Vargas Llosa's *Cinco esquinas*, a novel about life in Lima during the Sendero Luminoso attacks of the 1990s. The opening scene portrays a couple of wealthy women who find themselves trapped together by curfew and take the opportunity to give in to long-simmering desire for each other. Bomb blasts, police checkpoints, a night of elite passion. The cover image of long female legs was now coated in crushed scorpion remains. I wiped it off and tossed the body into the jungle before laying down and drifting off to sleep.

BAM!

I awoke with a start. A shotgun blast?

No, the roof. Someone was throwing rocks at my roof. I could hear stones bashing into the corrugated iron so it resounded like a rifle report—*BAM! BAM! BAM!*—before bouncing onto the earth and brush outside.

I grabbed my flashlight and ran out into the darkness, shining the light up into the tree. Shapes and shadows, shakings and rustlings, but no more blasts.

What had it been?

I lay in the hammock for a while trying to calm down. The night was dark and alive with birds and bugs and frogs, a trance of chirping and buzzing. The adrenalin slowly drained from my system and I crawled back into bed. Eventually I must have dozed, because now a catlike whimpering penetrated my cloud of sleep. I could see light through my eyelids—it was morning. The whimpering persisted as I emerged into wakefulness, motionless.

Then chaos erupted: animals screaming, legs scurrying, running along on the walls or the ceiling, the edge of the bed, I couldn't tell. It was like an Istanbul catfight, but there were no cats out here. An ocelot? A monkey chasing a rat? Whatever it was passed inches from me but I was still pinned in place by sleep. I screamed myself out of my paralysis and heaved myself upright, but the sound had stopped. Was it a dream? I jumped from the bed and slammed the covers this way and that. I looked up at the mosquito screen stapled underneath the iron roof. Did I see something?

I went outside and thought I saw a small body disappear over the peak of the roof, but from the other side there was nothing. I couldn't be sure. My breath steadied and the pulse of insects and frogs returned. I looked down at the sandy patch where I stood, just downhill from the hut, and it was overrun with black ants, more and more of them. By the time my eyes registered the ants they were crawling up my shoes and legs, inside my pants, biting me everywhere.

I bolted to the little porch in front of the hut and stripped and was sockless, pantless, madly shaking my clothes, killing ants, inspecting my body. The bites were tiny and stinging but finally subsided.

I checked my pants and put them back on, and just then Miguel showed up to give me my morning dose of ajo sacha.

¡Brak!

I showed him the ants and he walked over to have a look.

You know what you need to do? Urinate. You need to urinate around the edge of the hut. Make sure they go somewhere else. Sometimes these ants come through and eat everything. No one can stop them. They eat insects and leather and there's nothing left.

I told him about the animals and the shotgun blasts.

Choshnas, he said. Or smukis. Probably choshnas.

He took his walking stick and gestured up to the high tree above the hut.

It's a quinilla tree, he said. It gives fruit. It's the season.

He walked over and showed me the walnut-sized husks that lay in the leaves.

Choshnas are little monkeys. Smukis a little bigger.

He imitated the movements and sound of little monkeys.

They come out at night to eat fruit. The fruit and husks fall against the roof.

It's loud! I said.

You were scared, he laughed.

And then he told me about a dream he had.

It was the yanchama tree, he said. It fell on the hut and crushed it—Todo una mierda.

He splayed his arms out, palms down, to indicate total destruction.

The tree doesn't want me to blow smoke on it, he said.

And me?

You weren't in the hut when the tree fell. The tree was upset with me, not you.

He walked over and lay a hand on the trunk.

It was me who blew smoke on it, Miguel said. It's fine to be near the tree, to admire it and look at it, just don't blow smoke on it.

He left me alone and headed back up the house.

Before the next daytime ceremony, Miguel led us down into the thick jungle along the path that led to the plantain orchard to see chacruna. The bushes grew five or six feet high to one side, with elongated leaves, lozenge-shaped, coming to a point at each end. Trunks and stems were narrow, blotched with gray.

Miguel pointed out the green leaves that represented new growth and the darker, splotchier leaves.

These leaves are ripe, he said. We cook the ripe leaves.

Chacruna leaves were packed with DMT—the chemical that caused strong hallucinations—that's why when Miguel and Luis sang to it, they called it *pintorera*. Its compounds painted our vision, brought out the colored filaments.

I touched the waxy leaves of the chacruna leaf, thinking of the visions it contained. There were holes in the leaves where they'd been eaten by insects. I watched a peach-colored beetle land on a leaf. Would the beetle that now gnawed on the leaf hallucinate? Were all the insects around us submerged in visions? Many other plants were full of DMT, too. Perhaps that was the natural state of things. To emerge into linearity was the aberration. We were surrounded by a shifting natural world that saw us woven with bright and colorful threads.

I heard that elephants in Gabon eat the wood of the iboga tree, which is hallucinogenic and schools local youth in their mortality. You might wake in the night and find yourself surrounded by ecstatic elephants— snorting and stumbling—trying to navigate the land of the dead.

On the way back to the comedor, Miguel showed us a patch of chest-high reeds erupting out of the grass.

This is piri piri, Miguel said.

A cluster of slender green shoots, straight and sparse and pointed.

Mostly we cook ayahuasca with chacruna, Miguel said. The vine from the basin and the leaves from the mountain. We cook them for a long time together so the effects fuse. Then we might add other plants. Piri piri is used for perfume, but when we mix it with ayahuasca it brings music and sometimes laughter. But it can be strong, too. It's like a song—if you play one note it's like this—he sang a tone—but if you sing two notes it's more. If you sing three notes it gets stronger.

Pliny, I remembered, says elephants have been taught to dance, and once they were found rehearsing in the moonlight.

I went back to my hut and spent the morning wandering in the jungle looking at trees and vines, the occasional burst of flowers or mushrooms, one shape more extravagant than the next. The afternoon was rainy and I sat with Luis at the comedor watching water stream from the roof.

Jaguars, tigers, ocelots, pumas, Luis said. All kinds of cats used to stalk the land at night. When they kept chickens they had to guard the chickens. Or they would stake out at night with a rifle and wait for the cats. Sometimes though, they went up the mountain to hunt them. They would set off at nightfall and head up to one of the peaks. Luis described his father Liborio taking him along for the hunt. They walked into the forest around ten o'clock, creeping through the dark with a flashlight. Some hours later they were far up the peak when the bulb of their old flashlight popped. It was pitch dark. There was no way they could find their way down. They had no shelter and had to stay vigilant for snakes.

We stayed awake all night, Luis said. We took turns keeping watch until dawn. Then it started to rain like this.

Luis was twelve years old.

My father will come up this week, Luis said. Both my parents, uncles and cousins. It's the Fiesta de San Juan. All the families gather in their chacras to celebrate.

The rain let up and the night was peaceful. No choshnas came to eat quinilla fruit and pelt the roof with husks. There were no phantom animals or scorpions or armies of ants. The yanchama, by all accounts, was content. Thinking back, I find no signs to suggest the turbulence to come.

In the morning Miguel arrived with his satchel of supplies to set up the ceremony. He pulled a chair out of my hut and had me sit down on the floorboards in front of him. He lit a mapacho and smoked for a bit, pulled out the bottle of ayahuasca-piripiri, opened it and sang to it, holding his mouth close to the bottle. He blew tobacco smoke inside, recapped the bottle and shook it. Then he reopened it and poured me out a small cup. I drank it down, felt the thick and bitter substance descend my throat. Miguel blew smoke on my head and chest and hands.

Listo, he said.

We sat in silence.

Just stay around here, Miguel said. Don't walk out into the jungle. I'll be back in two hours to check on you.

Of all the ceremonies, my memories of that day are the most compact. I remember settling into the hammock intending to be very peaceful. I remember closing my eyes and feeling the medicine come on. The play of sunlight against my eyelids set in motion patterns of color—chacruna visions of yellow and orange, geometrical forms shifting and swirling on my eyelids. The next thing I remember I am screaming my lungs out, my arms and legs extended and rigid, stretched like a pole in the hammock, screaming at the cusp of nothingness. A phrase kept coming to me: *cusp of the passionate nada.*

I saw with blistering clarity who I was, who my parents were, the web that caught or sustained us, that held me in its grip. Products of the white heart of the American century, I saw how the redlined suburbs, the imperial wars, had blinded us and made us weak. I saw the effects on my father of inhaling the shuttered opinions of heartland bankers and business-men, what it had done to his health and happiness, to my mother. I felt the flicker of fear in her caring gaze. *Something was out there.* I saw how they'd done their best for me while I'd strived to separate myself, through study, through headlong and reckless departures. But thrash all I might, there was no escape. You can do all you want, I saw, but that won't change the node in the web you were birthed into. I'd clung to books and art and movies thinking I would find a north star. I'd aspired to elsewhere. Now, here, from one moment to the next everything had utterly abandoned me.

When you needed it, the phrase echoed through my head as I screamed. *What was there when you needed it?*

Religion, literature, countries and languages, the love of friends and family—useless. It was all stripped away and I was merely there, barely there, hovering in my futility, the futility of all human effort and striving but especially my own. I saw all the moves of my life as the thrashing of a dying beast on a one-way street, protesting the inevitable. Now I was on that cusp about to be doused, and when I was doused there would be nothing left, no memory, zero. Heading that way, getting closer, I was screaming. And it was in that plight, screaming until I could feel the screams reach my fingernails and toenails, the ends of my hair, that some other understanding began to arise. Here my family stories, America, my own strivings and failures, all of that fell away. I was in a tractor beam drawing closer to my personal end. I didn't know when or why I started screaming, but now that I was screaming I had to keep screaming. It was the scream that brought understanding across the horizon of noth-ingness into my body, so it could be something I know. I know nothing about death itself, I realized, about whatever was beyond that blankness of personal extinction, the zero of the universe, but I saw that anything worthwhile I might possibly understand emanates from that horizon, it made all the loves and failures and personal limitations and historical contingencies laughable and even noble, and as long as I kept screaming I could feel it pulse through me, could see the situation, the rare thing that was survival, the arc of a life in its fullness, of eras and continents and the end of things lit up in its reflection. I was not afraid exactly. It was the scream of doom but also the scream of roller-coaster weightlessness. The intensity of the sensation was so great that only through screaming could I maintain lucidity. Screaming allowed me to feel and understand and internalize what was happening. A part of me was perfectly calm, could even see the humor in the situation: me in the middle of life, amidst a global pandemic, with oceans rising, trapped in a country I knew nothing about, up in the mountains, the high jungle between the Andes and the Amazon, territory of poisonous snakes and jaguars and apes that feed on fruit at midnight, away from my companions who I'd utterly forgotten, deep in the virgin jungle, screaming my lungs out so it echoed over the valley, over the city where corpses lay on concrete, and I will scream, I thought, until I properly internalize whatever the plants, God or destiny or chance or delusion has seen fit to pour into me that day. And even when Miguel and Abuelita came to check on me and I saw Abuelita lean over me to dab my forehead with Agua de Florida and could hear Miguel's voice nearby, I didn't stop screaming. I heard Miguel say: Estás en un trance de ayahuasca. Va a pasar. And I saw Abuelita's ancient and beautiful face melt and reform and melt and reform as she leaned over me in her rich blue ceremonial shirt. They left to continue their rounds, checking on the others, and left me still screaming, all the atoms in my body electrified, and it went on until it stopped.

Miguel came to check on me later, and by that point I was seated on the floorboards in front of the door to my hut, plucking on a guitar Luis had leant me, and I was calm, completely calm, and happy to see Miguel.

You were right, I told him. It did pass.

Piri piri, he said. Sometimes it's strong.

So much for the music and laughter, I said.

Chucha, Miguel laughed.

He said I could take a shower and come up for lunch. Karen had made soup.

When I got up there I found Jonathan and Nelson chopping firewood behind the comedor.

Sorry to scream like that, I said.

But they smiled and laughed and waved it off.

Everyone else was sitting around the table. Luis asked how I was, and I tried to explain what had happened.

I looked into the mirror of death, I said.

Abuelita came around and put a hand on my forehead, laughing.

His lips were white! she said. He kept *saying: ¡Estoy muerto! ¡Estoy muerto!*

Everyone laughed. I didn't remember saying that.

El espejo de la muerte, Luis repeated, shaking his head.

They don't call it the vine of death for nothing, Miguel laughed again.

The rest of the day is a haze. I must have written in my notebook because I have these notes scratched on pages:

When all your legends have deserted you, when your resources are all used up, when you realize you've been operating on false premises, when everything you've learned has failed you, what's left?

I lay in bed thinking about it, trying to recover memories of what had happened, wondering what I'd managed to bring across the horizon of the passionate nada. Now that all my cells had been electrified, was I the same person I'd been the day before? What had all that done to my neural pathways, my endocrine system? And pondering the possibility of irreversible transformation, a moment returned to me: When it was over, when the screaming had passed and I was calm and alone and back in the hammock, I remembered reaching over to pick up my glasses, which I'd placed on top of the jug of drinking water when I lay down in the hammock. Through my disordered memory I can vaguely see myself reaching for my glasses earlier in the ceremony and not being able to find them.

Is that why I started screaming? I wondered. Was it a moment of panic, not being able to find my glasses—I'm thoroughly blind without them—and in the intensity of the medicine descending into terror? What if all those realizations that felt so important, the supreme wisdom reflected by the mirror of death, was nothing but me flailing in confusion: *where are my goddamn glasses!?*

I laughed at the thought. How absurd.

I won't tell anyone, I resolved. It'll be my secret.

Lying in the hammock after breakfast the next morning I found myself humming an old Mexican song. *Las Poblanas*—it's not a song exactly, but a traditional *son* from the south of Veracruz, a song-form devoted to mourning after turbulent times, it was sung for prisoners and people who died in the revolution. Prisoners used to invent verses and scrawl them across their jail cells, hoping to sing them at a village fandango when they were free. I remember a version our friend Joel used to sing, a truly gifted musician, a repository of stories from the region with a huge warm voice.

Ahora lloran poblanas
Corazón de melón
Por que llevó la muerte
Una de San Simón.

I'd traveled the region as part of a documentary crew. Joel led us through villages, to families he knew, recording old songs and poems and listening to people. As we drove the winding roads of Veracruz, sometimes he sat in the back seat plucking his guitarra media with a plastic comb, singing out the open window:

Ahora lloran poblanas
Corazón de manteca
por que llevó la muerte
una mujer Chichimeca

I found myself in the hammock by the yanchama, singing *Las Poblanas*, and I don't know why but I choked up. Tears welled up in me. I kept singing and the well of tears overflowed. It was as if all the screaming yesterday now had to be mourned, but each bit of mourning led to more song.

Ahora lloran poblanas
Corazón de sanango
Por que llevó la muerte
Al vecino Don Pancho

I was alone in the jungle and let myself go, singing and crying, and each shift from mourning to song produced bursts of energy, joyous.

And even as the tragedy shook me—the virus, the police killings, people driven to steal oxygen, us here, the ember in Miguel's eye—my tears were joyful, full of relief.

مع العسر يسر

Nafis had a line from the Qur'an tattooed in Arabic script across his back beneath his name—*after struggle comes relief.* That's what I felt—after struggle comes relief—and how good it was. Whatever had caused that encounter with the mirror of death yesterday, now it reflected the pure pleasure of being alive. I loved my parents, even myself. Everything was forgiven. I got up and walked down the path to the waterfall and I felt like the luckiest person in the world. For once to be able to walk through the high jungle like that, through the sapoina trees and all the growing vines.

O kako sam sretan bio!

I spotted a long feather on the ground, gold and blue and red, that Luis would identify as the tail-feather of a macaw. I picked it up and pinched it between my thumb and forefinger as I kept walking. I got to the waterfall and stood under the cascade. One of the big blue butterflies flitted by and I luxuriated in the cool falls, water and stone and the misty fragrance, everything growing and living and dying, and alone there I sang and cried and sang and cried some more, laughing at who I'd become.

It was late June, two days until the Fiesta de San Juan, and several more members of the Tapullima family were supposed to come up to spend a few days with us. In the mid-morning Miguel was at the edge of the comedor talking to the park ranger, the one who'd first informed us of the state of emergency.

When he left we wanted to know if it was a problem we were here.

No, Miguel said. We've known him a long time. He doesn't care.

What were you talking about?

He said he spotted a new waterfall. One he'd never seen. A big one. And it seems it belongs to us.

It's in Juliampampa?

Juliampampa is huge, Miguel said. It takes all day to walk across. That way—he waved past one edge of the clearing—after a long walk. It's difficult to get to. Nelson and Ermo will check it out after lunch.

Miguel's brother Pedro—named after his father and grandfather—arrived an hour later with a couple of cousins. Their brother Andrés came soon with his wife Estefita. Luis's parents were on their way up the mountain, too, but then a call came in. We were just finishing lunch and didn't know what happened, but the atmosphere tensed. Miguel was talking to someone, Luis someone else, Karen glaring at her phone with bloodshot eyes.

What happened?

Amigo Brad, my father got attacked, Karen said.

What?

One of the apes, she said. He was feeding them.

Everyone was talking and calling and worrying and it took some time to cobble the story together:

There was a primate reserve in the park. We passed the sign for it on the way up, just at the point where the incline steepens, where the last set of switchbacks begin. The path forked and one branch led to an area where some of the larger apes gather, where veterinarians or biologists can sometimes find them. Luis and Karen's father, we learned, was accustomed to bringing them food on the way up to Juliampampa. He'd been doing it for years. His wife Rosita waited for him while he went down the path—about ten minutes or so—to where the apes lingered.

Liborio had a bunch of bananas strapped to his back, intending to drop them down for the apes. These were machín apes, about four feet tall, not usually aggressive, but one of them had displayed some problematic behavior and the reserve staff had chained it up. Liborio assumed he wouldn't have to be too careful, but when he got there, he didn't see it in its usual place. Instead he saw two other apes. He recognized them, friendly as ever. He walked toward them, about to drop his load of bananas, when something jumped on him—the other ape, unchained, wanted to grab the bananas right off his back. In his confusion, Liborio jerked this way and that, waving his arms. This made the other two apes think their companion was being threatened. Soon all three apes were on top of Liborio, biting and scratching him. He managed to drop the bananas and get away, but not before they wounded him in sixteen places. He hobbled back to the path where his wife waited. Rosita, who always walked up the mountain barefoot like Abuelita, now tore off Liborio's shirt and tried to staunch the bleeding where it was worst, and she supported her husband as he hobbled down the mountain to exit the park and get to the hospital. That walk took three hours in the best of circumstances, longer when someone's injured and bleeding and in terrible pain.

Miguel, Luis, and Karen were on the phone all day, keeping us updated as news came in. By the evening, Liborio was stable, badly injured but out of danger. He'd be off his feet for some weeks. Karen showed us photos of his wounds—closeups of lacerations, blue mottled flesh caked with blood.

Keep your eye out for apes, Miguel warned us. They're not likely to come up here, but we don't want to meet them.

Do they ever come up here?

They did once, Luis said. A big one, a female. She smelled food and went into the kitchen and we had to keep our distance. You don't want to fight them. We waited and she left.

With all that had happened, I slept soundly under the yanchama tree. My tears had dried and there was no sign of violent apes, but it was not over yet.

The next day they had to plan the fiesta. Nothing elaborate. The tradition was to be out in the jungle with family and eat *juanes*, rice and chicken steamed in banana or bijao leaf, similar to Oaxacan tamales. Pedro had brought the juanes, but they still had to decide where to eat them. Perhaps they'd go to the new waterfall. Ermo and Jonathan came back from looking for it with footage of a high cascade pummeling a bouldered ravine, a pool deep enough to dive into from the rocks.

Shall we go there? Pedro asked.

It's too dangerous, Ermo answered. It takes rope, and even then—

I almost died, Jonathan interrupted.

He slipped and fell, Ermo went on. Must have been five meters. He was unconscious for a while. We were scared.

Chucha, Miguel said.

But I'm fine, Jonathan said. And he jumped around to show his good health.

Pedro decided they'd just go down to a place they knew well. That was the plan for tomorrow.

As for Miguel, Luis, Jonathan, Abuelita, and the five of us would have a ceremony. A night ceremony this time, in the maloca.

We gathered at sunset and drank our medicine—ayahuasca cielo. Rather than piri piri reeds, the third note this time was a plant called ayahuma—Quechua for *death's head*. It was a brain-sized fruit that hung from trees. Luis told me ayahuma was good for drawing out fears. Its effects could be direct, free of metaphor.

Miguel poured us out our servings, one by one, and blew out the candles. There we were, once again, in the darkness of the maloca. We sat in silence for an hour before Miguel started singing, and soon after he began, his voice modulating in the high range, Jonathan picked up the icaro. He didn't strum his guitar this time but beat a simple rhythm on his shakapa. His voice, which had been thin and sweet, had a new edge. His tricksterish mischief wasn't playful anymore.

Cielo-cielo-cielo-cielo, he sang like Rumpelstiltskin around the fire at midnight.

His shakapa altered from an easy heartbeat to a rushing, insistent pulse and his voice took on a punk snarl as he sang. He brought his rhythm to a stop, and Abuelita's voice soon filled the space, her meandering melodies and delicate rhythms punctuated by retching and hacking and spitting as Jonathan started to vomit. When she stopped and Miguel took over again, his powerful singing underwritten by seemingly boundless good humor, I felt as if I'd been puking, too. Miguel kept singing and for a while the atmosphere was light like that, a lightness that knew how hard it could be. He sang strings of syllables, keeping the beat with his shakapa, and Jonathan began to sing, too, his snarl unfurling beneath his father's lightness.

Waa-oowww waah-ooow La-la-na-na-la-la-na-na

Miguel stopped and let his son take over. Jonathan beat time with his shakapa, quickening the beat again, his voice swirling up into the falsetto range, broken up by aspirated laughter.

Ha ha ha ha wow wow la la la

He sang a few words addressing the plants, but soon his singing grew confused and he was caught up in his own energy, snarling and attacking, singing nonsense syllables over his insistent beat.

Da da di di da day da da Kuna yari medicina, ya muy na na ayaruna

Miguel picked up his drum and began to beat a singular, regular rhythm, whistling over the beat, then let the beat alone resound through the maloca. Jonathan quieted, but as soon as Miguel began to sing, his son's awful retching resumed. Miguel interrupted his rhythm to check on him.

Bring him some water. He's getting hot.

Ermojines, whose task was to sit sober in the corner and keep watch over us, brought him a cup of water.

Miguel asked Nafis if he could sing and soon some illegible syllables echoed through the maloca.

Aya so so ku—Si shi shi tu puy

Nafis said he'd been chanting on the boulder in the Shilcayo down at Las Coconas and begun to sing like this. At first he didn't know what it was, he said, but it felt like some kind of ancestral ante-language, so he just went with it.

Sho ee ma yoy ki ya ya

He began to shake his string of shells and sang in his ante-language, melodically at first, but then like atonal chanting. It had an entirely different quality than the big laughing tone he'd sang with during the last diet.

Miguel asked me to sing and I did my best. I had no idea what I was doing, but Luis handed me a shakapa and I tried to keep a beat and address ajo sacha, understanding it was the way to establish connection with the plant.

Miguel took over again—mercifully for everyone—and sang for a while, but stopped when Jonathan started to retch horribly, and for a while we sat in silence listening to Jonathan hack and retch. He was digging up a horrid sludge of pain from his chest, hauling it up in mining cars, trace by trace, but he was impatient and began to thrash and scream. Abuelita sang in Shipibo, her rhythm increasing, naming Jonathan in her verses, but his strangled hacking and retching continued. Miguel and Luis blew smoke on him. Luis spit Agua de Florida in the air above him. Abuelita stopped singing and went to confer with Miguel. What to do? Jonathan was writhing on the ground, still retching horribly. Luis exhaled slowly as if to soothe him, but there was no soothing him. Nafis picked up his shells and began singing again. Perhaps he could do something? He kept a gentle rhythm with his shells and spoke-sang his syllables over it. Jonathan was fighting for his life, emitting awful inhuman strangled screams. Mining pain a moment ago, now he was thrown down the pit. He squealed and screeched and writhed in agony.

Miguel came to sit next to me.

He needs to fight by himself, Miguel said. If I go too close to him he'll cling to me. He needs to do this alone.

My encounter with the mirror of death was still fresh in my body, and I felt I knew what Jonathan was going through. I could sense him relive his moments lying unconscious earlier that day, where he fell on the way to the waterfall. He was with his uncle the moment of the ape attack. If only he'd been there to help. He was in Tarapoto with the sick and hungry, the region's whole bloody history. It was the sound of vital energy encountering greater, immutable forces. Nafis's voice rose higher and louder and the retching stopped.

Perhaps he'd calmed Jonathan, I wondered, but no. Miguel asked Ermo to bring more water, then went out of the maloca for a second. I heard Nafis's voice:

Sing, Brad!

I found Luis's shakapa still next to me, and now it didn't matter whether I knew what to do or not, we all had to do whatever we could, so it was my duty to keep the beat on the shakapa and try to sing. I muttered and hummed and sang a few words and Jonathan was quiet for a second.

If I can give him something of what I went through a couple of days ago, I thought, perhaps it will help. Is there a way that who you are and what you've been through can be expressed like that? Carried across through the room into someone else? Can you calm a suffering soul? That was the work of the curandero, I understood. We were learning it now by force.

But it was beyond me to help anyone. When Miguel came back I could hear Jonathan semi-coherent, telling Miguel about his girlfriend who loved him and took good care of him, but whose family disapproved. Someone had bewitched him, he said. As he tried to speak his energy rose and he returned to writhing and shouting, trying to cast out some infecting glance.

¡Concha tu madre! ¡Largo de mí!

Miguel and Luis started singing together over him as he shouted.

¡Cuídame, huevón!

But it was no use. He was entranced, speaking to his lover's family, then to the rest of us in the room, Ermo and Luis, calling them brothers, calling his grandfather:

¡No les da caso! ¡Abuelito Pedro!

Miguel had seen Eszter help Szilvia and asked if she would go sit with Jonathan.

Eszter would tell me the ceremony had been beautiful for her up to that point. She'd been full of love. The plants—or some entities she understood as the plants—were teaching her about helping people, about how powerful it was to use your hands.

How do I do that? Eszter had asked.

One of her hands was resting on her sweater, balled up next to her mat. She felt her hand resting on the soft wool.

Just like that, the plants seemed to say to her. Just like your hand on the sweater.

She was having this teaching moment, and Jonathan was shrieking, ordering whoever was bewitching him to get away.

¡Lárgate concha tu madre!

He beat on his mat with his hands and sang in his demonic voice.

La la la la la la cuida me cuida me cuida me lárgate!

Meanwhile the plant-entities were communicating with Eszter:

This is healing. Healing can sound like this.

His screams rose and Nafis began cackling. Szilvia started laughing, too. Soon we were all laughing, except Jonathan who continued to battle and shriek.

This, too, is healing, the plant-entities murmured to Eszter.

Can I heal him? Eszter asked. Can I use what you showed me?

Not yet, the plant entities said. Just wait.

But when Miguel went to her—Esztercita, I got a message that maybe you can help him—she understood that yes, now was the time.

She sat behind Jonathan who continued to scream and lay her hands on him like the plants showed her, and part of his scream entered into her, but she was strong and laying her hand on his back just as she'd rested it on the soft wool of her sweater, through her strength and softness his anguish was metabolized.

We are all dead! I remembered Eszter's own trance the night before we learned about lockdown.

Miguel had several instruments scattered around his corner of the maloca and began to play soft melodies on a flute, then blew beautiful sad tones on his father's harmonica. Jonathan continued to shout at the invisible demons.

¡Concha tu madre! ¡Lárgate!

I went out to get some air and Miguel followed me. We sat on the bench in front of the maloca listening to Jonathan scream inside.

He's confused, Miguel said, saying whatever comes to his mind. Sometimes ayahuasca is like that.

I continued to feel sympathetic to Jonathan's madness. To thrash and shriek and say things that might be true, whatever came to mind, seemed an appropriate response to our mortal condition. Especially if you were a Nativo-Lamista kid from Tarapoto, reluctant heir to the traditions of Juliampampa, submerged in the paradoxical impulses of youth, trying to make sense of 2020.

I told Miguel I thought I understood something after howling into the void the other day. Miguel said he'd had nights like these, too. I asked if our experiences were similar, but Miguel said his connection to the plants was so deep and solid and grounded that there's an impenetrable bond between him and the land and the plants that goes back to the origin.

Right, I said.

Miguel went inside and I sat alone for a bit before Luis emerged, laughing.

You come here the first time, Luis said, and you see the beauty of the mountains, the maloca. You think: what a magical place. But after spending a lot of time here you start to feel how many things pass in and out of the maloca. You know what might happen during a ceremony—like this! All the beauty and terror, you sense it when you walk into the maloca. It's always there.

Luis said when Jonathan started to scream earlier in the night he'd known he needed to protect himself. He'd drunk a capful of Agua de Florida, taken five deep drags of tobacco, stepped outside, and vomited. After that he could stay calm.

The most important thing is to stay calm, he said. Because if you lose your calm you can get sucked right into the other's madness.

We stepped back into the maloca, Eszter was singing. Her voice sounded strong and confident. She was calm, too. And Jonathan was quiet, but then when she stopped singing he retched again, just once.

Little by little, it's going to pass, Eszter said.

She went back to singing, and Jonathan's shrieks now became moans and whimpers. He was still suffering, but we could tell, somehow, that the worst was over. Miguel began to chuckle lovingly, patiently, watching his son writhe in agony.

We sat for a while listening to silence punctuated by Jonathan's shouts and whines and whimpers. Eventually he stopped.

In the gathering calm, Eszter sang the last song of the night—by now it was the early morning. It was a Hungarian song, a lullaby her father used to sing to her in her childhood apartment along the Danube:

Paradicsom közepében, she sang, Arany szőnyeg van terítve . . .

In the middle of heaven
there's a golden carpet
A cradle rocks there
where baby Jesus rests

In his left hand a golden apple
in his right hand a golden wand
Whenever he waves it
forests hum and fields echo

A star now rises
    rousing all sleepers
A star now rises
    rousing all sleepers

Jonathan, Miguel, Luis, and Abuelita left the maloca to sleep, and the rest of us sat in silence with two candles burning. Akos lay in silence, but the rest of us eventually began talking and laughing over what had happened. At one point a moth flew close to my head, then circled again and again. I blew tobacco around myself, but it didn't dissuade the moth. It appeared in front of my face, getting closer—I could distinguish its body dusted with magenta and lavender. I kept still and waited until the moth was close to my face, then blew a quick gust of breath and the moth flew up and out of view. I went back to chatting with Nafis, laughing at the demonic screeches we'd withstood all night, but the moth reappeared right in the light of the candle flame—whfff—sputtered and fell.

I'd been thinking about all the plants mixing inside us—ayahuasca and chacruna, piri piri and ayahuma, bobinsana and yacushimbillo and ajo sacha, uchu sanango and chuchuwasha—how when the wave hit me the other day I could only scream with all my organism, against dying, against mortality, against the end of natural resources, on the horizon of the beyond, absolutely nothing, facing nothing nothing nothing—asaaaaaaaghghghg!

Now I thought: how surprised the moth must have been when I blew on it—turbulent forces unleashed against that weightless creature sent spinning up into the air, no doubt terrified, seeking its bearings, any kind of bearings. I've heard moths orient by the stars, an evolutionary artifact older than fire—is that possible? Fire resembles stars and scrambles the moth's orientation, so whirling through the air, overwhelmed and confused, the moth reaches out for whatever might orient it, heads that way, and gets burned.

When what you took for your north star turns out to be lethal—then what?

I once knew a Provençal sailor named Serge who built himself a sailboat and sailed across the Atlantic. It was in the early seventies when he left Europe. He passed Morocco, docked in Senegal, then crossed to Brazil, where on an island in Bahia he bought a small piece of land. He hired himself out to French tourists, captaining small sailing cruises through the Caribbean. Off season he came back to his island and built the house where he lived. The walls were high and beautifully whitewashed, modeled after houses he'd seen in Morocco. Inside it was simple—just a kitchen below an upstairs bedroom, an overgrown garden with a few chairs and a long wood table.

After he'd been on the island for many years, Serge came down from his upstairs room and surprised a couple of kids trying to rob the place. He shouted at them, trying to get them to scram, but one had a gun and fired at Serge as he came toward them. The bullet entered his right eye and lodged in the back of his brain. He staggered to the hospital, but the doctors were unable to remove the bullet. He would have to hope the wound healed on its own.

Serge went back to his house and lay recuperating in horrible pain. For months he lay thrashing in his bed or doing his best to stay still and recover. The pain brought visions, and through that hallucinatory period he had conversations with his dead father and repeatedly witnessed his own death. He saw himself anchoring off a small island, sitting in a drinking hall, going home with a woman, and as they made love through the night he reached off the bed and found his hand resting on a small child asleep on the floor next to them.

En fin, he said to himself.

He refused to wear an eyepatch, so his right eye was an open wound, often running with pus. Years later, when I met him, he still dabbed at it with a handkerchief as he passed me a joint of rough weed from the island. We sat across from each other at the table with a large bowl of mangos and bananas between us. Dabbing his right eye as he spoke, Serge told me stories of sailing life, the island, memories of an affair with a baroness on the Canaries, saying: You guys are going to have to make an emergency metaphysic out of a little Tao, Buddhism, whatever shredded remains of Christianity you can find. When darkness fell, two-foot fruit bats swooped down at the bowl, taking thumb-sized bites from the bananas between us.

I heard of an Istanbul taxi driver who got shot by a gangster through the left eye such that the bullet lodged behind his right eye, blinding both.

He said he forgot the face of his wife. He forgot the face of his children, but he couldn't forget the face of the man who shot him. That act of violence was the whole of his vision.

Dreams, imaginings, the warnings of blind seers. What's the difference between visions brought on by ayahuasca or by a bullet in the brain? Khaled's fever returning him to the jasmine vines of his Damascene childhood. Some Islamic dream interpreters distinguish *true dreams* from the disordered sequences of images that flow through our minds every night. They're rare, they say, but such truths are worth recounting, because the stories they contain are instructive.

Some say prayer is whatever we discover ourselves doing under maximum pressure, when life is at its hardest. But sometimes under emergency situations we flail and thrash and go numb. Terror might inspire us to pray, but we don't do it when we're overwhelmed; we do it afterward, anticipating the next wave, at moments of relative calm, knowing such intensities and difficulties may be heading our direction once again.

Miguel told me early in his training he'd had a vision of a snake—a huge writhing anaconda was coming toward him, getting closer. He reached for his machete and began swinging it back and forth. Then he heard his father's voice:

Don't kill the snake. Sing to it.

Miguel crawled inside the snake, singing, and looked out through its eyes.

In another vision he was walking behind a rooster, and the rooster was leading him into a cave.

He told his father, and Pedro said the rooster was the promise of power, a temptation to use plants to gain control over others.

You can become powerful, his father said, but eventually it will cost you.

The next day when I was back at the yanchama, Miguel showed up and found me kicking dirt near the base of the tree. I pointed to a blue swatch entangled with the roots. Miguel reached down and pulled on it until it started to come out. Bigger than it had appeared, it was buried under eight inches of earth. When he stood up he held a piece of blue cloth.

Clothing, he said. Probably my father's.

Sometimes Miguel hears his father walking through Juliampampa. He hears his boots clomping over the stones.

I told him he's lucky to have had such a father, who taught him so much and left him all these riches. He said yes he is, and he's trying to do the same for Luis and Jonathan.

I told him there was much to learn in all this, and he said Sí, hombre.

Once he had a dream, he said. He was at a private airport. There was a plane idling on the tarmac, and the door was open. There was a man offering Miguel a suitcase, saying: Let's go! Let's go to the city! But Miguel refused to enter the plane.

Alone that night, I stood watching the play of lunar shadows, feeling at home in my hut by the yanchama tree, the ceaseless sounds of frogs and insects and the distant flow of water and the fresh rush of wind through the jungle.

As I drifted off to sleep, my mind returned to the mirror of death. I saw the thin scrim that was the phenomenal world. You could find a corner that was fraying, and if you pulled at it a little, it might lift up, and that's when questions started to flow, one upon the other, an endless inquiry that was a disposition toward oblivion and beyond. Everything

I'd ever learned was useless, I knew, but the next day I'd follow Miguel through the jungle, asking about this vine and that, drinking whatever concoctions he gave me, as if I might find an answer.

I remembered a story by a friend of mine about a trio of Cairo gangsters. One of them had stashed the drugs somewhere, but then overnight turned into a goat. The others drove around the neighborhoods with the goat, inspecting the goat's reaction, looking for a sign, trying to find the stash. Their desperation increased the more they were unable to accept the obvious: the transmutation had been complete. The goat was not a dealer in the form of a goat, but just a goat.

Beyond the yanchama tree I heard birds chirping and saw them nearby, balancing on a branch, small birds with bright red throats. I followed their movements and it led me to notice another area of motion, more birds, two elongated hoopoe birds bobbing up and down on a slender branch, looking like birds from a dream, and then I realized they were in fact a dream—they weren't there at all. It was just a trick of light and the motion of branches. In the foreground I could see the red-throated birds flying and those were real birds.

I stood by a slender tree a little ways down the path near the first sapoina. I'd been standing by that slender tree for a while, looking past it into the jungle at imaginary birds, but just now I took a step back and realized it was full of fruit. It was loaded with yellow-green globes, a little bigger than a cherry, and each of them was so ripe they were splitting open, each globe had a droplet of fluid or sap, glinting in the light, about to drop on the forest floor. I'd been there all day and just now noticed.

How much else have I been staring at without noticing? I wondered.

Miguel found me standing by the yanchama tree as usual. He told me its sap is used to treat internal wounds.

They give it to women after birth, he said.

Internal wounds, I thought. The yanchama itself looked like a conglomeration of wounds. Ripped bark, gashes, tangles of vines like electric cable in knots, ancient and cracking, peeling back, mushrooms growing on it, a hole right through its center. As we stood there I heard a sound like a helicopter, and a large hummingbird appeared, hovering before Miguel and I, as if taking us in, before zipping off on its way somewhere.

Miguel said that one's called a runrun, and further down the path was a flightless bird called an umpalito whose eyes glow in the dark—Eszter had seen one the other night. The gerbil-rat was called casha ucucha.

Miguel left me thinking about imaginary birds and invisible fruit, of birds with glowing eyes and purring wings. Because they can fly backward, I'd heard, hummingbirds are associated with the ability to do the impossible. I knew they were creatures of these American continents. None were native to Europe or Asia. Some species of hummingbirds are only known by a few dried skins purchased from traders, never seen again. They were like earthquakes, I thought, which were native to earth. No seismic blasts shook Saturn or Uranus. Some humans had a delicate sensitivity and could feel earthquakes at great distances. I heard rocks thundering down the ravine at night. In the waterfall I feared they would crush me.

Perhaps the way Miguel sings to the plants we could sing to tension in the earth. Singing was about creating a relationship. We sing to the plants so we know them, know their moods and powers, and they know us. Then we might ask for help. It was like repeating the names of God— calling to the Sustainer or the Compassionate. It established a lifeline. I wondered if in the same way we could cultivate sensitivities. We could sing or chant the name *al-Sami'*, for example, the Listener, and hope to hear with the ears of the jungle. Perhaps we could hear ants idling in a pool of sunshine on the jungle floor, or hear the big poisonous isula ants patrolling the roots of the yanchama tree.

A hot and dry day followed and we idled in the shade of the comedor. Nelson and Ermojines dropped huge tree trunks to be chopped for firewood, then collapsed next to Jonathan in the hammocks. Karen checked with her mom to see how Liborio was doing after the ape attack. Eszter and Abuelita sat on the bench overlooking the valley. Miguel hung up his machete and disappeared into his room. Shadows grew and in the silence until nightfall, when we gathered again in the maloca. Without Jonathan this time who chose to rest.

This time ajo sacha appeared to me as a quick and humorous spirit—*bam-bam*—a sharpshooter. Thoughts would come into my head and—*swat!*—ajo sacha would crush them. It was like a little orange pistol at my side—*peeeeoooh!*—accurate and rapid and glowing and friendly and very deliciously garlicky. I'd had that garlicky taste in my mouth for two weeks.

Na-fiiiisssss!

Miguel asked Nafis to sing, but instead he stood up to dance. He moved around in the darkness and I saw creatures crawling on his back. I couldn't tell if they were friendly or not, but they were enjoying themselves.

Knowing that just outside the stars shone, the webs of interconnectedness flowed through the trees and mountains and uncountable insects, the tireless work of the leaf-cutter ants disassembling the world and carrying it into a little hole under one of the snaking roots of the ojé tree, rebuilding a replica underground there, turning the whole world inside out. Eszter and me and Szilvia and Akos—Budapest and Subotica, the end of the Cold War and NATO bombings, and there was Nafis, who'd been a US Marine, a firefighter in Canarsie, now cavorting with spirits in Juliampampa.—Na-fiiiisssss!—Thinking of Eszter's and I's apartment in Harlem, our windows on the back of the building overlooking the roof-tops of Sugar Hill with its circling pigeons. I sat on the floor with my back against the wall of the maloca, smiling as I felt the growing urge to piss, the need to stand up, the weakness in my legs, the ache in my back, and the simultaneous awareness of the relationships between Miguel and Luis and Jonathan, the lineage of the family from grandfather to father to uncle to Miguel and onward. Holding all these thoughts in my head was impossible, panic-inducing, but I found that if I lowered my awareness so I was holding them in my chest they could reverberate and coexist freely and redound in all their complexity. They could occupy the same space without crowding each other. There was enough space for all impressions and sensations, emotions and suppositions, whatever might flow in and out of that mansion of awareness with its countless hallways and endless rooms, all of which could materialize or disappear in the blink of an eye, expand or disappear as needed, be rebuilt or not be built at all, exist hovering on the horizon as a capacity as effortless as breathing out.

And when I did go outside to piss I stood over the wall where we puked when we arrived, land of bad spirits, that Luis had taken me aside to warn me against—Don't give them a chance, he said. They can pretend to be someone you know.—But I didn't care as I pissed off the stone wall, thinking Of course this is where the bad spirits breed. This is where we

puke our guts out when we arrive, unburdening ourselves of all our trash
and poison and pain, the subway rides and debt statements, algorithms
and bad faith and daily dishonesties, echoes of abuse and violence, the
booze and bad food and emotional residue, burning police vans and unex-
ploded ordnance, killings done in our name, harrowing unspeakables we
hardly know of that make us scream bloody murder into the night, all of
that oozing into the patch of ground so even when the rains come to rinse
it away it's still there, seeping in and breeding bad spirits, mixing with the
memory of civilization-altering calamities of the past, conquest and colo-
nization, rape and pillage and new religions, and it will take much more
rain and even more rain and tectonic shifts and a disinfectant cataclysm
more powerful than the virus to wash all that away.

THE MINUTE YOU LOSE
YOUR HEAD

There's a rapid insect-like tempo to growing plants. Their stillness is not passivity but acute concentration.

Take this narrow and hairy palm: its leaves jut first then hang like a mantis with a thousand claws. As an insect, it would gingerly inspect your chest before digging its claws into you, elongate a tendril into your jugular and suck the blood out of your vein.

But no. Its menace is playful. It's provocative, beckoning, the tips of its fronds dancing in chest hairs.

Another narrow tree sprouts clusters of huge thorns all up its trunk. A monkey would prick its feet trying to climb. Behind it the weaving duckbill pink of heliconia flowers. Yellow bamboo stalks jut from the earth like arrows in San Sebastian's chest. A sound system somewhere pumps a distant baseline.

Sticking my tongue out, the air tastes vaguely sour.

What's the first sense of approaching rain? A change in fragrance? Rising wind? Air pressure?

Always, always, always the sound of the river.

Back in Las Coconas, hours in the hammock, solitary walks up Prolongación Alerta to the gate of the reserve, past the closed down orchid garden, other closed down centers of empty bungalows.

La Baronesa—the tarantula that lives in the wall just here outside our bedroom. How comfortably we've learned to cohabitate by now.

When I pace the garden on the phone with Khaled, he stands smoking at his window overlooking St. Nicholas Ave. He tells me they're holding fresh corpses in the funeral parlor on his ground floor. Refrigerator hum echoes up the air shaft of his building. Cardboard boxes the size of coffins pile up under the tree downstairs.

We're not supposed to congregate outside, Khaled says, but whenever there's no funeral the neighbors sit under the tree like always. The cops drive by. They don't get out, just shout through their bullhorns: *DISPERSE!* And people disperse for a second then come back.

I paced among the heliconia flowers listening. A toucan alighted on a thin branch. Khaled told me a few days ago he was out on the street with his son.

I had Walid strapped into the stroller, he said. A neighborhood kid came running down Amsterdam, chased by a bunch of cops. The cops caught up to him and threw him to the ground. Other cops showed up. Everyone else pulled out phones and started filming. The reinforcement cops formed a wall around the cops wrestling with the kid on the ground. I found myself face to face with a young cop. His face was frozen, completely blank. He'd been utterly dehumanized, turned into a robot, but there was still a trace of fear. It made me understand something about the US military.

He tried to think what it was:

In Damascus the regime cops are just assholes. They know they've got all the power, so they're dicks. They're open about it. They're animals. These kids were like machines, but the shell is brittle. Anything could happen. I realized: These were the same kids rolling through Baghdad. No wonder.

Yes, I thought. A door bashed in, panic and paranoia. Can't speak the language. Never been anywhere and don't know how people behave, but armed and on edge. Shout in English no one can understand. People weep, terrified. A movement somewhere, then *blam, blam, blam!*

We hear missionaries brought COVID to the jungle. Setting up medical centers in isolated places, thinking they would offer care, they spread disease instead. It's not the first time missionaries brought calamities. I read that many missionaries who appeared in the 1950s were World War II servicemen who couldn't find it in themselves to return home. Americans and Italians vied for influence as if the war in Europe were continuing in Madre de Dios or Lamas and the weapons were lemonade, blueberry muffins, and T-shirts. They say uncontacted communities have fewer medicinal plants but also fewer ailments. Miguel knows about hundreds of plants. We learn about more every day. No doubt the legacy of conquistadores and missionaries and explorers, the rubber boom, all that intersecting with a living history with its own rivalries and conflicts and strains of violence and cooperation, competition and solitude, recent upheavals like the Sendero Luminoso, the drug war, wildcat mining, shamanic tourism.

But for now the only thing moving is the virus. And Abuelita, who showed up to tell us she'd received permission to travel home to Pucallpa on a special bus. She came one last time before heading to the station.

She held Eszter close, tearing up.

You're like a daughter to me, she said.

She sniffed and hugged her again, smiling through tears.

Eszter and Szilvia walked her to the gate of Las Coconas before she left. They would miss her.

131

Eszter sat drinking tea at the table outside our room. I lay collapsed in the hammock. These long afternoons, how long would they go on? We talked about Abuelita, about our situation. Were we perhaps happy here? Eszter laughed and her laugh was like home. It felt good to go through this together.

Miguel came later the same afternoon. He picked up a vial Abuelita left on Eszter's table.

Perfume?

Yes, Eszter smiled. Abuelita said it's what makes everyone love her.

Don't use it, Miguel said. I'll make you something else. We'll mix shimipanpan and shimipanpachana. It'll be good for attracting clients.

We went with him into town to buy ingredients. It was mid-summer in the northern hemisphere, winter in the south, but in the jungle it was dry season, hottest time of the year. We rolled through Tarapoto in the back of a mototaxi, jostling over the rutted dirt roads until we got to the paved center. The little regional hub was still locked down but people had adjusted. The market was open but guards armed with fever guns stood at the entrance, letting people in one at a time. You weren't supposed to linger in the square. It wasn't clear what impact any of these measures had on the spread of the virus, but the habits of it quickly became ingrained. Inside Las Coconas we lived in happy isolation. We'd only ever known the lodge empty, so that didn't seem strange to us. We were used to finding a spot behind a locked bungalow to make calls or zoom into a meeting, perhaps avoiding a distant whir of power tools as someone down the way worked on their house. We only strapped on masks when we left Las Coconas as we did today. We bought them off stacks on crowded commercial corners in the town center. Superhero motifs, sports teams. Eszter's bore a Shipibo design in whites and grays printed with colored dots.

Miguel instructed the driver to keep going through the center, past the cemetery to another market. Here it was not only fruits and vegetables and cured meats and salted fish like the main market. Right at the entrance a man sold jungle game like caimans and boas. And there were stalls with medicinal plants Miguel would use to make perfume for Eszter. He grabbed a few handfuls of herbs and chatted with the vendor.

Listo, he said, before heading home.

We walked through the heat of the afternoon idle and amused, Eszter with the bundle of herbs Miguel had bought. What would happen to any of us?

When we hopped in a mototaxi back to Prolongación Alerta, we told the driver to go up past Sacha Wasi. That was our landmark, we found. Everyone knows where Sacha Wasi is—the most famous center in Tarapoto, among the oldest international centers in Peru. We jumped out at the corner uphill from its locked gates. A high wall surrounded the extensive grounds. Now silent, free of patients. Only a couple of guys idled around the gravel entranceway, keeping watch.

Since our initial neighbors flew back to France, we'd wondered what goes on beyond Sacha Wasi's high walls. We'd learned it was founded by a French doctor named Mathieu Bastarache, who arrived to the province of San Martín in the 1980s and studied with local curanderos. He founded Sacha Wasi believing what he'd learned would help people from his native context. Soon addicts were arriving from Europe and beyond to rid themselves of habits, strip themselves of the accrued toxins of their Western lives.

But it was not only the attention of the sick and seeking he attracted. By the mid-1990s the French Ministerial Committee for Surveillance of

Sects kept a file on Sacha Wasi, describing the center's practices as combining drug use and brainwashing.

Though Mathieu had studied with the local curanderos, his methods were syncretic and idiosyncratic. His relationship with Miguel's father had been tense.

He thinks we're country witches, Miguel laughed.

While Pedro spoke of spirits that roamed freely, Mathieu diagnosed his patients with infestations that derived, he claimed, from bad drugs, bad sex, bad spirituality, polluted places or polluted people. He administered plant remedies and ayahuasca but also drew on practices from the Catholic church.

Miguel always asked for permission before a ceremony and thanked Nuestro Señor Jesucristo, but Mathieu sprinkled holy water and wielded a crucifix.

This syncretism dates back to missionary tolerance of shamanism, but recent observers who visited Sacha Wasi found patients calling themselves possessed, contaminated, inhabited by malevolent forces. They arrived with complaints of pain, chronic illness, sudden loss of a sense of life's meaning. Western doctors and therapists couldn't cure them, so they'd looked elsewhere.

I heard of a nineteen year-old Parisian student who arrived with eating disorders. French psychiatrists had prescribed antidepressants, anxiolytics, and therapeutic sessions, but she was barely surviving, could hardly complete her coursework. She saw a documentary about Sacha Wasi—it sounded serious—and feeling desperate, flew halfway across the world.

She sat for a ceremony in the facility next door to us. She was told to keep her back straight, not to speak or make noise or sing or touch anyone else.

Confront what emerges, Mathieu said.

He blew tobacco on her solarplexus, fontanelle, and palms, then recited a prayer, and this prayer brought with it its own history:

In the 1880s, a priest employed in the Vatican named Domenico Pechenino witnessed a peculiar event. Pope Leo XIII suddenly froze during mass, his gaze locked on some distant point. The pope turned pale, then collapsed as though dead.

He came to with a frightened look on his face. He'd had a terrible vision. Demons were gathering around Rome. The pope saw Satan approach the throne of God, boasting he could destroy the Church.

The Lord was not shaken but reminded Satan His Church is imperishable.

Satan offered a challenge. The serpent said if granted a hundred years and power over a number of worldly servants, he could bring ruin to God's reign on earth.

The Lord granted his wish—a hundred years—as if to say *go ahead and try.*

The transfixed pope saw all the gruesome events of the twentieth century: wars raged, murder on untold scale; mass descent into immorality, depravity. He saw believers turn away from God.

When he came out of his trance, Leo called his secretary and had him transcribe a prayer to St. Michael, which came to be called *Exorcismus in Satanam et angelos apostaticos.*

His prayer envisions a great battle, with the archangel as *leader of the heavenly militia.* He envisions a market, where God has bought humanity from the devil. He implores God to apprehend the *serpéntem antíquum qui est diábolus et sátanas,* and throw him into the abyss.

So that he may no more seduce the nations.

He calls on *every unclean spirit, every satanic power, every assault of the infernal adversary, every legion, every diabolic congregation and sect* to flee from the Church of God.

Leo emerged from his trance still terrified by his vision, had the papal secretary write down his prayer.

This is our only hope, he said. All priests must recite it at mass daily, even several times a day.

And so it was done. In 1902 a shorter version was produced, and priests continued to read out the so-called *Little Exorcism* through the upheavals of the Great War, the collapse of European empires, the atrocities of the Third Reich. Then in the 1960s the Catholic hierarchy met in the Vatican and made changes to the ritual: Priests would no longer perform mass in Latin but in the local vernacular, and they would prepare communion facing the congregation, not with their backs to them as they'd always done. Also—so it was resolved—they would drop the *Little Exorcism* from daily services.

Some Catholics were scandalized by this. It's not like Satan had ceased to ensnare humanity. How could we lay down arms against that insidious enemy?

As a teenager in my hometown of Kansas City, I'd visited old St. Patrick's church on 8th and Cherry one Sunday. The priests there refused to adopt the new style, which they considered an aberration and sacrilege. They continued to perform mass in Latin and face away from the congregation when blessing the bread and wine, imagining themselves lonely holdouts in the battle against apostasy.

Mathieu Bastarache, it seems, shared this dismay at the church's unilateral ceasefire. It was Leo's *Little Exorcism* that he recited over the Parisian student after her fontanelle was infused with tobacco.

It made sense in a way. Sometimes when the medicine came on it was terrifying, so intense, and you grabbed onto whatever was available.

Créator ómnium visibílium et invisibílium! you might cry, *liberate us and keep us safe and sound.*

Amen.

At Las Coconas, one afternoon, a skinny blond woman arrived—Nadia. She said she was Ivan's girlfriend, and she'd been trying to reunite with him for several weeks. He'd left her somewhere further down the foothills toward the Amazon basin. It wasn't clear how she made it to Las Coconas, but when she arrived she congratulated Teodora and Jorge for hosting a man as handsome and intelligent as Ivan. With her arrival and Abuelita's departure, there seemed to be exceptions to the continuing ban on domestic travel.

As for us, a friend back home had lost her apartment and asked to move into our place; now it was her watching the pigeons circle over Sugar Hill, which meant we didn't need to cover expenses while we were gone. Here along the Shilcayo, in the shadow of Juliampampa, we saw no reason to sign up for a humanitarian flight to New York.

Nadia and Ivan sat together through the evenings but slept apart due to post-dietary restrictions. She'd come from yet another center attracting international guests. We'd hear all about it later.

First, Ivan wanted to cook us dinner.

Having eaten nothing but fruit on his way to becoming pure light, now he was preparing salad, lentil fritters, even meatballs.

He reminded us the meal wasn't vegetarian by asking if anyone knew the English word for труп. He then held up his phone, its screening blinking a word in all caps:

CADAVER

He set out everything and invited the five of us, Teodora and Jorge.

It's my birthday, he said. In Russia it's traditional to offer food to your friends.

We wished him happy birthday and sat down to eat. His phone continued to blink. No one touched the cadaver.

A few days later we found Ivan and Nadia back in the kitchen.

What had happened to his diet of raw fruit?

They were going to fly to Europe, they said. They'd managed to get on a flight to Spain, and from there they could get back to Moscow. They'd arranged a driver who would pick them up tomorrow and take them across the Andes to Lima.

We leave at 6:00 a.m., Ivan said.

To celebrate, he'd bought an entire chicken and put it in the oven. Two hours later, as Nadia packed or otherwise retreated to her room, he was seated at the kitchen table by himself chewing on a chicken leg.

We woke up to early-morning scurrying and muttering around Las Coconas. We heard Nadia shouting.

Please, can someone help me?

The car was here and she was trying to load it up, but Ivan was still in his room. The whole chicken did not sit well with his fruitarian stomach. Rather than turning into light, he'd deliquesced into a pool of puke.

The last we saw of Ivan was Nadia escorting him to the car. He was hunched over, deathly pale, clutching his belly. It was going to be a long ride to Lima.

Akos and I sat in the kitchen in their wake, feeling like a storm had passed.

The human body is fascinating, Akos said. It's so mundane, but it changes everything. Every day you eat and sleep, but these processes, somehow, are the portal to new dimensions. Our emotions, but also our magic, all that comes through flesh, blood, sweat, piss, and hair. All the heavens and hells we see in ceremonies are just so many transmutations of beans and bulgur.

I was reminded of Lenin: *The truth is always concrete.*

I'd once visited a pathology lab with a med student friend in Budapest. The room spread with dead bodies, most of them fat old men now belly up on stainless steel tables. Evacuated of life but still utterly human, they were helpless sacks of gray flesh. The professor toured the cadavers quizzing students. Everyone in white robes, pausing before a sawed open chest to lift out a lung, so beautiful and blue.

What are these groove-shaped indentions on the kidney?

An assistant opened a skull and let the brains slop out. Organs of those gentlemen's visions now glistened in a metal bowl.

The Tarapoto bookstore where I found *El viborero* was dark and cool in the afternoon. It stocked mostly pirate copies of commercial classics, and I was always the only one perusing the shelves. I asked for another regional title, and the bookseller tossed me the 1942 novel *Sangama*, by Arturo D. Hernández, a little green, cheaply produced paperback.

Hernández, I read, was the orphan son of a criollo schoolteacher drawn by the rubber boom—a period of horrific rape and pillage for native communities. He was raised among underpaid indigenous laborers, joined a revolutionary movement, and was jailed at eighteen before he started writing.

Sangama opens with comic portraits of small town life along the Ucayali—petty fears and grievances, the corruption and hypocrisy of local officials. The title character is an old tracker of mixed parentage, skilled in indigenous practices and in touch with a network of isolated researchers who impart occult knowledge.

As he leads the narrator through the jungle, Sangama mocks Europeans who consider the jungle a place of savagery. The outsider, he says, wants to impose their customs, habits, and laws onto the jungle. And they must fail, producing "drama formed in error" by which they are stripped of their customs and themselves become savage.

He describes the jungle as a site of *civilized collectives*, where human culture emerged from dense entanglement. To coexist in such an environment requires sensitivity and foresight:

"No young tree manages to grow up to reach the realm of clouds and birds that didn't once look for the best route between the branches of the canopy."

I lay in the hammock hearing the bamboo clatter in the wind, the rush of the river, and paged through the books I'd found in town.

Rumrill's *El viborero* mentions the story of Penny David, based on David Livingstone Pent, son of American evangelicals born in Iquitos in 1931 who fled his family and went to live among the indigenous people his parents hoped to convert. Rumrill describes him learning Piro and Campa, smearing himself with red body paint and traveling the region preaching the return of old gods driven away by the White Plague, who abandoned the world to smallpox and syphilis to live in the pure kingdom of Axpikondiá.

"The terrible nudity of nothingness," Rumrill writes, "which burns the last word like a sun."

The historical David Pent, I learned, lived in an opulent hacienda along the Tambo River, its storehouses stocked with cotton and shotguns. He leveraged the hardwood from his farm to swindle North American investors, turning the funds over to the Asháninka he worked with. It was headquarters for a group of political extortionists controlled by the one-eyed gangster Inganiteri, also a secure compound populated by trafficked indigenous women.

In 1962 Pent financed a leftist congressional candidate and married a nineteen-year-old girl, despite her engagement to a local cop. The morning after the wedding the couple were shaken awake by colleagues of the jilted fiancé. The cops threw Pent in jail as a communist; he was soon deported to the US, and his wife of one day never saw him again.

The FBI tracked him. His brother heard he was working as a chauffeur for a Hollywood actor, then that he'd remarried in New Orleans. *The Militant* reported him appearing at the Socialist Workers Party's LA office raising funds to promote Peruvian land reform.

He snuck through the border in 1965. The Peruvian press had him collaborating with the Asháninka who'd joined the guerrillas, importing weapons via Bolivia one day, waiting tables in New York the next. His old friend Javier Dávila claimed to have visited him in a Pucallpa jail, where he appeared pink cheeked and freshly shaven, and later heard he'd been thrown from an airplane over the jungle.

His sister, who suspected he'd been colonized by Satan, heard he'd gone into diamond mining.

On a wire kiosk in town I found brightly colored paperbacks containing regional folklore. I lay in the hammock reading of whistling demons, comet demons, demonic spider monkeys, demons with matted hair, demons with enormous flowers or palm trunks for genitals. I'd read then ask Miguel or Luis about these stories.

The chullachaqui is a figure used to scare little children. Quechua for *crooked foot*, these are trickster figures, chittering and mocking shapeshifters. An empty receptacle jungle sorcerers can cause to appear as various bodies, their emptiness is their power. It was with the chullachaqui in mind that Luis warned me about the bad spirits behind the Juliampampa maloca.

They can appear as anyone, he said. Your best friend, your lover.

You need to look at the feet, Miguel said. Because a chullachaqui can take on any form, but one foot is always crooked.

The games of the chullachaqui are pure trickery. Being tricked turns you into a child. Your absurdity is revealed. In this way, the chullachaqui shows us to be as empty as they are.

Alone in the jungle on a moonlit night, a beautiful man or woman appears by the calm water. A night of sensuous joys and passions and exertions ensues. In the morning the ravished awakens alone, cramped and feverish.

Yakuruna—owner of the Yacushimbillo tree I'd dieted on—is a spirit in the form of a large snake that lives in the river. It avoids the rapids and stays where the riverbed evens out and the waters calm.

If you sleep at the edge of the pool or go underwater you risk being carried off by the yakuruna, who may be in the company of other species, four-legged animals with heads of fish. Taken by yakuruna, you lower into the pool, carried to the underwater city where the spirit takes its captive. You know you're close when the riverbank appears carved—scenes of musicians and banquets, travelers and merchants, ramparts and gates and flower boxes. It's a city of celebrations and pleasures, but it is wholly unreal.

Hunting in the jungle requires a particular skill, because you have to approach very close to the animal without alerting it to your presence, otherwise it's impossible to shoot it, either with a dart or gun. Scent and stillness—you come close, and you get one chance.

A plump bird alights in the forest ahead of you, a few steps to the left and you'll get a clear shot. You step off the path, but the bird moves to another branch, and another. Following with your gaze, you step carefully. Eventually, the game is yours, it plummets at the base of a tree. Thoughtlessly, you mark the trunk with your machete so you'll know your way back. But wait—you realize you've strayed far from your path. You have no idea which way it is. Darkness is falling. You need to find your way back. You set off in the direction you think is right. In the last glimmerings of the day, you see a familiar tree. Getting closer, you see your machete mark on its trunk. You've been walking in circles.

Where to go now? The only place to get a good look at the sky is along the river. You see the moon through the trees and sense a clearing, but it's still blocked by leaves and branches. Eventually you come to the banks, and the moon now reflects the river's calm waters. Overcome by the moment, you strip down and step in. That's when yakuruna appears.

Drama formed in error, switchbacks of fate, the Peruvian Amazon was a place of reimaginings. I came across no story more contradictory, perhaps, than that of Manuel Córdova-Rios:

In 1907, at the tail end of the rubber boom, Córdova-Rios, Iquitos-born son of a white rubber tapper, was hunting in the forest when a band of Amawakas grabbed him and carried him off to their isolated settlement. He was fifteen years old. The raiders presented Córdova-Rios to an elder named Ximu, who took him in and schooled the captive in his language. Ximu identified himself as chief of a community called Huni Kui—*the Chosen People.* He bathed his prisoner in herbal infusions and renamed him Ino Moxo—*Black Panther.* Ximu explained that his community was threatened with extinction by rubber tappers; they needed arms to defend themselves. As a white man, Córdova-Rios was able to put back on his white man's clothes and stroll into town to buy more guns— something no indigenous person at that time could do. The captive, once reborn as Ino Moxo, agreed to help. He taught Ximu's community to use a rifle and to tap and package rubber for trade. Before his death, Ximu revealed that his own son had been killed in a raid, and he had adopted Ino Moxo to succeed him. The Huni Kui survived under the white man's leadership, but eventually Córdova-Rios abdicated his chiefly position and returned to Iquitos.

Later in life Manuel Córdova-Rios was hired as a fixer by an American surveyor, F. Bruce Lamb, and they traveled the region mapping tributaries. The surveyor found that wherever they went, villagers approached asking for remedies; his fixer was seen as a great curandero. In 1971, the American published Córdova-Rios's autobiography—*Wizard of the Upper Amazon*—with Lamb himself as ghost writer.

I lay in the hammock and read of the young captive's initiation, a series of fasts and hunts punctuated by ceremonies with vision-inducing herbs. In his first ceremony, the newly initiated Ino Moxo witnessed "emotional involvements of undefinable content, confused elements, pure colors, and abstract shapes."

It was not until much later, after many sessions, he said, that he established enough control to attempt to describe his visions. But already after that first session he had a breakthrough with language. Previously struggling to understand and be understood in Amawaka, now overnight he gained noticeable fluency.

Wizard of the Upper Amazon contains accounts of quotidian details of Ino Moxo's acculturation. It describes dental remedies, use of tree resin to remove body hair, hunting techniques for toucans and tapirs. We learn that touching the skin of a boa brings luck. A hawk is the symbol of knowledge.

The book contains translations of transcriptions of icaros. The ghost-written Ino Moxo describes his teacher Ximu singing them in a high falsetto with a "tremulous obbligato."

spirit of the forest
origin of our understanding
illuminate our mind
bring us foresight
show us the designs
of our enemies
expand our understanding
of our forest

Listening to these songs, Ino Moxo experienced a pulsing hum, sexual sensations, and then emerged from his body, able to roam forests and mountains unencumbered by physical being. Time was elastic. Trees took on an aspect of "obedient benevolence."

Córdova-Rios paused his account to remind his listener that "the deeper we go into this, both written and spoken words of formal language become more and more inadequate as a medium of expression."

Under Ximu's tutelage, Ino Moxo's visions became an education in animal behavior, plant behavior, an introduction to all varieties of life in the jungle. He learned that tinamous titter at the approach of a jaguar, that the sadness of their call expresses a reluctance to sleep alone. The apprentice found he could visualize "shades of cinnamon, chestnut and dusky brown, colors that blended imperceptibly with the light and shadows on the leafy forest floor."

He saw, to his surprise, the male tinamou guarding the nest. This was no metaphorical vision, but simple insight into the birds' gender roles.

"Yes, he raises the children," the chief confirmed.

Roaming the night, Ino Moxo learned to distinguish gurgling from clucking from the four-note melody of the bird known as mother-of-the-moon. His ears sharpened until he could differentiate at a distance the rhythmic rustling of an añuje from the quick steps of a cashucucha. He also learned there were unidentifiable sounds called *yene*, "a spirit source no one could explain."

In another session Ino Moxo learned how plants could be used as medicine. He saw the method to stitch gaping wounds with polished palm thorns. He learned to influence plants with song. He learned that songs intensified or calmed his visions, guiding their course.

With time he found the acuteness of his senses remained even between sessions. He felt he could anticipate events and divine reactions of other people. In turn, he taught his companions how to sharpen an axe and machete and make heavy wooden mallets—the tools of the rubber trade. He taught them how to drain a trunk of milky latex sap.

When he first went to a trading post to sell the latex, he wondered whether Ximu had brought him under some kind of mind control. It was June 15, 1910. It had been two and a half years, and he found in himself no desire to return to the society from which he'd been abducted. In the company of other traders, he ate feijoada and drank coffee—his first salt and sugar since his capture. Like Ivan after his chicken, Ino Moxo suffered the consequences the next day, but returning to the Huni Kui, he ate smoked jaguar and jungle fruits and was restored.

When Ximu died, his body was laid out on a platform lit with burning resin, and the community chanted in mourning. In his teacher's absence, Ino Moxo grew into his role as chief. He learned to suss dynamics in the community, when to release tension in drunken euphoria, when to call rivals to hash out problems face to face. When someone was sick, as shown by his teacher he used sleight of hand to make them believe he'd sucked poisoned thorns out of their body. Soon they would be cured.

The Huni Kui shared a memory of expulsion from their native territory by rubber prospectors. An event of horrific violence, parents had seen children's skulls bashed in, their daughters and mothers raped. It was indelible in the collective memory. Ximu led the survivors to the territory where they now lived. After his death, the community urged Ino Moxo to travel with them to revisit those forsaken lands, a kind of pilgrimage. Only then could he understand what they'd been through. When they arrived they found the prospectors' settlements abandoned, whoever had terrorized them was gone. The rubber boom had come to an end.

Returning from their pilgrimage, Ino Moxo narrowly escaped a couple of poisoned arrows—from raiders or members of his own community?— and began to wonder about his future with the Huni Kui. He prepared the vision-inducing brew and sat alone to drink it. Color patterns appeared, but the vision grew dark and menacing, vipers coiled around him. He began to discern subtle patterns in his heartbeat. He sensed the involuntary impulses that controlled his bodily processes. He floated off into "a boundless, hideous void" without spatial dimensions.

"A feeling of uncontrollable rhythmic acceleration toward some impending disaster plunged me, helplessly, into an indescribably agonizing purgatory of the mind."

He confronted enemies, saw his mother die, met the spirit of Ximu, and united with the spirit of his feline namesake. When he came to in the morning light, he felt whole, fearing nothing, but when he returned to sleep in the village, the terrifying visions continued. Nightly, now, his anguish was relentless. Only when alone could he find calm. He was still staving off such bouts on his next trip to the trading post.

I'd carried my book to a bench near the fruitstand around the corner from Las Coconas, and I stopped now to consider the feeling of uncontrollable rhythmic acceleration. I'd had my own nights where visions and voices were coming at me fast. As beautiful as ceremonies could be, there were times when I felt throttled, writhing, caught in the grip of a force so powerful there was no escape. Sometimes it felt as if layers of irony were being ladled one on top of the other until the meanings amounted to ranting madness.

I looked around at the dirt roads of this neighborhood called Villa Autónoma, wondering at the outrageousness of a community kidnapping a white man to resist white encroachment and ending up making him their chief. Was any of this true? The layers upon layers of irony, when they came, could be more excruciating than nausea or physical pain. You knew all that would pass but the hastening mental figures felt like a terminal race toward destruction. But now I was at the edge of Tarapoto considering the stories of Ino Moxo from the safe distance of words on paper.

When Córdova-Rios made this next trip to the post with his blocks of rubber, on hardly more than a whim, he said, he cashed in his goods, boarded a launch, and sailed downriver to Brazil, disembarking in far away Manaus. He reaccustomized himself to clothing, to seasoned food, to speaking Spanish. Overwhelmed by the big central Amazonian port city, he booked passage upstream to his father's house in Iquitos. As his vision had foretold, his mother was dead of flu. He did his best to settle back in to life at home. He was twenty-two years old.

When narrating the book decades later, Córdova-Rios had had no contact with the Huni Kui but retained his training from Ximu. He possessed invaluable insights into the natural world, knowledge of plant remedies, and an uncanny sense of what was to come. Wherever he went, the sick seemed to flock to him.

"I am able, sometimes, without knowing exactly how, to help them."

The story of Ino Moxo found its way to César Calvo, an Iquitos-born poet living in Lima, who resolved to return to his hometown, seek out the old man, and see what he could learn. Along the way he visited other famous curanderos, sat with them, and drank medicine. The next book I read was his 1981 account of that excursion, *Las tres mitades de Ino Moxo.* Calvo's record of encounters and visions is offered in the voice of a fictional brother—as if it were impolite to narrate one's visions directly.

More than fifty years after his abduction, Calvo finds the now elderly Córdova-Rios in an ordinary Iquitos home, and the two of them spend several evenings together. The curandero says he sees his capture not as violation but revelation. Ximu offered him a true identity.

Ino Moxo offers the poet a theory of language, developed through paradoxical living. Beyond his own shifting identity, it was written into the land itself. The Amawaka lived on jungle islands that appear and disappear as rivers change, surrounded by plants that switch gender from one day to the next:

"To understand and name a world like that," Ino Moxo tells Calvo, "we also need to speak like that. A language that sinks or rises without warning, forestations of words that are here today but wake up far away."

"Our words are like pools in which different waters mix: waterfalls, the drizzle of other times, oceans that were and will be ash. Our words are living beings that walk on their own volition, animals that never repeat themselves, that never put on the same skin."

When you can speak like that, Ino Moxo says, you are capable of curing illnesses: "there is no error, and no miracle."

Hearing this, Calvo reaches for his box of matches and sees that it is the head of a deer.

How can he light his cigarette with the head of a deer? he asks, knowing it is also a box of matches.

Miguel brought Nafis, Teodora, and me up to Juliampampa; the rest needed to be online. We came up to rake and clear and harvest and plant. Even in dry season like now plants grew at a rapid pace, mice ate through windowscreen, termites feasted on beams and boards. Even the simple huts required constant upkeep. Usually visitors come once a month, so it paid to bring up several family members and feed everyone while they work the land and take care of the place. But now in lockdown there are few visitors, and so, as Miguel said, se está volviendo monte.

We walked up, crossing the Shilcayo fourteen times, cleaned the maloca and watched as Miguel cooked bobinsana for Teodora, who was going to complete a short diet while we're here. He put three or four kilos of bark in a huge pot and cooked it on the fire at full boil for four hours. Then he pulled the bark out and let the mixture sit overnight. This morning they strained it and it was ready to serve.

We had a small ceremony, just the five of us. I sensed entities in the maloca—tense coils of energy bouncing around. They passed right through the field that was my body. I knew if I tensed against them they'd get caught and I'd be overtaken by fear and anxiety and anger and begin to cry out and thrash and scream. As long as I stayed calm they passed right through me and I was fine. It happened over and over again through the night.

Miguel called the ceremony to a close and asked us questions.

Why do we get old?

We sat around talking, as usual.

Miguel showed a picture on his camera—an ad for a ceremony in Asunción: *El Curandero Mashti*. I hadn't thought about him in weeks, but there he was dressed in the robe he'd worn for his photo shoot in the maloca.

He has my father's feathers, Miguel said.

Sure enough, Mashti wore the crown of feathers he'd borrowed from Miguel that evening.

Este wawki, Miguel shook his head, using the Quechua word for brother.

How did he get to Paraguay? I wondered.

He was in Las Coconas before he went, Teodora said. He stayed with his boyfriend.

Boyfriend? Miguel was confused.

But Teodora said yes, he came with a guy and they spent a few nights together in one of the rooms in Las Coconas.

Este wawki, Miguel shook his head again, seeing the truth for the first time.

And observing Miguel take in the news of Andrés's sexuality, I felt I understood more about what was happening.

I knew Andrés grew up at the edge of Tarapoto, in a crisscross of dirt roads not far from Las Coconas. His parents owned the neighborhood liquor store. He'd worked for Miguel's father until he died, and then, as he said, he grew wings. He began to travel the world as a curandero, convening all kinds of people.

I might criticize his insufficient experience, at least by Miguel's standards, and his manipulation of Herta. I might scoff at his nickname, his silly robe, his cooption of Pedro's feathers. But I had to grant that for Andrés it was the most readily available way out of Tarapoto, away from the macho culture that would never understand him. Holding ceremonies in Tulum, in Berlin, he could explore who he was. He could be free. The medicine gave him wings, and who were we to say he might not possess vision?

Nafis and I spent the days threshing and raking, clearing paths and replacing screens in huts. In the afternoon we sat at the long table at the comedor and relaxed. Today there were other visitors. A friend of Miguel named Daniel had come up with a group of biologists. The lead researcher was a wiry Italian woman.

There are bees up here unknown to science, she said. We're going to gather specimens and collect wild honey.

A porter had accompanied them. He dropped his burden and sat with us. Nafis asked his name.

Hitler, he said.

Nafis asked him to spell it.

H-I-T-L-E-R.

The German? Nafis asked.

Sí, führer, Hitler said.

Years later, when the biologists published their findings on new species of stingless bees, I came across his name in the acknowledgments. I didn't imagine Hitler's parents celebrating genocide—who knew what it meant to them? But the name spoke of human legacies migrating across the world, moving in all directions, warped and misinterpreted, woven into new realities with untold consequences. It was a reminder of those interlacings, how they stretched and morphed and made the world.

Miguel told us that Daniel ran the animal care center at the edge of the park, the place called Urku. We'd heard of it. It was where COVID, having migrated across the world, first struck near us, and we passed it on our walks up Prolongación Alerta.

He has a tiger, Miguel said.

Daniel said it was an ocelot. He'd found it injured and nursed it back to health. Now it was better, but he knew if he released it someone would kill it. He was trying to figure out what to do. Meanwhile the ocelot paced its cage, looking at Daniel with its beautiful eyes.

New and unknown bees, I thought. Wild honey. I'd heard that neurons functioned like swarms of bees—chattering to each other, exchanging stories, thinking together. I knew the Qur'an claimed that bees, alone among animals, possessed the power of prophecy.

In the morning Miguel served me a cup of medicine—straight aya-huasca with chacruna, no added piri piri or ayahuma. I found that if I took my glasses off and softened my focus, patterns and forms began to emerge—swooping, constantly moving shapes like water or oil on a pane of glass. The movements were within or among or inseparable from the plants and birds and bugs. I sat for hours on the stone just past the yanchama tree watching these flows and forces running and streaming, beading up and shifting, as if the fabric of reality were that oil on glass. Imaginary matter, silk threads.

I felt thrilled by this, as if I'd discovered something. I could feel a rise in my chest, a kind of pride. I thought now that I'd seen these forms and shapes I would always see them, even when I couldn't see them, because I knew they were there. But there was an edge to my enthusiasm, as if I were taking credit for these visions rather than simply receiving them. I had to remind myself to calm down.

Miguel arrived and found me staring into the empty air and I told him what I was seeing.

Those are spirits and powers that exist in the jungle, Miguel said. If you ask permission, you can communicate with them.

I turned to look at the yanchama tree enveloped in vines, ancient and masterful, woven from these silk threads. I looked at the bark and moss, the trees within trees, and wondered if swathes of history, in minute detail, weren't written on the yanchama tree. I was aswim in the mental liquid that holds together all that happens.

The southern face of the trunk was riddled with hashmarks from machetes. Was it a way to gather the medicinal sap of the tree? A mark to find your way? Perhaps it was a thoughtless, even tender interaction with the tree.

Miguel stood as usual with his palm on the bark, looking up.

My father said it had maybe fifty more years, he said.

Miguel indicated for me to sit in front of my hut, and he gave me a limpia. I felt the insistent beat of the shakapa's dry leaves on my head and face and shoulders and palms as he sang. Afterward we sat on the floorboards of the hut. He told me about his grandfather Pedro, his father Pedro, his brother Pedro, about an earlier relationship he'd had—Jonathan's mother. They'd been together twelve years. Now they're not together but they're all right. He's been in his new relationship thirteen years, but she's diabetic and she won't come up and work with the plants. And her diabetes is advancing.

What can I do, he said. I can't force her.

So he comes up alone. More and more he comes up alone.

I went to see Nafis and found him still euphoric under the plants' spell. He was shaking his shells and calling out to family members, teachers, everyone who'd ever helped him. His face was livid with joy as he enumerated his gratitude. Finally he landed on Allah—

The creator sees me!

He turned to face me, sure I'd understand.

Allah sees me!

I could see Nafis hurling through space, from his Canarsie basement to war zones to contracts in Tokyo. All the while watched by God.

Of course, I said.

I was reminded of the moment I'd imagined scratching at the fabric of reality until it peels up, revealing what's beneath. Even if what's revealed is another layer, and it's clear that below that is another and another, the matter of lifting up the scrim automatically, somehow, I thought, reveals

155

the source—you're alone with the bottomlessness, the whole apophatic blast. Staring into the whirlwind, it seemed, you look out for any still point. The Ka'aba encircled by worshippers—you see it. That connection is made and it changes everything. One still point, the creator, all the ka'abas, stillness everywhere.

A storm came over the mountains and pelted the roof with rain.

In the evening we sat around the table at the comedor. We watched Daniel and Hitler bag beans from the beanfield. We watched the sun set over the ojé tree and the bobinsana. The toé bush was in full bloom and its dizzying scent mixed with smoke from the cooking fire.

Is it true that plants can read their surroundings? I asked the biologists.

The Italian explained that seedlings understand what will happen to light, where it will move and what will block it. They seem to see in advance how other plants will grow, prognosticating the state of the canopy years into the future. Some plants can distinguish between shade cast by a corrugated iron roof from shade created by a tree.

I remembered Sangama: it takes sensitivity and foresight to survive out here.

Even if plants can't necessarily tell the future, I thought, a vine that can encircle a tree, depending on it for structure and sustenance, keeping it close without strangling it—blooming and withering, extending tendrils, enwrapping, dropping fruit or seeds or saplings—that's the intelligence of civilized collectives.

So if we feel in our visions that we're seeing the future—Ino Moxo's uncanny sense of the impending—this might be an aspect of plant intelligence seeping into us.

But the biologists said it's not only the sense of what's to come. Plants have senses—they register the chemical make-up of the air around them, the texture and solidity of what they come in contact with, they sense magnetic fields, gravity.

Roots are explorers, they said. They're sensitive and alert—touching, listening, smelling the air around them. Plants are exposed bodies. All that's most sensitive and vulnerable is at the surface.

The yanchama, maximally sensitive and entangled, must have great knowledge of its place in the world. And do I know my place in the world? I wondered. Or better yet: what do I know about my place in the world? And now that I'd registered this imaginative skein that interweaves reality, what does that tell me?

Taking this moment as a case study—us, here, now—what do I know?

Is that what *plight* means—to grasp one's place in the world?

Ino Moxo says words are animals and language must reflect sudden changes in the course of the river. But up in Juliampampa it's not so much the river that shifts—the Shilcayo is serpentine, but it's too steep to shift the way a river can in the Amazon basin. Here, instead, there's wind and rain, light and darkness, distant rumblings, rocks falling, earth pushing up, pressing together, sliding apart, striking and slipping. Standing on rocky earth we might feel tension, the myth of solid ground, rising up through our feet and into our brain, gathering in the back of our throat before we speak or attempt to sing. Here language must be steep and seismic. Not that it must be, it is whether we like it or not.

If the stillness of plants was acute concentration, what about the stones that surround us? We know plants aren't really still but move with light and heat and humidity. Stone movement is slow, slow, then cataclysmic.

When I used to spend time with Manhattan diamond cutters above Forty-Seventh Street, they'd tell me each stone has a song. They glue a stone into a dop and lower it against a spinning plate called a scaif, and the stone emits a high whine. After years of polishing you can hear imperfections in the grain of the diamond's carbon lattice. Those subtle imperfections are valuable; they're what gives the stone *life*.

If it were merely a matter of corralling light, gathering and concentrating light, there would be no point in listening. Perfect equations are bright but lifeless. Life comes with subtle inefficiencies—that's the stone's poetry and its poetry has value, also its history and heritage and legacy and the stories that accrue to it. It's not simply a matter of dreaming things into existence, because the dream is shared.

Luis had been coming by Las Coconas in the afternoons to teach us a few words of Quechua. By now when Miguel sang I could follow many of the phrases he often repeated, freely mixing Quechua and Spanish:

Ñukanami kayariki, he would call a plant to come.

Yaikurimuy la maloca—Enter the maloca, we're waiting.

He would tell the plants to cure our bodies, guard our spirits. He would call to the mountains, the jungle, the jaguar pacing the peaks.

It's up there, he'd tell me in front of the maloca at night. He would indicate the high peaks above Juliampampa, marking the jaguar's movements with his walking stick or his mapacho—back and forth, back and forth—looking out under his glasses with the hint of a smile.

He sat me on a rock—Sing, Brak!—and as I tried to sing he imitated me until we were both laughing.

Don't sing like that, he said. I'm telling you this because I love you.

Now he started to sing and I followed him, then tried to diverge but keep his pace and structure, so our melodic or semi-melodic lines were intertwined.

Keep your cheeks loose, he said, and your tone high—delgadito.

He sang in his own thin, searching manner, showing me.

That's what the plants like, he said.

He sang syllables, a few phrases in Quechua. Then we sang nonsense together for a while.

Like the foot of the chullachaqui, I was learning that the song could be twisted. The transformative power is in sounds that don't declare but hover at the edge of meaninglessness, that turn away from meaning—either singing gibberish or repeating syllables until they lose their semantic depth—forbid the mind from alighting anywhere for long, remaining unfixed, conditioning the mind to stay searching, opening outward.

The song was a discipline. It reminded us we're still finding out what the world is, how things are, what the laws are. We're aswim in the unknown and half-known, the almost seen, the haze and murk of our limitations, our position in the unfolding. But the discipline was also going someplace, and the language urged us forward so we didn't dissolve and spiral off into the haze and murk that lie within. The songs oriented us and stabilized us, one word was enough to offer direction.

What if those Baghdad marines had walked around singing ¡Graci-as! like Nafis?

Here on the stone behind the Juliampampa maloca, I realized, Miguel was trying to show me how language and sound come together to summon spirits. Searching and loose so when they come they come in clouds of meaning, swarms of bees, fungal tips, and plant roots. Great swarms of neural bees are summoned when we call to someone or something. We say *O mama bobinsana come cure my body and guard my spirit!* And what comes are those clouds of sensitivities and intelligences. We summon through language and sound and we summon through affection. The plant recognizes our affection and returns it, returns it with greater force and generosity and patience, because that's its nature.

Before we went back down I walked alone toward the high cataracts. Past the third sapoina, near a deep puddle, I saw a frog I'd never seen before, the size of my thumb, all black except a pale-yellow patch behind its head and reaching halfway down its back. I squatted down and got a good look at its glistening skin before it hopped away.

Miguel and Teodora would stay a few more days, but Nafis and I needed to reconnect, so we went down from Juliampampa alone. It was the first time we'd made the three- or four-hour walk without guidance.

We stood at the top of the hill carrying our own packs this time.

After the first crossing, Miguel said, there's a fork. Don't go left up the hill but stay to the right. When you get closer to the bottom, don't veer off but follow the river.

With that much instruction, we set off. It felt good to be on our own in the jungle, to feel at home in the cordillera. Nafis hadn't brought his bag of dried coca leaves, but we gathered some fresh leaves right off a tree and were buoyant and talkative as ever.

Nafis had been struggling with his firehouse. His supervisors did not believe he couldn't come back.

They think I'm down here scratching my ass, he said.

The city was still shut down, there were few fires. Most firefighters were at home. But still, the department expected him to find a way back to New York.

I'm down here doing something they can't understand, Nafis said. And I find myself thinking things over.

He said lying in bed after the burn last year he'd begun to wonder about his future as a firefighter. Now he finds himself in Peru, with Miguel, and the idea of returning to the department is not appealing.

They said I better come back if I want to keep my job, Nafis said, so I said fine: I'll resign. But then they hit me with this—he started laughing—I need to come back to sign my resignation letter in person—just to sign!—and I need to do it by the end of September. Otherwise they won't give me my pension. Are you kidding!

We made it to the first crossing and went to the right as Miguel instructed. We managed the fourteen crossings without getting lost, stopping to drink the crystalline water Miguel showed us the first time up. We followed the river to the gates of the reserve and walked down Prolongación Alerta. We passed Daniel's Urku center, the Hilton maloca at Serpentina, the closed down orchid garden, and made our way to Las Coconas. We found Akos and Eszter at work, Szilvia playing with the cat, the toucans flying from one tree to the next.

It was summer by then and Ramadan was about to start. Nafis was gearing up for the fast. I was not a convert, but I'd studied Islamic theology and participated in all-night dhikr rituals, which meant I'd repeated the conversion pledge countless times. Nafis and I's banter often turned to Islam. In different ways it helped us both understand what we were going through.

Would it bother you, I asked, if I observe the fast with you?

Be my guest, brother!

Nafis said he'd be very happy to have the company. So for those twenty-eight days we woke before dawn for suhur. I boiled quail eggs and Nafis threw mangos and avocados into the blender. We ate and Nafis talked. He told me about his father, about moving from Youngstown to Atlanta as a child, about joining the military, ending up in New York as a firefighter.

How long was your stretch with the department? I asked.

Five years, Nafis said. I was in the academy for a year. I hit top pay in 2019.

It was odd to have had the image of firefighting and firefighters in my mind since I was a kid. I pictured frantic action interrupting endless games of chess. How was that life?

You have intelligent people there, Nafis said. A lot of military guys—Rangers and Seals—but also doctors and lawyers and engineers. It was their dream. They wanted to be firefighters since they were kids, because their father or uncle—it's a family industry.

We ate cubes of melon. I kept peppering him with questions about firefighting. We were here about to dissolve into immateriality. I thought of Jonathan screaming and it was like he'd been saying *Douse me!* What could more concrete, I wondered, than fighting fires? I wanted to know what it did to you to be in that state of immediacy. How did you get good at it?

Nafis spoke about it with the fluency of seasoned experience.

You have to understand the job, he said. You have to understand the systems, how buildings are built, what your tools are. You need to understand techniques and procedures. That stuff is paramount. People spend a lot of time studying, discussing tactics, drilling. You need to think on your feet, you need awareness of your surroundings. The ideal firefighter is compassionate, empathetic, selfless.

This last expression made me imagine firefighters like a religious sect. But mostly it was just a bunch of guys engaged in firehouse banter.

All day long you talk about the job, Nafis said. If somebody messes up, gets hurt, is too scared to go into a fire, as long as there's somebody to tell that tale it'll get told.

I'd participated in prayers many times, but I'd never learned to pray properly, so over that first day Nafis taught me to pray. It was moving to be taught to pray, even if I had mixed feelings about it. Who was Muhammad to me? I thought about it each time I repeated certain passages. But through the endless hours in the garden, the repetitive days pecking at the computer or reading in the hammock, it was good to have that structure and solidarity. It was the backdrop for weeks of morning conversations. I wanted to know about getting burned, which I knew was one of the reasons Nafis had come back to see Miguel. How did it happen?

He told me in the middle of his divorce he'd had to get out of the apartment he'd shared with his wife. He was adrift and in need of money. On top of the fire department, he was driving Uber and Lyft and picking up contracting work and sometimes sleeping in his car. In that blear he'd ended up sleeping through a run at the fire department.

I was in the shithouse, Nafis said. I got brought into the office, had to speak to the captain. Now I'm *that guy*, you know: you missed a fucking run. *What if somebody got hurt? What if somebody died?* I was apologetic, but they wouldn't let it go. So every night I got put on night watch.

I listened. I could imagine those guys, what it felt like in the shithouse. I'd known military guys in the Balkans. But somehow as obvious as it was, I had trouble imagining a firefighter getting burned.

It was three in the morning and we got a call, Nafis said, fire in a third-floor rear apartment. We got to the building, we went in: a one-bedroom place with a living room right off the entrance. There's the kitchen, bedroom's in back. I've got the fire extinguisher, I'm in what's called *can position*. We're supposed to search for life and find out where the fire actually is, communicate to the engine so they'll know where to operate. It's the kind of job where you could end up with a medal. We go inside. There's a couch on fire in the living room. I move past it toward the doorway to the kitchen. Since I have the can, my role is to protect the other two firefighters who are with me. One guy's got the irons—he's responsible for forcing the door. The other's the boss. The three of us are on the fire floor. We need to check if there are people in the back bedroom. We have to go past the burning couch in the living room to do that. And there's no firehose. We've called down but there's still no line in place. The couch is burning, a window has failed, and I'm in can position, using the extinguisher to mitigate the heat and protect the two firefighters while they inspect the back. I do that until my can is getting low, and there's still no line in place. The fire is starting to push over our heads, and that's never good. I'm already feeling like I'm getting burned. And then my can is out and there's still no water. I can feel the heat gathering, I know my arm is burned in one place already. So the only thing we can do is push deeper into the apartment. The heat is starting to build. This all happens in a matter of seconds. We're calling for water, trapped in the back of the apartment. The situation is bad. It's getting crazy hot. I thought I don't want to die here, but I wasn't panicking. I remember my breath training from the academy. The minute you lose your head, a bad situation just got worse. Stay relaxed. I'm burned. It is what it is. The water comes and it's out. I checked around the floors, ceilings, all the things you do when a fire's out. Got downstairs and changed out the equipment, finally asked about going to the bus because I knew I was burned. When another firefighter realized later, he said I should've called out I was cooking because from second- to third-degree burn is quick, and the damage is much worse. But I was playing the game, *earning my stripes and burning my stripes.*

The way off the shit list, it seemed, was to show efficacious stoicism in the face of being burned alive.

We downed our blended mango so we could pray before dawn. Nafis made the call to prayer, and the beauty and melody of his voice echoing off the bamboo was uncanny, as if it came from a body beyond him.

I was still translating the *Song of the Banu Sasan*, the perfect counterpoint to fasting. Between listening to Nafis, trying to memorize suras to recite during prayers—*after struggle comes relief*—I meticulously reworked that ode to blasphemy:

> We're those strutting studs who giggle and flirt through
>   Friday prayers
> and every saucy beggar queen prancing like a thoroughbred while
>   her husband looks on
> and all the throbbing hard-ons at Eid
> O God—make it rain on the Banu Sasan

THIS COULD ALL BE YOURS

Rivers of the dead. Waves of human bodies, naked, coursing through. I knew some of them, even if I could hardly see their faces. I discerned a jaw, a neck, curve of hips, a familiar thigh. We'd been close at other times in other places, gone through things together, known struggle and relief. Lovers, old friends, family members—our fates were intertwined. But now they were among the dead and flowed through the darkened space with all the others. Where their eyes were unobstructed we gazed at each other in recognition, nonverbal knowingness poured between us. The river moved on and they made their way and I remained, at least for now. I could only blow a kiss and wish them well.

Diaphanous, playful, brightly colored beings now dangled just near me, woven from smoldering gems and moth wings, clusters or concentrations of almost imaginary matter. They tittered softly and flubbed their lips, pulsing in a humming mist, an undercurrent of shadow cast by light that might be firefly flickers or the patrolling night watchman's flashlight through palm fronds sharpened to bloodletting points. At first the creatures appeared light-hearted, as bewildered as I was, but each carried in its center a knot of trouble, a knot that might loosen and open, suck you in and spit you out elsewhere. You could leave this life and go hopscotching through time, see unimaginable things, converse with creatures made of pure mathematics, subtle meanings, all the colors of doom.

A sleepy hiccup from the mouth of a great frog, bubbles popping out of simmering glue, with a filter shift the background replaced the foreground and a deep and dark and massive but compressed clod, as much mind as air, now asserts a readiness to swallow and digest. Keeping soft and still so as not to disturb, the slightest flicker of attention, impulse to blink without blinking, might be enough to set it off. But no, it retracts, and like that the clod is gone and for now we're safe. Though still there were lurkers in the garden, corners of swill and grout and gust and lurch that want and watch and wait.

Ramadan had come and gone and then summer was over, too. Nafis, Akos, and Szilvia weren't around. Eszter said she'd talked to too many clients that day and couldn't deal with more stimulation, so decided not to come. Jonathan was back to his old ways, driving his mototaxi around Tarapoto, hanging out with his girlfriend, avoiding ceremonies. But Miguel invited me and I went, back to Serpentina's Hilton maloca. It was Luis, a couple of Russians, a friend of Jorge's from Lima and two friends of Miguel's from Tarapoto—Nurse Rosita and Efraim the barber.

Efraim worked in the peluquería where Miguel went to have his hair buzzed. He knew Miguel's reputation as a curandero, and as he adjusted the shield on his clipper he dogged Miguel to invite him to a ceremony.

When will I get a chance? I want to know ayahuasca!

He was in his late twenties, in distressed white jeans with a black t-shirt stretched tight over his broad chest. His hair was in a neat fade with a line cut just above his ear. He joked nervously with Miguel as we settled into our spots.

Rosita worked in Tarapoto's main hospital. Miguel had known her for years. She'd balled up her scrubs at the end of a long shift, showered, and come straight to the maloca. Her black hair, streaked with gray, was tied loosely at the base of her neck. She hardly spoke and didn't move from her mat all night. She drank her medicine then sat in place, shoulders shaking gently, tears streaming down her face. Eventually she lay on her back and was still.

I'd heard from my emergency room doctor friend, who'd accurately foreseen the civilization-altering pandemic about to line up the sick outside his hospital. By now he'd accustomed himself to walking through corridors thronged with hacking and dying patients. He described holding up the phone to an already motionless parent's ear so a son or daughter could say goodbye. His eyes glazed as he went on to the next case.

Stolen oxygen, organizational collapse, her own private matters—I had no doubt Rosita had things to cry about.

The medicine hummed through me and I felt sensitive and patient, not craving greater intensities tonight.

Efraim, on the other had, said he felt nothing and asked for more, but a half hour later the medicine hit him and he began to wail and rant. He'd imagined Miguel's life a shower of money and foreign women, thought the plants would open him up to all that. Instead Efraim connected to the pain in Miguel's eye, his wife's diabetes. He summoned his own fear and longing and anger, his rage at privation and injustice and the fucking limitations of life, not to mention all the fried food and bad booze he'd consumed. He sat howling and snarling as Nurse Rosita cried silently next to him.

I stepped outside, where Luis was perched on a step with his head in his hands.

They think we go up to Juliampampa with a bunch of foreigners and get rich, he said.

I could feel Efraim's miasma as the weight of envy on Luis and his family. A girlfriend's mother thought her daughter had hooked up with that Tapullima boy so now she must have money—she's lying when she says she's still broke. Tangles of desire and vulnerability and sweetness and jealousy and shame, with no centralizing strength. So many people lost, traumatized, in danger. Many, as Miguel said, had hoisted the white flag.

The medicine was stable in me while I sat and listened to Luis. He described the future he saw in Tarapoto: wife and child and more children and more struggles and misunderstandings, more stress about money, more jealousy, anger and fights and divorce. It was like a blanket falling over him. He felt the need to escape and escape now.

If I could just go to the beach by myself, he thought, have a break from this reality and see what's what.

The Russians had wanted to escape, too. They spent all night in the empty grounds outside, singing to each other. I went back in where Efraim continued to bellow in self-pity.

What have you done to me?

Somewhere if not down the river of the dead then at least down the Shilcayo Valley through Tarapoto, down the Marañón and Ucayali and all the other tributaries gathering in the big open basin of the rainforest, with its wide rivers of uncertain trajectory and elaborate volume, lazing through lowlands full of silt and sand and soil, somewhere there, I knew, lives the piraíba—a catfish as big as a car. Mostly it rests on the river bottom as water flows past. But then it shifts, whipping its tail and stirring the murk. And when it stirs the murk, no one can see anything.

Efraim's miasma was not the bitterest of the season's appearances. There'd been a night Nafis and Szilvia witnessed with me. After vibrating next to Jonathan as he confronted death, Akos occasionally preferred to sit ceremonies out. Eszter had planned to join but just as we were leaving she said she was exhausted and decided to stay at Las Coconas.

Eszter sabe, Miguel would joke later.

Szilvia and I had talked many times about ceremonies we'd shared. What did she make of all this?

We sat drinking tea as the daylight waned over our walled garden, talking about biology. When she talked about her work Szilvia was straightforward and serious; her slight accent fell away with the familiar vocabulary of science:

Biology offers tools to study cells and tissues, she said. We used to use radioactive labeling to grasp molecular mechanisms. Now live imaging lets us study cellular processes in real time. A new kind of microscope allows us to see things in a new way, and that's how we make discoveries.

As with Nafis, these conversations spanned weeks and months. Before a ceremony we sensed the waves of intensities about to sweep over us. The need for calm gave our conversations weight.

Plant medicine is a powerful microscope, Szilvia said. It might help us gain insights into incurable diseases, like autoimmune conditions we don't understand the cause of. A lot of diseases have some emotional aspect: some misfire stored in the body, a malfunction biology can't explain. We can't measure pain. But we know it's real. We can measure local inflammation or some other associated biomarker but might not grasp the causal link.

I wondered if lately she'd thought more about such unknown links.

Plant medicines keep you open-minded, she said, and that's good for doing science. When your research contradicts what's known, your experiment might be trash or you might be about to revolutionize the field.

She told me about her own research, which was on Huntington's disease.

It's thought of as a late-onset neurodegenerative disorder, she said. It usually appears when people are fifty or sixty years old. But we used stem cells to engineer tissue corresponding to stages that precede brain development, and we already found differences between healthy and diseased samples as early as two weeks after conception. The evidence suggests the disease was there all along.

She took a sip from her tea and went on:

Many clinicians were absolutely resistant. It violated their training and what they saw before their very eyes: *People develop symptoms at sixty! You're telling us they were already sick in their mother's womb?* But these findings can help people get care early, before symptoms appear, and that could change their lives.

She thought for a second:

It's good to be open to whatever you encounter, even if that means witchcraft.

She uttered this last phrase through laughter—*witchcraft*.

Before lockdown Szilvia was managing several experiments at once. She planned out her day so from 9:00 a.m. to 9:00 p.m., she was literally running from place to place in the lab—starting processes, comparing results, entering notes. The current experiment looked at fibroblasts from a mother and her three children. The mother was fine, but the children all exhibited the jerking movements characteristic of Huntington's disease. How did it develop in them and not her?

The cellular material rested in culture medium inside petri dishes. They'd taken skin cells and stimulated them in such a way that they transform into what's called induced pluripotent stem cells. They were less stable than embryonic stem cells—which they also used—but these induced stem cells were better able to capture the genetic environment occurring in patients.

Hands in sleeves inside a protective case, Szilvia pipetted a few microns of a chemical cocktail into the petri dishes to instigate cell differentiation. With this cascade of effects various aspects of the cell's DNA were expressed—division followed division and certain cells took on the qualities of, say, a pancreatic beta cell.

Around the lab were cells or cell clusters at different stages of differentiation. Szilvia positioned a microscope in order to see what was happening at various stages, under various conditions. Some microscopes increased contrast, which allowed her to see a cell's overall shape. Some lenses reduced depth-of-field to such a minute layer she could see a cross-section of the cell. Because of the instability of the simulated stem cells, mutations might invalidate results. But if all went well, in around a hundred days, they'd have a neuron.

What condition was it in? If it had degraded, when? Could they identify a variable that caused the degradation? If they could determine the conditions or series of variables under which future neural cells start to degrade, they might learn how to halt or even reverse that process—find a cure.

To cure a disease was a noble goal. Of that Szilvia had no doubt. And despite any misgivings she might have, there was something captivating in the process of watching cells divide and differentiate, the intelligent unfolding of minute structures.

Whenever I looked into a microscope or cared for cell cultures, she said, it was like sitting in a monk's chamber. It was a pristine place of perfectly executed experiments, beautifully captured images, precision down to the micron.

She saw the world through protocols and lab practices. She knew somehow she was using scientific training, all the overplanning and urgency, to avoid other things—chaos, ambiguous emotions, everything that's nonlinear, not logical, not measurable, not quantifiable. In order to elude all that she had to do more and more.

I was working fourteen-hour days, she said. I was exhausted, cut off and numb. I'd leave our apartment like *gotta get to the train* and then I'm in the train like *gotta get to the stop* and then I'm like *gotta get to the fucking lab* and then I'm at the lab and I'm like *gotta get home*. There was no moment to take a breath and savor the miraculous work that was happening.

After managing for a while like that, constantly striving for perfection, it was becoming untenable. She sensed the walls of her chamber starting to crack. That's why she wanted to come to Peru. If she and Akos were going to embark on the next phase of life together—who knows, start a family—she was going to need to shed some habits of mind and open up.

And through the diets and ceremonies, the pandemic, ruminating through these long days in the jungle, what Szilvia had long suspected became clear to her—it was more than ambiguity and uncertainty she was avoiding, her absorption in her work rested on a sea of painful experiences she'd been suppressing all her life.

The medicine made her sick and dizzy and nauseous. Sometimes she thought she'd pass out. She would shake and cough, but through that something would clarify or be revealed.

I saw myself as a child, she said. I felt what my parents were going through, who they were to each other at the moment of my conception. It was a powerful realization, full of pain and grief. I saw how war colored my childhood.

Szilvia was born in 1988 in Vojvodina, an ethnically Hungarian region of Serbia, which was then part of Yugoslavia. Within a couple of years that would all crumble. Peaceful towns not far away would become corpse-strewn ruins, concentration camps, mass graves.

I was a baby when war broke out in Croatia, she said, then Bosnia. Our Bosnian cousins showed up in the middle of the night, terrorized, and stayed with us for months. A few years later Tomahawk missiles dropped all over town. I was still a kid and I remember it vividly—air raid sirens and explosions and everyone panicked.

When I was six years old, Szilvia said, my mother saw I wasn't eating and took me to the hospital. The doctor said I had advanced pneumonia and was on the verge of death. Luckily a round of antibiotics cured me. But in a ceremony I understood I was suffocating in grief. I'd absorbed so much pain those first few years of life, it was as if my organism decided: *Okay, thank you very much, this is not for me.*

Violence was everywhere, she said. My father taught his best friend's son to fire and clean a rifle, and the three of them went hunting together, shot and butchered animals together. Then when the boy was a teenager, my father showed up at their house and found his best friend, his wife, and his mother shot to death, blood splattered across the living room. The teenage son was sitting in the family car in front of the house with a gun in his hand, shaking. He hardly knew what had happened.

My father told me as a teenager he dreamt he got shot and felt himself sink into death. He became fascinated with guns. When he got his first gun he started reading about near-death experiences. What does it feel like to get shot?

He told me he wasn't afraid of death, Szilvia said. And I don't know why but I'm not either. I was magnetized by the mystery of death. I wanted to understand it. I always wanted to know the truth about things, and that led me to science.

The search for truth, for a cure, for wholeness. Szilvia was even-tempered when she spoke but glowed with intelligence and commitment.

After the first diet I felt good but with so many things stirred up, she said. I was doing my best, ruminating on impressions and memories, fighting with pain, regret, and rage. Living with sensations in a new way. All the sudden I *feel* all this shit. It was so much. It ripped me open, everything was pouring out. I felt an urge to shout it all out, until one afternoon I really began shouting—you must have heard me—I shouted until things fell into place. All the painful realizations vibrated inside of me and inspired feelings I'd never felt before—spaces of immense beauty and stillness.

That night, leaving Eszter and Akos back in the Coconas kitchen, Szilvia, Nafis, and I walked up the road together and once again settled into our places in the Hilton maloca. Other than Miguel and Luis, there was Teo-dora, a cook from Tarapoto with a big smile named Manuel, a local friend of his named Nimay. Manuel brought a guitar, which I hoped he wouldn't play, and sat chatting with Nimay after they got settled. There was another Tarapoteño named Alberto and a guest of his from Lima named Claudia.

We took our seats and Alberto began talking about the maloca. He was a large man with a ruddy face. He was a lawyer but said he also worked with a construction company, the company that had built this maloca, no less. He'd never been out to see it. He was impressed by its lacquered floors and carved wooden entranceway, the high quality of materials and crafts-manship. He and Claudia had met in a hospital in Lima—both had tested positive for COVID. She'd had a five-day fever. Alberto had been asymp-tomatic. But it was early on and he had to go to the hospital anyway.

He and Claudia got to know each other, and when she found out he was from Tarapoto she said she wanted to come to try ayahuasca here. Alberto said: when we're out of the hospital I'll take you. That was four months ago. Now here they are.

Claudia had abstained from meat and alcohol for a week to prepare herself. She was looking forward to the ceremony.

Alberto said he was excited when he learned Miguel was holding a ceremony. He knew him by reputation as a great curandero.

We're just humble people, Miguel protested, as if it were important to disabuse Alberto and Claudia of such notions.

Manuel had sat with Miguel before—they knew each other.

How's the restaurant? Miguel asked, and they joked about life with-out tourists.

This is my friend, Manuel nodded toward Nimay.

He had a soft expression. By his appearance he could be nativo like the Tapullimas. He was dressed in a yellow T-shirt and nearly matching shorts.

Miguel said hello and asked if he had experience with ayahuasca, if he'd prepared for the ceremony.

He answered in a quiet voice, said he'd taken the medicine once but it hadn't been a good experience. He was looking forward to trying again. He said he was a strict vegetarian, didn't drink or smoke.

That's good, Miguel said, then indicating Teodora, Nafis, Szilvia, and me, he said: these are family.

He served everyone and Luis blew out the candles. Again we sat in darkness as a ceremony began.

Not more than twenty minutes passed when the silence was broken by Nimay moaning—My leg!—He lay clutching at his left thigh.—It hurts!—He moaned and whined in pain.—¿Qué están haciendo?

Miguel began to sing, but Nimay's whimpers and moans escalated. Miguel's singing faded, started up again, then faded to silence. Luis began to sing but Miguel stopped him. We sat in silence listening to Nimay, who was thrashing and pounding on the floorboards as if possessed.

What was happening? Where was the quiet man we'd been sitting with a moment ago?

Miguel sliced a lemon, which should reduce the effects of the medicine. He tried to squeeze it in Nimay's mouth, but Nimay grabbed the wedge and threw it against the wall. He turned to Miguel, his eyes livid, and began shouting, telling Miguel he's a fraud:

¡Engañas a la gente! ¡No sabes nada!

He turned to Teodora and began commenting rudely on her body, shouted racist epithets at Nafis, and called me *¡flaco huevón!*

An hour before he'd been a peaceful person. Now he was like an angry drunk staggering through the D train at 2:00 a.m. who you avoid making eye contact with. The slightest glance became an invitation to violence.

Miguel's lemon and sugar had no effect on Nimay. The only thing that might mitigate the situation was to turn on the lights. That might keep his visions from getting worse. So Luis flicked the switch and we sat in the Hilton maloca with the lights on, listening to Nimay hurl insults at everyone, especially Miguel.

¿Qué maestro eres? ¡No sabes nada!

Miguel and Luis sat without singing. At one point reaching for my water bottle I touched the shakapa on the floor, and I noticed Miguel's glance shoot over at me: ¡*silencio!* Nafis began quietly to sing in his antelanguage at one point but Miguel stopped him.

Nimay continued his ranting and wailing.

Manuel tried to talk to him.

Alberto tried to appeal to his asshole nature:

¡Yo también soy cabrón!

Nimay quieted for a moment, listening to Alberto. Maybe Alberto was making him better? But then he went back to screaming. It grew louder, more violent.

If the best ceremony could turn filth into song, pain into wisdom, Nimay's medicine transmuted healing into bile, generosity into theft. Whatever had taken control of him tonight was like an intestinal enzyme that turned all sustenance to poison, fed off anything that passed through, so the only solution was a complete fast. Whatever it was, we needed to starve it until it died. The only lesson for us was not to think we had the answer.

Maybe if *I* sing to him. Maybe *I* can say the right thing.

But no, everything was rendered poisonous, food for Nimay's demons. I remembered Jonathan again, and myself when I was screaming in the high jungle. Sometimes the only thing to do is to bear witness in silence.

So be still, don't engage, accept that this thrashing would continue as long as it continued. And it continued through the whole ceremony. Nimay thrashed and thrashed. There was nothing else to think about. Just his pain.

After several hours, Miguel called us up one by one to sit in front of him for limpias. Now he sang and he shook his shakapa even as Nimay continued to rant.

Before the start of the ceremony I'd thought about my intention for the night—sometimes I took a moment to do that. Tonight I'd asked for insight into the book I was working on, into creative work in general.

When it was my turn for a limpia I sat in front of Miguel. He sang into my face his now familiar icaros—*sinche sinche medikoini*—taught to him by his father and grandfather and ayahuasquero uncle, pouring his heart into it as he beat my head and shoulders rhythmically with his shakapa. At one point he pulled from his pocket what I recognized as his grandfather's mouth harp. He sat facing me playing the mouth harp, plucking at it, saliva flying out of his mouth. I could feel his intensity of focus. From behind I heard Nimay—*¡Qué maestro eres! ¡No sabes nada! ¡Es engaño puro!*—shouting insult after insult, calling him a fraud, while Miguel gave everything he had.

That's your lesson, I thought. If you want to be an artist, you have to be prepared to sing your heart out even in the face of insults and scorn.

Finally after several hours Nimay relented and grew quiet. Miguel called the ceremony to a close.

Returning to his senses, Nimay suddenly saw what he'd done, who he'd been. He went around to each of us apologizing, begging forgiveness.

Amigo, Miguel said. I don't think you should take more ayahuasca.

Later Teodora told us Nimay was a Krishna. Not a convert, his parents were Krishnas. That's how he was raised: vegetarian, peace and love. I didn't know anything about Krishnas, but I wondered if it were a lifetime of repressed negativity or bile cultivated through disingenuous goodwill that came bubbling out of him that night.

Alberto said he'd learned a lot. Claudia, who'd lay prone with a sheet over her face all night, thanked Miguel and said goodbye.

When everyone had left but the Tapullimas and us, Miguel said: I know that lawyer.

Many years ago, he told us, when his father Pedro was using Juliampampa to hunt, raising a few plantains and potatoes and beans and inviting dieters one or two at a time, a Frenchman—a friend of Mathieu from Sacha Wasi named Immanuel—came and asked to use the place. Pedro said okay, and Immanuel built a handful of huts and a maloca and began to bring groups of foreigners to Juliampampa. But then someone from the reserve alerted Pedro that Immanuel had filed paperwork trying to get the property deeded in his own name.

Pedro asked him to leave, but the Frenchman refused.

I built all this, he protested. It's mine.

Pedro began receiving letters in threatening legal language, warning him to immediately evacuate the land or face heavy fines.

Now Miguel and his father hired their own lawyers and fought back. It was expensive, nerve-wracking, and lasted more than a year, but eventually they prevailed. Immanuel had to clear out. He brought up a crew to disassemble the huts and the maloca and carry everything away.

He didn't leave a single board, Miguel laughed. Not even a nail.

Miguel couldn't forget the name of the law office Immanuel's threatening letters came from. They were from Alberto.

I guess he didn't make the connection, he shrugged.

We asked why he didn't say something, but Miguel just laughed.

As we were packing up our stuff, Luis gave another reason for the difficulty of the ceremony:

It's not only the lawyer or Nimay, he said. There's something in this maloca.

Luis told us this piece of land used to be an orchard owned by a friend of the family, where his grandfather used to stay when he traveled from Lamas to Juliampampa. Pedro would spend the night here, then the next day go up the mountain. At some point this friend was murdered—they say it was his son who murdered him. Or someone coming after his son who murdered him by mistake. After the murder a rich Russian bought the land and built the center and the maloca—with the help of Alberto's construction company. When the maloca was finished the Russian invited a group of Shipibo curanderos to inaugurate it. According to Luis, they left a force-field here—the energy is jealous.

And as nice as the retreat center is, Luis said, dieters complain they hear someone cry at night—the ghost of the murdered man.

We do our best to clean it, he said, but sometimes whoever uses the maloca has to suffer a little.

It's a wonder we had many beautiful nights here, I thought. It was the site of Nimay's demonism, Efraim's miasma, and it was where Miguel picked up the rotten smell of the virus. But on other nights we had joyous, beautiful visions that lifted us up out of the plague year, our limited lives.

Fraud, murder, dispossession. Stumbling back down the hill, I asked Szilvia how she'd survived this most pleasureless of ceremonies.

I was fighting other demons, she said. Or I don't know what was coming from outside and what was coming from within. But I felt something coming from my family. I felt forces showing me how to manipulate people, some witchcraft.

She said she'd had to imagine herself close to the plants she'd dieted on: as if she were embracing ajo sacha and nina caspi in order to resist. Because the demons knew her, she told me. Something to do with her father's family, generations of conflict.

I saw my great-grandfather after World War I, she said. He was a fierce man. He was drawing a blade across someone's neck, a Serb.

He killed him? I asked.

No, it wasn't murder, she said. It was a duel. He had to draw blood in the name of justice. It was a code. They were showing me how things were done. It was the whole weight of the past that I felt. They were coming to me, offering me power. It was like the tests Miguel told us about.

There was so much talk of hexes and curses and brujos in the world of the medicine. Who had made Miguel's father Pedro slip and fall to his death while walking up to Juliampampa? Who had caused the ember to fly into Miguel's eye?

It was a world of competitive magic, sabotage, and sorcery. A legacy now appeared to Szilvia, as she thought back on stories she'd heard growing up.

None of this is exotic, she realized. It's part of a heritage.

Where I grew up, she said, we all talk about spellcasting. At least my family does. We call it *vracskaz*—a word that's half-Serbian, half-Hungarian, like the region—someone who does it is called a *vračar*.

Here began Szilvia's tale:

My grandparents split up before I was born, she said, but they had kids together and remained in each other's lives. Every year on my grandfather's birthday, my grandmother used to bake a cake and gather the family in front of grandfather's house to celebrate. She was always first to go inside, carrying the cake herself. This ritual continued even after my grandfather married another woman.

One year the family gathered as usual, and just as everyone was about to march inside to congratulate my grandfather, my grandmother realized she'd left the cake in the car. She went to get it and my aunt entered the house first.

A month later, my aunt got very ill and began to lose weight. Soon she was down to forty kilos. She went from doctor to doctor all over Hungary and Serbia but none of the doctors could help her. Eventually she came across a Macedonian woman who was throwing beans, a kind of fortune-teller. She said something had happened, she'd been vracskazted and needed to see vračar to get the curse lifted. She sent my aunt to see her mother.

She's retired, the Macedonian woman said, but maybe she'll help you.

So my aunt went to see the old witch, Szilvia said, and the witch said my aunt had crossed under an accursed threshold.

Here's what you need to do, the witch said. You need to fill three jugs with water from three wells and bring them to me. The water needed to be from artesian wells—spat out of the ground by pressure, not raised in a bucket—and there were three such wells in our town.

When my aunt came back with three jugs of water, the witch had her hold each of the jugs above her head while she dropped lead into each one. She told my aunt to bathe in the mix of three waters and then gather the bathwater.

Pick a tree, the witch said, and pour out the bathwater at the base of the tree.

My aunt did as she was told, Szilvia said, and poured out the bathwater at the base of a huge old cherry tree in front of their house. I remember the tree because it produced a lot of cherries that we picked each spring as kids. I was seven or eight years old when this happened—my aunt poured out the bathwater, and the tree dried up and died. All of the sudden it was being cut down. We kids kept asking what happened, but no one told us.

Soon my aunt started to gain weight and regain her health, Szilvia said. Eventually I heard more of the story, as older relatives told it to me: The woman my grandfather married had been jealous of how happy it made my grandfather when my grandmother waltzed into the house every year with a cake. So she went to a vračar and had them make something. You put it over the door, and whoever walks through next absorbs the hex. My step-grandmother knew my grandmother always led the way with the cake, so she placed the hex above the door in anticipation. Then my grandmother forgot the cake, my aunt went first, and she ended up getting sick instead.

My grandmother was very frail. She probably wouldn't have survived the illness my aunt had.

Family members talked about seeing my grandfather the night he died. He appeared in front of one of my uncle's houses, trying to reveal my step-grandmother's plot, claiming she'd poisoned him.

Then when my step-grandmother died, they said she dried up just like the cherry tree. It seemed like the old Macedonian witch had passed the curse back to her.

Stories like that were part of growing up, Szilvia said. None of it holds up to the rigors of science, but it was part of my world. I was fascinated and intrigued by those stories. Even though they involved sickness and death I didn't find them terrifying. I was curious. Death was a portal to somewhere but no one knows where it leads. There had been so much sickness and death around, anyway, that wasn't enough to scare me.

I didn't believe in witchcraft exactly, she said. I didn't know what to believe. Before I studied biology I was a pharmacist. I worked in a pharmacy in Serbia. It was a way to take control. But now plant medicine makes me reconsider my family's witchcraft stories. It's not the same as what happens here, but I can tell all this to Miguel and as far away as that world might be, he says *yes, of course.*

The temptation during the ceremony was to combine Vojvodina witchcraft and plant medicine into a powerful force. It was like a voice saying *this could all be yours.*

Miguel warned me this might happen, Szilvia said. He said *They'll come to you and promise you things. Everything will be beautiful. But you'll know better. You're strong.*

Szilvia said she saw there are certain things—many things—you can only understand down that path. The temptation preyed on her thirst for knowledge. The truth about things lay that way. You have to get your hands dirty to fully realize.

But I said *No!* she said. *I'm on the side of helping and healing.*

And then she saw New York, the pandemic spreading like war. She saw how many others, like her, had arrived to the city from places wrecked by conflict: Yemeni, Syrian, Palestinian, Congolese, Salvadoran, on and on and on. She saw hunger and confusion and pain stir through the multitudes, every corner.

People have always been desperate, she realized, trying to one-up each other, sabotage each other. If they think witchcraft will help they're willing to use that, too. My family is no different.

She saw herself as a child surrounded by madness and pain and death.

How can I interact with energies like that? she asked. During the ceremony I just sat and coexisted with them, and I started to feel incredibly strong and peaceful, something new I hadn't had access to before.

Stories arrive in fragments, she realized, in little packets, explosions of feeling, jags of storylines. When they fall into place a huge change happens all at once.

Unless there was a ceremony, we cooked every night in one of the outdoor kitchens. We took turns shopping and planning. Eszter and I had always cooked together, mastering the choreography of many tight spaces over the years. This outdoor kitchen at Las Coconas, a range under a roof with its expansive counter and long table, was a luxury. The four of us took turns prepping and assisting each other, experimenting within restrictions and with the sometimes unfamiliar ingredients we found. We bought orange-headed river fish called gamitanas, wrapped them in big, pungent bijao leaves from the edge of the garden, and lined them up on the grill. We gathered wood from the grounds and grilled endless peppers and eggplants and tomatoes. Akos became expert in making naan. We cooked fesenjan with chickens from down the street. Eszter improvised Persian rice colored with turmeric instead of saffron, even managed to recreate the crunchy tahdig with a skillet and a towel. Szilvia learned to make delicious desserts sweetened with dates scrounged from the dry goods store in Tarapoto. Over those months in Las Coconas we ate every date they had. When they ran out Miguel brought us wild honey, which was even more delicious. We came together after our days of solitary walks or work sessions or trips to the market and cooked in the cool evenings, sat around the table like the family we'd become. Nafis preferred to eat chopped fruit in the middle of the night but he'd often sit with us, too, and the table would resound with our laughter.

Akos after a day of advertising would let out a sigh of satisfaction:

Ah, the simple life.

No one wanted to leave, but pressures were mounting. Nafis's department still threatened to withhold his pension if he wasn't back by the end of September to sign his resignation. Szilvia found out her lab was about to reopen, which meant she was going to need to be there.

Wasn't there a way? Akos asked. Couldn't we put it off?

They were protected for a time by the fact they weren't US citizens— they were the lowest priority for evacuation flights. They got news they'd secured seats while Nafis and I were up clearing Juliampampa with Miguel, communing with Hitler and the stingless bees. I remember a wistful expression overtaking Miguel when he heard they'd be leaving.

When he came down Miguel held a goodbye ceremony, the last time the five of us would sit with him together. We gathered in Serpentina, but this time there were no demons. No one thrashed and wailed.

Nafis asked Miguel if once he returned to the US he could serve ayahuasca to others.

It's okay, Miguel said. Start slowly, gain experience, but yes.

He called out *¡Maestro Nafis!* with a laugh, and Nafis sang. His big and open and generous spirit returned as he sang for a while to each of us.

Szilvia grabbed a shakapa and shook it in appreciation of all that had happened. Akos was sad to abandon the simple life.

The next afternoon, back at Las Coconas, Akos and I shared a mapacho in the kitchen where we cooked. We'd shared mapachos overlooking the valley from Juliampampa. We'd shared countless walks into Tarapoto to shop and prep for another meal. We'd sat on the Shilcayo boulders through idle hours of the afternoon, chased monkeys around the kitchen holding out miniature bananas. I'd talked to him after some of his most difficult medicinal encounters. I'd come to value his tender humor, his subtle and intelligent observations.

Now that he and Szilvia were leaving I wondered what he saw when he thought about his time here.

I see myself leaning on the porch railing up in Juliampampa, Akos said, looking out over the mountains—the most beautiful view ever. I see the maloca and the old ojé tree, the benches in front of the comedor. I see Abuelita sitting there doing some embroidery, the spaces between her toes from walking barefoot. I see neon orange mushrooms growing on the tree nearby, and the jungle canopy off to the distance. So many birds. Eagles overhead. I see us all seated in the maloca and Miguel comes in the door—he'd gone out for a piss or something and now he's back and walking to his spot he starts dancing. I can hear his laughter, see his smile.

There was a day ceremony when Miguel came to give me a limpia, Akos said. He'd been working in the field all day. Instead of his usual nice clean ceremonial clothes, he was sweaty, in jeans and a work shirt. It's not like he wasn't taking his role seriously—he gave me all his power—it was just that to him, I realized, tending to us is no different than making sure the beans are planted, the plantains are harvested. He'd check around the hut to see if a board is broken or a screw is sticking out somewhere, make a mental note to come back and fix it.

I see Nafis on the boulder, such a beautiful person, sitting cross-legged on top of the boulder in the middle of the river. I hear Luis's voice—can feel the shyness in his singing, his internal battles. I can hear the progress he's made just while we've been here, how he's changed. He looks different now than he did when we arrived. He's matured. He was like a teenager and now he's a young man.

And myself, Akos laughed. Before we came here I was a guy working in an office on Canal Street. You know—it's not what I want to do long term but it's okay, nice people. I'd been successful in ways that were unthinkable when I was younger, but still. We had an outwardly comfortable life but I sensed a simmering shame and anxiety, a feeling there had to be more. Then I'm here, and in one of the first ceremonies I was looking straight down the barrel at insanity. I saw the spiraling roulette of my biggest fears: rejection, mental breakdowns, letting people down. There was a spotlight chasing me, ready to expose me in the worst way. But then something changed.

When I was around three years old, he said, I had a series of episodes where I'd be overcome with vertigo and click out for a few seconds. My eyes would go blank, like I'd lose touch with what was going on around me. It felt like the laws of gravity had been lifted. I began to wonder what was real, to feel I needed to test things. This happened without warning, and no one around me was able to explain what was going on. I began to relive these experiences—that isolation and unease, not trusting the ground below me, seeing faces looking back at me with fear and anxiety, mockery and impatience. How much of my relationship with the world was formed in those moments? One after another I sorted through them, and as I did I felt the spotlight fade and turn off. There in the dark I felt the earth where it was, and now even with these visions flashing in my head, the pandemic, all our plans scrambled, in the most basic way I did know which way was up.

And that carried a powerful sense of orientation, Akos said. I saw three entities somewhere, calm as Buddhas, and they were generating the universe. I saw the cosmos as a self-generating system with droplets of consciousness repeatedly introduced, which spread and developed in ever greater complexity. It was not something beyond me. I was part of it. I could feel those droplets rise and expand through me, eventually reaching a level far beyond my ability to conceive. But sensing and knowing that changed me right away. I heard Szilvia struggling and purging. Eszter was with her, and I approached and was just projecting calm, which was how I needed to be at that moment.

He leaned forward now, before he went on.

Our next time up in Juliampampa, Akos said, I wrote out a five-point plan—*How to be a better Akos*—and put it on the wall of my hut. I looked at it every day and I could feel my anxious mind relent, as if I'd undergone a permanent change. I felt excellent.

That was the mood I was in the day Jonathan fell from the rock and lay unconscious. I knew nothing about it at that time. He'd almost died a few hours before. Now he was right next to me in the maloca. The terror took him and he screamed and writhed, and I sat with that energy all night.

He took a breath, remembering, before he went on.

I can sense the presence of death, Akos said, not as an abstract biological concept but an entity I know from experience. A close friend of mine jumped from his apartment building in Budapest, and I came across his body just as he bled out on the sidewalk. I was with my grandmother on her death-bed—I know when death is near. The night of Jonathan screaming it occurred to me that death was coming for him right there. I saw us at his funeral, all of us looking at his grave, shattered, carrying a wound for the rest of our lives. Then when he started to feel better, when he finally quieted down after those hours of terror, a thought began looping in my mind: *You're next.*

It was like I'd been infected, Akos said. I saw my own death, people around me, people I love. Anxieties simmered and swelled. I saw gas chambers, piles of bodies. The scent of all that was in the maloca. That force, incredibly powerful. I felt if I make one wrong move, just a slight move of the body, if I lose focus, it will suck me in and feed and grow— *what happens if it gets out of control?*—then it's thousands and millions of corpses and there's nothing we can do about it.

When it was over and you all started talking, he said, I was confused— hadn't you all sensed how close death had been? I staggered up to my hut and lay down, thinking: *I came here to face my fears and instead I just absorbed new trauma that has nothing to do with me.* I kept hearing his voice, laying there in the dark. The sun came up and Jonathan's screams still echoed in my head.

I kept thinking: *This was not necessary for any of us. This could have been avoided.*

I walked down to breakfast without sleeping, feeling beat up and exhausted. A day before I'd been on the cusp of a new life, but now a chance flow of events had derailed me. Then after breakfast, Miguel was like: *Come with me.*

He took me to the maloca, sat me down and started to sing and shake the shakapa and give me a limpia. I was not in a ceremonial state of mind, but the way he sang, with every beat of the icaro, with every word, patterns of fresh energy filled my—*body's* not the right word—*self*, more like. It was beyond physical.

I was not on ayahuasca. I'd just had breakfast. I was sober. But whatever he was doing, he was able to lift me out of ordinary consciousness.

After the limpia I slept, and the experience faded. I still didn't know what Jonathan or I learned from all that. Now looking back—what I can say is, I saw that from the madness and solitude and fear to the serenity of the Himalayan universe-generators, there's no separation.

Akos stopped and we sat in silence at the table in Las Coconas. Night had fallen and everyone else had gone to their beds. There were no monkeys around, and the tarantulas were in their tarantula nests.

As I lay in bed I thought of Hortobagyism, the religion of devotion to the little flower of comic death.

Before they were scheduled to leave Miguel came in the morning and set a huge drum of water by the banks of the Shilcayo. We spent the day chopping plants. We chopped rosa sisa and chiric sanango flowers, mango leaves and leaves of mishquipanga, ruda, and mucuri. We dumped it all into the drum of water. Finally Miguel added a few sprigs of rosemary. We let this mixture steep all day, and in the heat of the afternoon he called us down one by one, scooped up gourdfuls of water—cold and redolent of all the herbs and flowers—and dumped it on our heads and chests. At the end he blew tobacco all over us.

Listo, Miguel said, sending us off to lay in our hammocks, wrapped in towels and caked with chopped plants, which dried until they fell from our skin.

Miguel gave us this same treatment at the end of each diet, but now, before Akos and Szilvia, and soon Nafis, would leave us for New York, it had the quality of bundling them up in jungle freshness for the trip.

We'd grown close over these unexpected months together, our impromptu family created by circumstances. Akos had become like a younger brother. Nafis had taught me to pray. Eszter and Szilvia had imagined a short trip together and instead we were flung into a whole new world.

If I think back to that now I might get dizzy, Eszter said.

Seeing their bags piled up in front of Las Coconas, knowing all their mixed feelings, I wondered if I was jealous of their return. Would we all meet again somewhere? Miguel came by to blow more tobacco smoke on their bags to ensure their safety. Morning came and they were gone.

Las Coconas became very quiet. With Akos, Szilvia, and Nafis returned to the US, Eszter and I turned around and it was just us. The tide had ebbed and we remained on the beach. It was comfortable like that, familiar. Eszter spent a few hours a day with clients—most of them locked down in New York, though some had retreated to other places. I continued work on my book and my Mae West research—"*I had touched the hem of the unknown, and being me I wanted to raise it higher.*" Shopping trips into town, walks up Prolongación Alerta, the trance of daily life deepened. I sat for long minutes watching La Baronesa motionless in her tarantula nest. Eszter once found her inside, on the table next to her bed, but mostly she was tucked into a nook in the wall a foot off the ground. I lay in the hammock for hours overlooking the flowering bush where Jaru hunted, the yellow bamboo, the rush of the river. It had been two months since our last diet. We'd come off our dietary restrictions. We could eat red meat if we wanted, feel the delicious burn of the ají amarillo or other chilis from the market, share a bed like lovers, like the married people we still were. Occasionally in the afternoon I read on a bench under the tree in the neighborhood nearby and drank a cold Cusqueña lager from the shop.

My excursions into regional literature eventually led me to Alejo Carpentier's *Los pasos perdidos*, which portrays a Latin American composer and musicologist living in New York, recruited for an expedition into the Amazon to collect instruments. Soon he's traveling through an anonymous country with place-names like Los Arcos or Puerto Asunción, where Mexican desert plants like agave and peyote are listed among *stupificants of the jungle*.

At the beginning, the narrator repeats familiar romantic demonizations of the jungle, a place where "a malignant pollen in the air—fairy dust, unseen rot, hovering mold worked with haste and mysterious designs to open what was closed and close what was open, to mangle calculations, misreckon weights, corrupt all guarantees."

He quotes Goethe, who described *nature* as a site of "mad and febrile commotions."

In the jungle, the narrator encounters trowels used to pulverize an unidentified seed "whose intoxicating powders are inhaled through tubes made from the breastbones of birds."

There were remedies from "nux vomica, mallow root, tartar emetic."

The musicologist arrives with a cosmopolitan, sexually adventurous girlfriend from New York, but under the spell of the jungle, he drifts from her. He finds himself reconnecting to the lost Latin America of his youth, and he's attracted to a local woman named Rosario who he imagines as a more rooted, elemental companion. They bathe together in the river and are soon united. As he travels upriver, his desire to return to urban life fades. He'll make his home in the jungle with his elemental mate and write elemental music that arises from mud and vines. He'll care nothing for worldly success but will submerge himself in this newly discovered world that is also his original home.

In a village where they stop for a while, he encounters Nicasio, a leper who rapes and mutilates a young girl. The narrator has a gun, and aims at Nicasio, convinced it's right for him to kill the wretch. But at the last second, "inwardly, I resisted, as if once I pulled the trigger, something would change forever."

Soon an airplane sounds overhead and lands nearby. Airmen appear—a search party looking for the narrator, who's been reported lost, perhaps kidnapped. The musicologist resolves to return with them—his party has been traveling for weeks but by plane the city is only three hours away. He'll bring the musical instruments he's collected, finish a piece he's been composing, then return to the jungle village, commit to Rosario and give himself over to native existence.

But when he returns a few weeks later, Rosario is off with another man. The world he'd felt accepted into had evaporated into illusion. He is terminally associated with the modern city, barred from that transformative, revelatory existence he'd glimpsed.

It's impossible not to suspect the fatal moment was his encounter with Nicasio. If he'd killed the leper, would he have still boarded the plane? *Something would have changed forever.* Perhaps he'd have been bonded to his new reality. Instead he balked and was returned to his habitual banality.

Though perhaps his inability to shoot the leper was a reflection of deeper forces, what made him what he was, which couldn't be changed from one moment to the next. Is it a story of failure, of a man who misses his sole chance to transform himself and recover his full humanity? Maybe not. Maybe it's a story about life as it is, as it's lived, where transformation arrives via mistakes and errancy, never the way one planned or expected or would have even know to want.

There are memories and images and experiences, I thought, that can't be understood with the head, that can't even be understood by the heart, or not by the heart alone. It requires the sensing membrane of the lowest of the low—the soles of the feet—to inch through what happened. The mute, unexplainable reality of it.

Would you shoot the leper?

Lying in the hammock through the long afternoons, wandering the neighborhood's dirt roads, sitting in comfortable silence or laughing with Eszter as we ate our evening meals, I wondered what was real in any of this.

I stepped into the kitchen to find a tall, thin foreigner with straw-blond, shoulder-length hair dressed in a plain T-shirt and harem pants sewn from expensive-looking cotton. His spoon was in our jar of wild honey.

Excuse me, I said.

I explained it was a gift from a friend, and he apologized, but I noticed a significant amount had already disappeared.

Damn this fancy hippy with his hand in our honey jar, I thought.

He said his name was Oleg. He'd come to Tarapoto looking for a place to stay. Everything was horrible but then he'd called his friend Ivan—maybe we knew him—and Ivan told him to come to Las Coconas and this was the nicest place he'd seen since arriving in Peru.

Later Oleg was not alone but in the company of Yana, a tall woman in banana-yellow pants, and a small woman with high Central Asian cheekbones named Zina. They sat smoking and drinking tea and bantering in Russian.

They all came from a place called El Cristal, they said, a center outside Yurimaguas, the next town over, an hour or so from here. That's where Nadia and Ivan had come from, too. At one point they'd all been there together.

Ivan is very generous, Oleg said. He flew me and some others to Peru. He's been giving ayahuasca ceremonies in Russia.

Ivan has been leading ceremonies?

Yes, Oleg said, the past year. We were together in an ashram in India, and then we went to Spain where he works with iboga.

Imagine all over the world, I thought, people with no idea what they're doing administer these powerful substances, each with its own history and context, its own politics. Was such scandalous hubris and confusion unique to our time?

Oleg explained that Ivan was the son of an important Moscow family, raised to take over huge contracts managing natural resources. Ivan, it turned out, was some kind of oligarch.

He was always out in Moscow, Oleg said. Huge parties. And you know—parties in Moscow are real parties. His thirty-fifth birthday was legendary. Cocaine, orgies, days on end. But when he pulled himself together at the end of it he said *I have to change my life.*

Ivan left Russia for India, Oleg said, he spent months living in an ashram, meditating and practicing yoga. He met a Peruvian ayahuasquero and resolved to come here. But first he traveled to Gabon to undergo an iboga ritual. And then he brought the shaman from Gabon to Spain. He resolved to dedicate his life to helping people, providing access to these two avenues of great personal growth.

I remembered Ivan saying *You can be a small magician, or you can be a big magician.*

I thought of death entering the maloca as Akos had described, Teodora alone with a cup of medicine and a speaker. I thought of all the medicine might do, was no doubt already doing, in the hands of the blithe and inexperienced.

I wanted to know about this other center where they'd been. The only center I knew was Juliampampa, which seemed not so much a center as the Tapullimas' family hideaway plus a few guest huts. There was Sacha Wasi with its exorcisms, Serpentina with its curses. What happened in El Cristal?

Oleg said it was a huge area of jungle, perhaps a hundred hectares—as big as Juliampampa. But Zina said no. It was perhaps thirty or forty hectares.

It was run by a curandero named Don Quique, who they talked about with reverence. I wondered if we sounded the same when we talked about Miguel.

Don Quique was from the region but not indigenous, Oleg said. He speaks no indigenous language and claims no particular authority. He was introduced to the plants and the plants tell him what to do. The plants tell him how to run the center, where to build a new structure, what diets to give people, how to handle money.

There are as many as forty people dieting at a time, Oleg said. And there are twenty or thirty people working. There are cows and chickens and many dogs. There's a big concrete dormitory where everyone sleeps in cots, very close to each other.

Separated by at most a sheet, Zina said. You can hear all the sounds, smell all the smells of the other dieters and workers.

There's a big central kitchen, Oleg said, a place you cannot believe exists, everything black and burned. People might be rendering fat or cooking broth or grilling meat or making other things. It's absolutely filthy.

When you first see it, Zina said, you think: This is the worst place in the world. But then you realize there are people who never leave the kitchen, who stay in the kitchen day-in day-out.

Not because they're working, Oleg said. Because they like it.

Quique receives dieters from Peru and from all over the world, they said. Many Russians and Europeans. When they arrive, the first thing that happens is they go to a consultation. Quique assesses you and assigns you a number of *chips*.

Chips?

That's what he calls them, Oleg said. It means the number of ayahuasca purges you need to go through.

Most people have five or six, Zina said.

I had two chips, Oleg said, which was a miracle.

For most people, they said, your first five or six mornings you stand at a little window and someone slides you a big soup bowl with a half-liter of pure ayahuasca, no chacruna, which makes you dizzy and nauseous. You sit on a bench with whoever else is there in this big space that is not a maloca.

People might be fixing the roof, Oleg said. There are children and animals and people talking and laughing. You drink your bowl of ayahuasca, you probably puke, but because there's no chacruna you don't have DMT visions. You rest and repeat until you've gone through all your chips. Then you're clean.

Clean?

Free of psychological trash, Oleg said. So you can move on to the real work.

Everyone is required to complete a ten-day ojé diet, Zina said. According to Quique it's dangerous not to complete it. He asks everyone to sign a contract affirming they understand and are determined to complete this diet.

Ivan left halfway through his ojé diet to come here, Oleg said.

I realized Ivan used to leave halfway through ceremonies, and only did half a diet at Juliampampa. With all his extremes, he seemed to lack follow-through. I mentioned Ivan abandoning his path to becoming pure light in order to eat a whole chicken.

When I talked to him now, Oleg said, he was in Moscow. He said he was done with plant medicine and wants to live on breath. But it sounded—he laughed—more like he was back to his old ways.

I remembered Ivan's blinking phone—*CADAVER!*—and wondered what would become of that broomstick with eyeballs. I was glad Oleg seemed to have a sense of humor about him.

But now I wanted to know about the ojé diet. What was it like to drink the medicine of that beautiful tree I knew so well from Juliampampa?

It's a bowl of milky white sap, Oleg said, as thick as glue. You drink it and you feel knocked out all day. After ten days like that Quique gives you another plant to diet on. I took chiric sanango.

He gave me ajo sacha, Zina said.

There are many diets, Oleg said, sarsaparilla, uchu sanango, toé.

But only the roots of toé, Zina said. They don't use the seeds, which are psychedelic but very dangerous. And you can drink ayahuasca if you want to, but it will always be the same as at the beginning—no chacruna, and not cooked down that much. It's very watery. Quique says that's the proper traditional way to drink ayahuasca. Because if you drink it with chacruna, you have strong visions but then it's over and you're back to normal. But with pure ayahuasca it's like it never starts and never stops.

He considers the mixture with chacruna a cheap and impure innovation, Oleg said. He only serves it on New Year's Eve.

Like a party drug?

But usually there are no visions, they said, no ceremonies.

There are no icaros either, Oleg said. Instead there are speakers hung from posts around the area, and they play Sanskrit mantras all day.

Well, Zina said, five times a day.

In order to ensure everyone hears the mantras, headphones are forbidden. Sanskrit?

And everyone is required to carry an umbrella at all times, rain or shine. You don't want to be in direct sunlight.

Mandatory parasols?

Quique has arranged it like this, they said, because the plants told him to. He's just following orders.

Zina said everyone in the community starts to talk about listening to the plants. Everyone is always attributing their desires and decisions to the plants.

Why did you shoot the leper?

The plants told me to.

When you want or need or are asked to eat, Oleg said, you get in line, and the lines can be long. You might stand in line for two hours—with your umbrella, listening to mantras—and then you come to a small window off the kitchen, the most unthinkably disgusting place in the world, and someone pushes you a portion of something—a single potato, a burned piece of fish—and you accept it, no questions.

Quique emphasizes a philosophy of total acceptance, Zina said. And living in this way is part of that. He adheres to no doctrine, no religion, no system except this idea of total acceptance of whatever the plants tell him.

He never gets upset, Oleg said. He never raises his voice, is always in a good mood, energetic, always accessible if you want to talk.

Talk about what?

Soon after the state of emergency, Oleg said, a flu swept through the place and everyone got it. We didn't know if it was the virus, but everyone was sick and feverish. Quique gathered all of us and gave us a strong dose of ayahuasca and we were better very quickly.

We closed the gates, said Zina. Sixty people inside the center and we were cut off from the rest of the world and we stayed like that for months.

I built a pravila, Oleg said—an ancient Russian technology.

He pulled out his phone and showed me a series of pictures.

I saw images of Yana, their silent friend right here in her banana-yellow pants, strapped into a torture device of some kind.

Oleg explained:

A pravila is an installation of four poles with pulleys and a rope system with cuffs that attach to your wrists and ankles, a sleeve that goes around your head. And all this is connected by a system attached to a winch, so the ropes can be pulled tight little by little. There are infinite configurations, but the point is traction. You can have your spine pulled, your limbs pulled, your body put into all kinds of positions, your neck pulled.

Pravila, I understood, meant *ruler* or *corrector*.

You built it? I asked.

Yes, Oleg said. I brought some of the supplies with me.

There in the pictures I saw Yana stretched out in the pravila, head in a balaclava, arms and legs pulled in various directions, suspended in the air.

Step into the corrector, my dear.

It was great for her, Oleg said. It cured a problem with her lymphatic system that had kept her from being able to regulate her weight properly.

I lost fifteen kilos, Yana said. I never felt better.

When I described all this to Eszter, she called it *fascist hippie hell.*

The three Russians had been at the ceremony where Nurse Rosita wept and Efraim the barber wailed out his envy and frustration. They sat outside all night, in a lighted area fifty feet from the maloca. When I went outside I could sometimes hear Zina's melodic voice as she sang to her companions.

At some point in the night she disappeared, and the next day she was gone from Las Coconas.

Oleg explained she'd entered the maloca at Serpentina and immediately sensed dark and painful energies—this was before I knew about the murder, the jealous energies of the inaugural Shipibo curanderos.

She's had bad experience with curanderos, Oleg said.

What happened?

I don't know, he said. According to Quique, it's better not to talk about bad things that have happened—it gives them power. All I know is that she'd avoided ayahuasca for three years. She'd been to El Cristal before and thought of it as a place to clean herself, so she went back.

She was interested to try ayahuasca outside of El Cristal but she was scared, Oleg said. From what I'd heard and what I saw Miguel is a good curandero, but she immediately had a bad feeling. She wanted to walk back to Las Coconas right away, but the guard wouldn't let her leave.

She said she realized she'd become one of those crazy foreigners walking around on ayahuasca, Oleg laughed.

She sat outside all night listening to Rosita cry and Efraim bellow. The next day, after the ceremony, she'd asked Oleg for some pure ayahuasca from El Cristal—he'd brought some with him; it was in the fridge in the kitchen. He served her a big cup and she drank it and vomited and afterward she said she felt better.

She was clean again, Oleg said. But she wanted nothing more to do with Miguel or any curanderos for that matter. Now she wants to leave the jungle.

Oleg stayed with us for months, but Zina planted suspicions in him that first night. In time they would grow.

When Miguel next came to suggest a ceremony, we asked if there were other malocas. Could we leave the bad energies of Serpentina behind?

Miguel said sure, and instead of walking up the hill we drove in several mototaxis to the other side of town. We were dropped off along a rough dirt road. To one side was a big concrete rectangle with a shipping container in front of it. A sign read PENITENCIA.

But that was not where we were going. To the other side was the entrance to a closed down center. We walked for ten minutes to a maloca that was labeled Tambo Ilusión.

As we got set up, I went for a piss. There was a frog in the toilet bowl.

Rosita was with us again. She told us the virus was getting worse.

At the beginning it had been a pulmonary infection, she said, but now it might show up as a digestive tract infection.

Like last time she cried throughout the ceremony. She was in the mat next to me and her gentle cries accompanied me through the night. Several hours into it, a pack of dogs started to howl. An electrical storm rose. The medicine was like those electrical flashes, lighting up an empty stage.

What have you brought? its emptiness seemed to ask.

I could hear Eszter's voice start to murmur across the maloca. I couldn't hear what she was saying but I could tell she was in a deep trance. She told me later she'd been giving birth. She was giving birth to the world over and over again, the world passing through her body. She birthed the world hundreds of times. And the world she gave birth to contained all the babies she'd birthed when she worked as a birth doula, when she'd gone through the burning door, all our miscarriages, all the needles and unsuccessful remedies, all the pain and confusion and frustration, all the swelling capacity in her, the space in her hips for birth, the space in her heart for care and witnessing and restraining and guiding and letting go, cycles and connections and fatalities flowing through her over and over and over, swelling and bursting and leaving, life after life after life. The dogs howled and the sky lit up and Rosita gently sobbed and Eszter gave birth.

When she described it to me later I wondered what effect all her birthing might have had on me. Perhaps through the river of the dead I'd seen some of those entities pass as well, faces that looked at me with recognition. My fate was enmeshed in that endless birthing, too. I was tied to her and to those wisps I'd seen in the dark, who knew me.

I'd witnessed one woman give birth in my life—the wife of an old friend of mine who I was also close to. Eszter had been their doula, and I'd helped them get to the hospital when it was time. At the last second they dragged me into the room and I stayed until the end, cradling one of the mother's feet to give her leverage as she pushed out the baby. Parenting, care, and heritage may be shared, but watching that heaving and crying and pushing there was no question that birth was something a woman did alone.

But here in the maloca Eszter's births were her births but I was part of it, too. It was a life we'd imagined together that would never be, and all the sorrow and confusion and disorientation and pent-up energy cycled through her and it felt endless, like it would never stop. She would eternally be in that loop. But no, eventually it came to an end. And when it came to an end, she told me later, she felt calm and clear, capable of acting in the world. A friend of Luis's was with us, and he was writhing in distress. Eszter heard him and got up and sat with him and calmed him. She knew what to do.

Miguel asked me to sing and not knowing all that had happened, in the best way I knew how I sang to ayaruna, the spirit of the dead. I could taste a slime tinged with shame and loss dripping down the back of my throat. I felt bereft and spent and also humming with deeply colored currents.

Eszter sat with Luis's friend until he stopped writhing and Rosita's tears eventually dried, too. The dogs relented and the storm abated, the curtain fell in the theater. We stumbled up to Penitencia and rode back to Las Coconas and slept.

When I checked the news in the morning, it was all images of Beirut. Battered blocks, broken windows. Friends posted pictures of houses and neighborhoods damaged.

Khaled said he'd learned from a video his mother sent, footage shot off a boat. The city seen from the sea, peaceful at first, then from one moment to the next an enormous, unexplainable explosion. I saw the whole Eastern Mediterranean red with blood.

TIGER TRAP

Threadlike roots, bone colored, delicate tendrils. A prehensile antenna searching straight up, listening and wavering, so thin it almost doesn't exist.

A narrow tree trunk curves over a boulder then extends vertically—palpating and pushing off the rock. That slow give and take, squeezing and lifting. Varicolored mosses proliferate, overlapping with pale lichen splotches. Cicada shells everywhere.

A creature lands: blunt proboscis, bulbous bottle-green body. Looking around with its enormous eyes and nose, a lost Marx brother in oversized boots. Where did it come from? What's it looking for? Quicker than the eye, its mottled back explodes into a pair of wings and it flies off.

Bright sun filters through the canopy, the air sparkling orange and yellow and lavender, trees in unison reaching out and up.

A trick of the slope makes the yanchama appear tilted as its bundle of intertwined forces thrust into the earth, rising up in thick and spiraling strands, stretching and twisting in strength and pleasure, chin lifted in abandon, neck tendons exposed to the light.

I step around the base of the tree and glimpse a gnome-sized ghost-creature nestled inside it, some imaginary elf-goblin suckling on its organic matter like a drug addict or binge eater. Lapping and guzzling, intimately absorbed—I can feel the deliciousness of the real to an imaginary creature.

I see it quickly as I pass, wonder whether I should stop for a closer look, but think: no, better leave that creature alone.

We signed off as COVID hospitalized the US president, his doctor and chief-of-staff contradicting each other, clearly lying. Perhaps he'd get better and come out strong. Perhaps he'd get worse, be defibrillated and left unable to campaign. Perhaps he'd die. Whatever the outcome, the US meltdown showed no sign of abating, a bubbling over after centuries of lies and denials, power grabs, hoarded resources, unheard of concentrations of wealth. California, Oregon, and Washington burning. Syria still in throes. Egypt and Iraq. Ethnic cleansing in Nagorno-Karabakh. Peruvian president Vizcarra about to be impeached, government on the verge of collapse. Turmoil in Bolivia, Colombia—Venezuelan migrants hiding on mountain passes and isolated beaches in Peru. Bolsonaro selling off the lungs of the world across the border in Brazil. Whole swathes of rainforest set to be razed or to burn like the west coast of the US, like Beirut. The approach of the US presidential election meant the nauseating effect of the news would only intensify.

To disconnect from all that, my God, not even to think about it.

Eszter, Miguel, Luis, their cousin Alvis and I, along with Oleg and Yana and a friend of Jorge's named Jean-Paul made the walk back up to Juliampampa in early October. Jean-Paul was a native Limeño newly resolved to extricate himself from the city. He was compact and sinewy, with bright eyes and dark, close-cropped curls, carrying a copy of Byung-Chul Han's *La sociedad del cansancio*. It was Jean-Paul who passed me Calvo's book on Ino Moxo. He'd been coming to Tarapoto for years, so when he made the move out of the city he set up in Las Coconas to begin daily trips to surrounding villages, looking for a corner of the jungle where he could start a new life. He'd been with Miguel and Luis for a couple of ceremonies. He was with us the night of Efraim's miasma—he stayed in the maloca the whole time.

I wanted to watch how Miguel reacted, he said.

This would be his first diet.

Oleg and Yana, not put off by Zina's departure, were interested in listening to plants beyond the strictures of El Cristal.

After the ceremony in Tambo Ilusión, Yana told me she'd relived her teenage years one by one—thirteen, fourteen, fifteen, sixteen, she counted—going through the various stages of punk rebellion.

Miguel told me he'd received a message to give me a mix of tree bark. He called it siete palos, though in fact he'd mix bark from eight trees. His younger brother—Luis's father Liborio—had recovered from June's ape attacks and helped bring our stuff up the mountain. When we emerged after fourteen river crossings into the clover-covered clearing and dropped onto the bench in front of the comedor, we met another Tapullima brother—Cruzildo.

A couple of years older than Miguel, Cruzildo's left leg had been amputated below the knee. He'd set off two hours before us, crutched up the mountain, and was already perched on a rock by the cooking fire when we arrived. A wiry, older man was with him: Antonio, father of Miguel's longtime partner Judy. Antonio had worked with Miguel's father. They used to walk through the jungle together identifying plants and preparing remedies. Antonio knew Juliampampa as well as anyone, knew where all the medicinal plants grew wild in the jungle. Miguel asked him to come up before us to gather cuttings.

Miguel called Cruz *El Cojito*—The Gimp—and Antonio *Cochito*, an affectionate Quechua-infused term for grandfather.

¡Cojito! he cried out. ¡Cochito!

I went to drop off my stuff by the yanchama, where I already felt very at home. I was relaxing in the hammock when Antonio walked by with an armful of humid reddish bark. He had a strong back and powerful arms, though he must have been over seventy. He said the bark was from a bachuja tree. I followed him back past the shower with its palm gutter and up the steps to the comedor. He went straight to a thick shrub near the shelter where they cook plants, and he shoved the bachuja cuttings inside the shrub. Miguel said that would keep the bark from drying out.

It should still be humid when we cook it, he said.

Piles of bark surrounded the fire. Antonio identified some purple-brown wood as bolaquiro. Cocobolo was chocolate brown. Remo caspi was pale and hairy. Miguel said they'd boil it all together for five or six hours, until forty liters of water cooked down to four and absorbed the wood's color. I'd drink those four liters over the next two weeks.

I began to ask about the medicinal qualities of different bark. I was already familiar with nina caspi, but Cruz, seated on a boulder, grabbed one of the abraded roots.

If you drink too much booze and your dick won't stand up, he said. This will help.

He held up a curled and drooping finger at his crotch to illustrate.

After another round of rosa sisa and boiled tobacco, puking off the rock below the maloca, feeding the bad spirits, I was back sitting with Cruz around the fire. When he finished cleaning ajo sacha for Eszter, he pulled out a block of wood and began carving it with a knife.

Making a new base for my crutch, he said, showing me the one he walked up on, all worn away.

Luis's sister Karen wasn't with us this time. Neither was Abuelita. Which meant Luis would do the cooking. He showed me a navel-high plant in front of the comedor, dead and dried up.

Lengua de perro, he said. I like to bathe in its leaves after ceremonies.

What happened to it?

Ermo saw Abuelita pour hot salt water on it, he said.

To kill it?

She wanted us to hire her son, Luis said, but Miguel said we don't need another curandero here. I guess she didn't like that, because she poured salt water on a few plants, to kill them.

Terrible, I thought. Abuelita?

When Miguel visited me at the yanchama to give me a cup of siete palos, he asked me to help him cut and remove a plant. It was waist high with thick, scaly green stems and broad leaves. Miguel said it was called bactina negra—it's used for sorcery and revenge.

You bring something that belongs to a person, Miguel said, or a photograph, and you put it under the plant. You score it along here— he indicated the thick stem—sap drains out and congeals on the object. Then the person gets sick, something bad happens to them.

Sounded like Szilvia's Vojvodina vracskaz.

Miguel said the real trick was to get someone else to do it for you.

Keep your hands clean, he said.

Abuelita, it seems, asked Luis to put a photo of her son-in-law—who knows why—but Luis refused.

I was furious, Miguel said. I want nothing like that up here.

I guess Abuelita's time at Juliampampa has passed, I said.

Sí, hombre. Miguel shrugged. If she used the plants only for healing she'd still be with us.

Eszter was heartbroken to hear this news about Abuelita. Eszter considered her a true teacher. It was like losing a mother.

She was an orphan, Eszter tried to understand. Mother of seven, grandmother of many more. She never had enough. Survival is what she knows.

But Eszter had to admit there'd been a lightness to the ceremonies with Abuelita gone.

I think Miguel's more comfortable, she said.

I remembered Eszter and Szilvia commenting that Abuelita used to pester them for money, sometimes even in the middle of ceremonies. No doubt she did the same with Miguel.

A complicated person, Eszter said in attempt to regain her equanimity, but I love her.

But even Eszter with her signature generosity would struggle to understand Abuelita. She would dream of her at times, feel her not-always-benevolent presence in ceremonies.

After a morning in the plantain orchard, Alvis appeared with the body of a black snake over his shoulder—a shushupe, feared viper of the jungle. Alvis spotted it harvesting fruit and hacked off its head with a machete.

Miguel held the head in his hand, a cork-sized plug of wood propping the snake's mouth open, exposing impressive fangs. He placed the gruesome figure on a boulder in front of the comedor. We passed by it all day.

Mortal, Miguel said, imitating a snake striking. *You're dead.*

In our second ceremony, as Miguel gave me a limpia in the maloca, he began calling the trees he was giving me—chuchuwasha, urku chuchuwasha, bachujita, nina caspi, remo caspi, bolaquiro, ukshaquiro, cocobolo. By now I found my knowledge of Miguel's ceremonial Quechua was good enough that, although I understood nothing when he and Antonio chatted around the cooking fire, I could understand almost everything when he sang. But now at the end of the limpia he started saying words I didn't understand. When he finished I asked what it was.

I was listing vines, he said. It was a message—now you're drinking the mix of trees, and the next time you come to Juliampampa we'll give you vines. The names of different vines were coming into my head: *murkuhuasca, tamborhuasca, acerohuasca.*

I asked if any of them grew around Juliampampa and he said yes, Antonio knows where they are.

The next day Antonio offered to lead us on a walk, so we five dieters, Miguel, Luis and Antonio set off together. We walked down the path from the comedor and were about to turn into the thick jungle when we came across Cruz. He'd set his crutch to one side and was on the ground, crawling, pushing himself up with one arm and slashing his machete at underbrush with the other. He was clearing a place to plant coffee.

¡Cojito! Miguel called as we passed.

Antonio stepped into the thick jungle and began hacking at vines and branches with his machete. We spent the next hour or so following the strokes of Antonio's long blade, slowly advancing through the vines and brush and trees. We stopped at a tall, elegant and narrow tree with a trunk that appeared woven from coils of arm-width fibers, it's pale and hairy bark already familiar—remo caspi. It gets its name, Miguel said, from oars they make from its good strong wood.

Remar is Spanish for *row*, and caspi is Quechua for *tree.*

We use it to propel canoes, Miguel said. It helps you steer through turbulence.

There was a nina caspi tree further on.

Remo caspi and nina caspi are related, Miguel said. Nina is Quechua for *fire*. We use the root.

The tree had bright orange pods dangling from it.

It protects the spirit, he said. If an enemy comes for your spirit, to grab your soul, nina caspi defends with its fire. If an enemy lights a fire inside you and you haven't dieted with nina caspi, you can't defeat that fire.

We walked further into the jungle until we came to a bachuja tree, similar in size to nina caspi, with elegant reddish bark and exposed roots like a walking tree.

La bachujita is a very good tree, Miguel said. It has big strong roots and its power protects you. It can be either male or female. We use both. It makes you *mareado* a little.

He used this same word to describe the effects of ayahuasca, derived from the word for ocean; it was also the word for seasickness.

When you're at sea, Miguel said, you can be dizzy, see colors. If you diet with it before making a child, you might make a very strong child.

We went further and came to a larger tree with knobby bark. Miguel lay a hand on the trunk.

This is chuchuwasha, he said. This one that grows in the mountains we call urkuchuchuwasha. There's another one from the valley. We use both. The one from the valley regulates the blood. If you're very pale, it strengthens your blood. It gives you energy. It helps women—it regulates the menstrual cycle.

They sell it in Tarapoto, Antonio said.

They sell it at every corner, Miguel said, mixed with alcohol. But who knows what the guy at the corner is selling.

And what about this mountain chuchuwasha? I asked.

It protects the spirit, Miguel said, moving his hands around his chest and head.

In ceremonies I saw chuchuwasha as a joyful and steadfast guide, sloshing happily through rivers of puke.

Onward, the plant seemed to say. Have no fear.

We continued through the jungle, now stopping at a plant Miguel identified as huayracaspi, a tall thin tree that waved in the wind. It was not part of the mix. No one was dieting on it.

If you diet on huayracaspi, he said, you can go up, up. You can almost fly.

We passed other plants on our walk—there was curarina sacha that served as a painkiller, mishquipanga with its pungent leaves for plant baths. We passed a leafy vine called hampihuasca:

If you want to seduce women, Miguel said, you come out alone and gather its leaves. Pick older leaves if you like older women, younger leaves if you like younger women.

We also passed huascorenaco, tamborhuasca, and acerohuasca, three of the vines Miguel would serve me on my impending diet of vines.

We passed a large tree whose trunk, around six feet off the ground, suddenly swells to twice its normal size. Miguel said it's called lupuna.

It's a powerful plant, like a bactina negra. You place a photo of someone into its roots, and that person's belly swells up and they die.

There are always more plants, Miguel said.

At that he stopped us, lit a mapacho, and blew smoke all over us.

Always, he said holding up his little cigar, when you're deep in the jungle—*mapacho*. Snakes smell you coming and you don't surprise them.

It couldn't have been more than five minutes later that I noticed Eszter and Yana step past a bright green snake, coiled and still. I saw they wouldn't step on it and didn't say anything. We all passed safely and then I stopped Miguel.

Maestro, I said. Víbora.

He turned and looked out from under his dark glasses. Antonio stepped closer and hacked the snake with his machete. It uncoiled but was soon chopped in half.

Uuuuh! Antonio said.

Miguel paced over anxiously, looking at it.

Loro machakwuy?

Sí, joven. Loro machakwuy. It jumps from the tree like this, Antonio gestured a snake leaping from a tree at your neck.

In twenty-four hours blood starts to come out everywhere, Miguel said. If it bites you, run downhill. You won't make it all the way, but hopefully someone will help you get to Tarapoto and the hospital.

Now the snake was dead, but anxiety still clouded Miguel's face.

I need to warn El Cojito, he said. He's crawling around on the ground. There are snakes.

He paced for a moment, visibly disturbed by the image of Cruz snakebit while clearing brush. It was a reminder of how far we were from medical help. The plants were here but the plants couldn't overpower loro machakwuy venom.

Miguel's anxiety was scattered by the sound of rain, which picked up and soon we were tramping through a jungle downpour, doing our best to head to shelter.

Miguel led us to a path I'd never been on, which connected to the comedor from below.

Here we had the cocal, Miguel said.

Cocal?

A coca orchard, he waved his hand over the hillside. We had a few hundred plants. We worked it for three years. We took the leaves down and Cruz synthesized cocaine. He's trained as a chemist.

I remembered Miguel mentioning that.

We did good business for a while, he said.

But then Cruz got jumped at the base of the mountain, beaten and robbed. Betrayed by a *peon*—as they called day laborers—someone from the community. Soon after, the Tarapoto police appeared in Juliampampa. Cruz was arrested and spent six months in jail. While he was gone, the municipality sent someone up to fumigate the plants.

Mama coca is one thing, Miguel said—he always called it *mama coca*—but the drug is something else.

Yeah, I said. I know.

I never tried it, Miguel said. Jonathan has.

Is that how Cruz lost his leg? I asked.

No, Miguel said. That was something else.

We sat for a ceremony that night.

Antonio had cooked enough of the siete palos mixture that Miguel, Luis, and Cruz were also drinking it.

Buena medicina, Luis said.

Eszter was dieting on ajo sacha, Yana and Jean-Paul on bobinsana, and Oleg on chiric sanango, which Eszter had dieted on in June. Oleg, still in his long draping t-shirts and brushed cotton harem pants, stayed in a distant hut up the hill from the yanchama. Where my hut looked down into the depths of the jungle, his looked up at the high peaks that surrounded us, enswathed in mist.

Chiric sanango was like a grandfather, Eszter told him, wise but severe. But he was kind to me.

It can make you very sensitive to light, Miguel said.

He told Oleg to bring dark glasses, and throughout the two weeks we were up in Juliampampa, Oleg often appeared late to meals and sat alone at the end of the table, silently gazing out over the valley in his dark glasses. Sometimes Yana spoke to him but he said little to us. Whenever I asked how he was doing he said *Very deep.*

Unlike most medicinal plants, chiric sanango brings visions. Oleg said unlike the rapid chacruna visions they would linger. He could even zoom in and inspect them in greater and greater detail.

During that night's ceremony, he said, he saw little crystallized bundles of negative emotions hanging in the air. But these weren't potential wormholes like the knots of trouble I'd seen, they were threatening.

If you look at them, he said, they start to gain strength. They get bigger and come closer.

He spent the night trying not to look at them.

Cruz was with us, too. I'd seen him before the ceremony standing in front of the comedor blowing tobacco smoke into one of the big, pungent toé flowers.

Luis said someone stole a bottle of perfume from him and he was asking the plant who stole it.

But when I asked Cruz he said something different.

There's a female, he said, that gives me horns. But I'm going to diet well and go down the mountain refreshed.

When the medicine hit him he pushed himself up on his hands and sang, impassioned and mournful, calling the tall trees to protect him and give him strength.

I felt a rising wave of nausea gather and stepped outside to see if I might vomit, but no. There was nothing. I went back inside still nauseated. Feeling my way back to my mat in the dark, I knocked over my stainless-steel water bottle—clang!

I felt sick and weak and incompetent, moaning and twisting on my mat. Whatever it was was stuck in my guts, unwilling to come out. I swooned with the waves of nausea, feeling weaker. Through all the ceremonies I'd sat in, I'd never asked for help. I knew Miguel was there. I knew if I needed him he'd do his best for me, and there had been times when the forces were excruciating. But I always hung on through the vicissitudes, perhaps gone outside to take a few puffs on a mapacho, but I'd never called out for help. But now, maybe, was the time. Whatever was in me was stubborn and wouldn't let me rest and I didn't know what to do.

When Miguel passed by and asked how I was, I gasped, struggled to speak, finally was able to tell him something was in me that couldn't get out.

Miguel, I said. ¿Me puedes ayudar?

He looked down at me and placed a hand on my shoulder.

Brak, he said. Ponte fuerte.

And he walked outside and left me alone.

I laughed almost bitterly—of all the wise and teacherly things he might have said, all he had for me was a measly *buck up*. Then suddenly I could feel the puke rising, I grabbed a bucket and bitter liquid poured from my mouth. I heaved a few more times and emptied my guts into that piece of plastic. When it was over I sat panting. The nausea was gone. There was no story behind it. Whatever it was had left me, and I felt better.

Without a word Ermo snatched the nearly full bucket of puke from in front of me and emptied it outside the maloca. I was a little embarrassed for him to do that but grateful. There were tears in my eyes from strain, and I lay back now, exhausted.

I heard Eszter's voice as she started to sing once again the *paradicsom* song—the lullaby her father used to sing to her about Jesus in heaven. Her voice was deep and beautiful. *Paradicsom*, the Hungarian word for paradise, was also the word for tomato—you could eat a *paradicsomos saláta* in the summer. And as Eszter sang the lullaby about Jesus in paradise, she remembered herself as a child along the Danube, listening to her father's voice and wondering why baby Jesus was inside a tomato.

Toward the end of the ceremony, Luis asked me to go outside and talk to him. We sat on the step in front of the maloca. He said all night long the plants had been testing him.

I could either die or learn, he said. So I learned lessons about what it means to be a curandero.

Ayahuasca opens a path like a tree, he said, with a thick trunk, and only at the top does it burst into flower. That's where you can work, but along the way you're shown magic, witchcraft, the power to deceive, to manipulate people, even to kill, and you have to decide what you want, to hone your intent. That's what the plants were doing to me tonight.

He was forced to face the envy of others, the need for money, to understand what he really wanted.

I felt that I want to be a true curandero and help people, he said.

He said in his vision he was walking through the land of death, and I'd been with him. I was singing to death and accompanying him.

I reminded him of the last diet when I'd screamed bloody murder all afternoon.

I know, Luis said, but now you were singing to death and we faced death together.

I couldn't help but be honored.

When this is all over, he said, wherever you are I'm going to think of you, light a mapacho and blow smoke for you. Maybe you'll see me in your dreams or visions.

We went back inside and before Miguel closed the ceremony, Luis had me sit in front of him and gave me a limpia the way Miguel does, beating me with the shakapa and singing in the style of his family.

What wealth, I thought, to have a family song. To have your grandfather sing and say: this is how it's done. You keep your voice delicate and searching, because that's how you connect. To have your father blow that song into your mouth, beat the rhythm into your back. This is how we do it. To possess that legacy, so that when they die you can sit in the mountain and sing and they are in your body, resounding out over a landscape that knows you.

At the end, when the Tapullimas and Jean-Paul had gathered their things and gone to sleep, when Eszter and Yana were passed out on their mats, I stood outside sharing a mapacho with Oleg.

We stood under the stars, watching mist gather on the peaks and lights twinkle in the valley.

He said he was happy he'd come here.

Different than El Cristal? I said.

Oleg said after two months in El Cristal he left and traveled further into the jungle.

Some people came from a community called the Aguaruna, he said. They live in deep isolation, hardly interact with anyone. They bring

Quique his ayahuasca. Quique needed someone to go with them to get more, so I volunteered. We walked several days, then came to a river. We paddled down the river in a canoe, slept by the shore a few nights, then carried the canoe through the jungle and paddled some more. Eventually we came to the Aguaruna village—simple huts around a clearing. Everyone mostly naked.

At night he saw fireflies the size of hummingbirds, with orange LED patterns on their bodies.

They drink pure ayahuasca, Oleg said. They grab pieces of vine and twist them until they crack. They throw them into a huge pot of water. After an hour, they drink it like tea.

He explained it's a warrior tradition. Guys compete to see how many gourdfuls they can drink before they fall down.

Some guys could drink twenty cups, he said. I could drink six.

We finished our mapachos and stood gazing at the night.

The Aguaruna took me fishing, Oleg said. They make a medicinal paste and smear it on a rock. They go to a place where fish gather, and they place the rock in the water. In half an hour fish float to the surface, alive but unconscious. They gather them with their hands.

Fishing, he laughed.

We lit fresh mapachos to blow smoke on ourselves before walking back down to our huts. On the way I passed Luis, who was already up starting to prepare breakfast. He said when he lay down to sleep he was still at sea, having visions.

How was it? I asked.

Ya pan comida, he said.

I slept through the night submerged in sounds of birds and frogs and insects, the yanchama towering above me, sheltering imaginary creatures seeking succor from the real. Birds that hum and whir like aliens landing, birds that let out a quick and loud siren blasts like police cars getting your attention, birds that myew like lost and hungry cats. In the morning I heard springtime chirps as Miguel came to give me a cup of siete palos. I drank it down and he left me. I lay in the hammock, my body vibrating with all the plants coursing through me.

Walking up the path, a gust of wind rose and leaves began to fall from the canopy, yellow-green palm-sized leaves. I stopped to watch and followed one with my gaze as it wafted down and balanced on a fallen trunk. Out of the corner of my eye I saw a dragonfly. When I turned and focused, its body was completely transparent except a faint black edging—a mere sketch of a creature.

It began to seem that everything in the jungle was on that cusp—florid, proliferating, as conjectural as the reflected world I saw on the forest floor. The year, the time, me and Eszter and Miguel, we were nothing but foam on someone else's daydream. We walked the forest floor, our hearts pumped, we interacted, coming into view like the hoopoe birds I'd imagined among the trees. From another perspective we were nothing but a trick of light.

A grasshopper landed: black body with emerald and electric blue stripes. It leapt and transformed into a white sail, a parallelogram flying through the air. When it landed ten feet away its sail furled so quickly it's like it was never there. Again the animal rested, hardly noticeable. Looking around, these white-sailed grasshoppers were everywhere.

Here we were, I thought, among bees beyond science.

I got to the comedor to eat breakfast as mist descended from the mountain. It began to rain and with the rain we heard orange-headed ispuitinos grunting in the distance. Luis said they were happy about the rain.

When it rains, he said, they sit on top of the trees with their beaks open to the sky. When raindrops fall in, they cry from happiness.

The next morning was a day ceremony. Miguel and Antonio had prepared a new batch of medicine. Ayahuasca and chacruna, but this time the third note would be mama coca. Miguel poured a cup and left me alone in my hut.

At the onset, the flow of time altered, slowed. Like an old film print projected at less than twenty-four frames a second, continuity lapsed and individual frames came into view. The yanchama tree—massive and intertwined with everything else as it was—flickered in and out of existence, created anew at every moment.

When it stabilized, I stood up and stepped closer. I wanted to be near the tree. I wanted to lay down on the forest floor, but I knew I couldn't just lay down on the forest floor among the bullet ants and tarantulas. I had an old Turkish towel in my bag somewhere. I was very much at sea, but I had enough presence of mind to sense that if I spread that towel out on the ground and blew smoke everywhere, I would be safe for a while.

There was a spot of earth to one side of the tree relatively free of underbrush and roots, mostly just soft soil, and I thought that was the right place to lay down my towel, but first I needed a mapacho. Ah, I had one in my shirt pocket. Great. I lit the mapacho and blew smoke around the forest floor, careful not to blow smoke on the yanchama itself. I wanted the yanchama to be pleased, to feel I was being considerate, not to smash my hut like in Miguel's dream.

As I was blowing smoke, feeling the soles of my feet on the soil, I felt the medicine course through me, a rising wave. It felt excellent. The embrace of mama coca was like a lesson in delight and pleasure. It had none of the hard edge of a cocaine rush, but I could feel the relation. No wonder it's addictive. Who wouldn't want more and more of these waves of light and joy?

I finished blowing smoke and knowing I'd need my half-smoked mapacho later, I wanted to set it down somewhere where it wouldn't get wet and dirty. I squatted down next to a dry root rising out of the earth. There was a green leaf on the root, too, a leaf that had fallen or been blown and landed on the root and was balancing there, and as I set down my mapacho, balancing it gingerly so I could go back to it, I saw a black millipede emerge from beneath the leaf. I didn't know whether it was poisonous or not, but the millipede crawled out from under the leaf, seemed to stop and look around, then continued on its way.

Now that I'd blown smoke around the relatively clear patch of forest floor and set my mapacho down on the dry root so I could go back to it, I spread out my Turkish towel. I was ready.

I lay back, let myself fall to the ground. Whoosh. It was a delight to lay back like that, just let gravity pull me to the ground. Like a child somersaulting, feeling the thrill of balance momentarily scrambled. After all the preparation I was laying back on the towel on the forest floor and I bent one knee and crossed my other ankle over it and like that I could look up at the yanchama, stable in the world next to me even though just before I'd seen it created anew at every moment. Now it appeared in all its grandeur and complexity—Aguaruna warriors could drink twenty cups of ayahuasca but the yanchama had been standing since the last end of the world, it's huge trunk or trunks rising up with its surface like a modern city built over an ancient city, like Rome or Istanbul with their layers upon layers of past civilizations. The yanchama was like that—whole epochs had come and gone and left their mark on the body of the yanchama. Its body was inseparable from that history, that record of minute events and broad sweeping changes: a million life forms, trunks and vines, trees within trees, dangling fronds and moss and lichens, mushrooms and insects. Through the eyes of the medicine all the lifeforms pulsed and throbbed with vitality, with cycles of living and dying, with material intensity that was inseparable from imaginings, my own and anyone else and no doubt the tree itself and all the creatures that made a home there or passed by there. And to understand the yanchama—not to understand that would be too much to ask—but even for a second to witness the yanchama meant taking in the multiform complexities and cycles of the material world throbbing and pulsing with its infinite inter-relationships as well as the flits and shades and delusions and insights of the imagination. And at the same time it was simply gorgeous and excellent and it was enough in life to have for one second gazed at the yanchama tree rising up from the mountains of Juliampampa.

I lay on my back in such reveries and let my eyelids fall shut and watched the play of sunlight through the canopy against my closed eyes. The colorful patterns of chacruna and the insistent lucidity of mama coca and the deep sense of connectedness of ayahuasca coursed through me and interacted with whatever was in my mind and body, whoever I am or have been. Somewhere there, for a moment, my whole organism dissolved into blue light, completely dematerialized into the ether of conjecture, relationality without substance, an equation with all values set to zero. It occurred to me I'd arrived at a surgical theater. It was in this state, I supposed, that a skilled curandero could rebuild the body on the knife's edge of vision, cure disease without error or miracle. The hum at the base of being, where solar systems were invisible but audible—anything seemed possible from that state. And I lay like that, a puddle of sensory aware-ness, throbbing and pulsing like the lichens, my mind a hall of inchoate wonderings and half-formed thoughts and appreciations, until comparisons and narratives fell away.

I was roused by a drop of bitter phlegm gathering in my throat. I wanted to drink water. In one movement I uncrossed my legs, sat up, and opened my eyes. And I found myself eye to eye with another creature. Gazes locked, bright black eyes staring at me, a visitor. It was a red squir-rel with a bushy tail that had come down and was perched on the trunk of the yanchama tree, its claws dug into the bark, balancing perfectly, and staring straight at me. For a moment we held eye contact, me and the red squirrel, and many thoughts and emotions swirled in me before the squirrel turned and hopped down off the trunk of the yanchama tree and disappeared into the jungle. I could see it's bushy red tail appear and disappear as it hopped and then climbed the trunk of another tree deeper in the jungle and was gone.

Alone again, I got up and grabbed the half-smoked mapacho I'd left balanced on the dry root and blew smoke around the towel so I could stay longer without being bothered by anything poisonous. But now I didn't lay back, I sat and stared at the yanchama and I found myself gazing into a large void, a gap in the trunk, an opening covered in vines. The trunk stretched and split open, giving view to the dark and mysterious heart of the tree, unmistakably vaginal, spilling out vines, rising up from a mess of decaying leaves and moss, a consummate tarantula's nest from which new sprouts shot up.

I sat staring at it and then at the bark and moss and lichens and every-thing around, wondering what was written on the tree here, thinking now my own mind and imagination and memory would be written on the tree, too. I remembered sitting with my friend in the center of Mexico City, just north of the Zócalo off Garibaldi where a pink sixteenth-century chapel rises out of a concrete plaza surrounded by houses with a few alleys receding this way and that. I imagined my friend in Mexico City now during the pandemic, how angry at me she'd been when she heard I was going to Peru.

That's the stupidest thing I've ever heard, she said. I can't believe I'm even talking to you.

We often went on insomniac walks through the city and she took me to that square with the chapel, *la capilla de los muertos*, where people condemned by the inquisition spent their last night before they were executed. Which meant that chapel was charged with those memories, the experience of people knowing they had one more night to live, at least we were charged by those thoughts, thinking of people condemned to death, their last night. What went through their heads?

We walked off toward an alley and a couple of kids stopped us, indicating we shouldn't walk down the alley we were about walk down.

Ahí roban, they said.

And my friend let out a chuckle with her eyes so bright and answered: ¿Me lo juran? And continued down the alley as if nothing could please her more than to be robbed by the robbers of that alley.

Now as I sat on the Turkish towel by the yanchama tree I remembered or imagined our friendship. I wished I could spend the day with her, the city empty, and we could walk through the empty city and get to that square and sit down on the ground with our backs against a wall and look out over the empty square and the capilla de los muertos and not say anything about the memories of the people who'd passed their last night there or the kids who would rob us if we kept walking the way we were walking.

Surely the capilla de los muertos was written on the body of the yanchama, I thought, and me and my friend in the square. I was here in front of the tree and I was also there. I was alone in the jungle and I was also with her. I was in my memory and I was also in my imagination, appreciating and savoring and regretting, and even regret was a pleasure.

I continued my walk through Mexico City with my friend and we passed through the Colonia Guerrero and the San Rafael and Cuauhtémoc until we got to the Glorieta and there by the Glorieta was a cantina we used to go to. We passed through the underpass, the big open space created by the intersection of Reforma and Insurgentes and a couple of guys passed by, so drunk and high with their arms around each other and they stopped to ask for a light, calling my friend *amor*, kids from the northern suburbs, from Satélite, out for a night in the city, exploring or just enjoying their sexuality, feeling urges in their bodies. I can hear how they spoke but can't imitate it, just that they called my friend *amor*. And coming out of the tangle of the metro into a cracked concrete alley between some old buildings dark and stinking of piss, looking for the cantina in the middle of the night, we came across a couple pressed against a cement wall surrounded by piss and vomit grinding against each other, male-female-trans, jeans falling and skirt hiked up, hips pressing and fucking and all of that right in front of us as we stood somewhat taken aback. Three guys came out of the cantina and one of them looked at the people fucking and said: ¿Están cogiendo? And one of his friends laughed and said: No, están bailando cumbia.

I laughed remembering that line, realizing all of that was now written on the body of the yanchama, too.

The feel of an insect on my arm stirred me from my reveries, and I got to my feet thinking I better blow some more mapacho smoke around, but then I changed my mind—I'd blown enough smoke already, because even if I didn't blow smoke right at the tree the way Miguel had done, I should be restrained. I went to get my shoes and stood looking through a gap in the canopy at the distant mountain for a moment, then stepped out past the yanchama and was staring into the jungle in all its density when I heard footsteps behind me and it was Miguel.

Brak!

He asked me how I was doing and I said excellent, I'm here with the yanchama. I pointed out the vaginal opening and told him I've been looking inside and seeing my life. Miguel looked at the opening, too, at the tangle of vines, then lifted his walking stick and poked one of the vines.

Huascarenaco, he said.

It was one of the vines he planned to put in the vine mixture.

Your next diet.

He told me how the others were doing, everyone was well, and he began to whistle and shake the shakapa he had in his hand and he started to half-sing—ñukanami kayariki—and I could see it dawn on him: time to do a limpia. He looked around for the best place. First he had me sit on one of the stones nearby but that wasn't right. I indicated the towel and he thought that was a good idea so I sat on the towel and he stood in front of me beating my head and shoulders with the shakapa, singing to the trees and vines and mama coca in his reedy voice, delgadito, as he says, how the plants like it.

He left me and I was alone and I walked through the jungle a bit, aware the ceremony was coming to an end now, and when I got back to the tree I looked down at my colorful Turkish towel and saw it covered in dirt and twigs and thought: time to hang it up and clean it, so I picked it up and as I did that I could feel joy coursing through my body. I was barefoot again, stepping on the soft earth I'd covered with the towel. Now again there might be millipedes or poisonous ants around. I needed to be careful. But I was happy to be careful. I stepped gingerly back toward my hut and lay the towel over the railing and I thought: there's so much delight in these simple acts. It was still the effect of mama coca, I sensed, a reminder of what it means to savor and enjoy things. It was to be respected, not abused. I remembered standing on Avenue C in 1996 before I left New York, a stupid kid waiting for Felix to pick me up so we could circle the block, I'd hand him some bills and he'd hand me an eightball of cocaine. Three and a half grams, I remembered—was it still like that? If you buy three grams you get a half gram for free? Three and a half grams brought a felony charge at the time, so for sharing that risk with the dealer you got a discount, a gift baked in bitter ironies. I remembered Felix's silver sedan slowing and me getting in and driving with him through the East Village. I didn't buy a lot of cocaine. It wasn't really my thing. But when I did I called Felix and he came, always in a new car. I remembered buying that eightball for my going away party right before I left New York, thinking it would be for the summer when it turned out to be for fifteen years. I sat in my triangular room on Attorney Street, with the little wrought iron fire escape one story above the stretch of warehouses, the Parkside Lounge which is still there. I thought of that chunk of cocaine, that eightball with its felonious discount that we crushed up on a little jewelry tray with its brass edging and its mirror. Everyone I'd met that year in New York was there and the cocaine made us delighted. Parties made me feel overwhelmed then but there I was about to turn twenty-two, Luis's age, surrounded by people I'd met that year on film crews, and with the help of cocaine I could feel happy and comfortable at that party. Because before there had been bathrooms and floors and alleys and knives and running up stairways and that was just me because there was also the wanton destruction of whole cities and countries and traditions and ways of life from people chasing that first spark of delight.

Cocaine, I thought, and now this.

I beat the towel free of debris, walked to the split-palm gutter, and stood under its flood of cold water. Butterflies fluttered by and leaves drifted down, the majesty of the ferns and boulders and trees rising. Black and yellow caciques cawed as they swooped between branches.

When I was back up at the comedor I sat with Oleg and he was talkative today, so as full as my head was with stories now I listened to Oleg's stories. He was my age and had seen wild changes: the USSR's collapse, from Gorbachev to Yeltsin to Putin, from command economy to tanks in Red Square to oligarchs in Marbella and Saint Tropez. He was from Moscow but recently he'd been living on the beaches of Vietnam. He'd studied finance in Moscow, he told me, and after transition he'd worked trying to reconfigure companies, reimagine the economy. Then he was hired by an English investment company to analyze assets. He was sent around Russia to inspect companies, see how they were run, what kind of state of collapse they might be in, what might be salvaged, who could be hired to run them. At some point he learned of a gold mine in Siberia. It was still productive but it was unclear how profitable it might be. His English bosses told him to check it out, so off Oleg flew to Siberia, a town along the Chinese border. He found rickety carts and old concrete constructions and a village of drunks, no one over fifty years old. But the mine was still productive and if run properly would turn a profit.

His English bosses said: *Great, we'll buy it. You run it.*

Now Oleg had to rent an apartment in that miserable gray town on the border with China and go through staff lists and see who he could keep on, who he could fire. He had to convince new employees to relocate to that godforsaken place and once it was all up and running he still had to fly out there once or twice a month to oversee the operation. He saw a lot of bad life and early death, but he was paid well and began to take holidays in Southeast Asia.

There are whole stretches of Vietnamese coast, he said, where everyone speaks Russian.

He began to spend a month or two at a time on the beaches of Vietnam, where his goldmining money went very far. He cohabitated with scorpions and cobras, which turned out to be good training for here, and he learned to kite-surf and began giving kite-surfing classes.

Every day I was flying over the ocean, he said.

His Russian wife came with him and the two of them spent months at a time on the beach, far from the dungeons of Siberia and the bad lives and early deaths of the goldminers. His wife was a fashion designer and they began to make contacts in Vietnam. Soon she was drawing designs for elegant beachwear and Oleg was helping. They sourced quality textiles and connected with manufacturing facilities—big rooms full of people at sewing machines—and they began producing clothes from his wife's designs.

All I wear now are clothes we produced, Oleg said, indicating his long T-shirts and brushed cotton harem pants.

He and his wife were spending more and more time in Vietnam and less time in Moscow and when the contract with the English investors was up Oleg quit, no longer to manage the Siberian goldmine. Now he lived full time in Vietnam making clothes and kite surfing. He only went to Moscow to set up deliveries and distribution of clothes. If he traveled anywhere else it was to India to spend a few weeks at an ashram doing yoga. When he and his wife split up he went back to the ashram for a longer stay and that's where he eventually met Ivan who offered to fly him to Peru and El Cristal. And now he was here with us.

We'd finished our bowls of saltless soup after the morning's ceremony, the embrace of mama coca still palpable but slight. Soon it would be gone.

Having sat mute going deep with chiric sanango, now it seemed Oleg couldn't shut up. He told me more stories about his first months of lockdown, strapping the denizens of fascist hippie hell into the corrector he built, until he finally left to go further into the forest.

At the edge of the Aguaruna village, he said, there was an old man. I don't know how old he was. He was healthy but his face looked ancient. He said he was over a hundred years old. The guys in the village would drink their ayahuasca tea and see how long they could stand up, but he was the only one who cooked ayahuasca longer and used it for medicine. He stayed by himself outside the village. The guys took me to him because he cooked the ayahuasca I took back to Quique. I drank ayahuasca with him once—no chacruna, so no light show like here, but it was very powerful.

This mama coca today was very powerful, too, Oleg said, but what I saw with the old Aguaruna shaman was different. It's hard to say—I realized however far you go there's always someone further, someone who might show you a different plant, more powerful magic. You stop eating meat and live on fruit. You stop eating fruit and live on breath. You stop breathing and—

Pchhh!

Our conversation was interrupted by a rifle shot.

Miguel set off down the path toward the plantain orchard. I excused myself from Oleg and followed him.

Did you hear the pigs? Miguel asked.

I caught up to him as we made it to the orchard, where the last few days Alvis and Antonio were clearing dead trees and propping up fruit. The fruit gets so heavy as it ripens it can topple the whole tree. You have to cut a heavy stick with a forked branch at one end, almost as big as the tree, and wedge it into place so it supports the weight of the fruit. Like anything up here, if you leave the orchard alone it quickly becomes overgrown. Vines will shoot out of the ground, seeds will land. It will be unrecognizable. The work to clear the soil around the plantain trees was ceaseless.

But now when we arrived at the orchard we saw Antonio standing with a shotgun and Alvis, shirtless, hunched with his machete over a wild pig.

Got one, jovencito, Antonio said to Miguel as he watched Alvis work.

Every year they come through in herds of fifty or sixty, Miguel said. They eat everything. Even shushupes.

Some people come up—*bam, bam, bam*—kill dozens of pigs, Antonio said. We kill one.

Alvis had decapitated the pig and began sectioning out the body with his machete.

Para cholos, Antonio said, and Miguel and Alvis laughed.

What? I asked.

Para tribus, Miguel said. Comida para indios.

And everyone laughed again.

Will you eat it? I asked Miguel.

No, he said. I used to eat it. But once I became an ayahuasquero I stopped.

We looked down at the flesh glistening in the sun.

The grease, he said. The plants don't like it.

Alvis and Antonio gathered sections of meat, Miguel and I helped them carry everything back up to the comedor and set it down by the grill. Soon the air smelled rich with roasting meat.

Luis watched us. He wouldn't eat it either.

Comida para tribus, Miguel repeated, and Luis laughed.

Miguel told me people used to look down on Quechua—*indios sucios*—but now for Luis's generation that's changed.

Miguel spoke Quechua at home and learned Spanish at school. Luis spoke Spanish at home and learned Quechua at school.

Now we're all proud, Miguel said. But still he laughed and his laugh had an edge honed in defiance.

Tribes eating pigs.

I walked with Miguel as he made his rounds that afternoon inspecting the empty huts, taking mental notes, as Akos said, of needed repairs.

Miguel told me Cruz had moved into one of the lower huts to complete a three-day treatment that required isolation.

He thinks it'll help him with his women, Miguel said. No one is happier than Cruz when he's with a female. He works two jobs so he'll have an extra twenty soles to give his girlfriend.

We both laughed. Miguel asked about Eszter. How was she doing? How were we? I told him we were well. She's happy here.

I had a vision that she'll work here, Miguel said. She's gaining power.

I believe it, I said.

Eszter would be happy to know he'd said that.

Miguel stopped at a place along the path where there was a mesh bag stuffed with a glass bottle, a backpack, a belt.

My uncle's belongings, he said. We left it here when he died.

What a memorial, I thought. When I die, what junk will I be carrying on my person that day? My wallet and keys, a phone, whatever book I was reading.

Some say we'll see our friends and family again, Miguel said. We'll meet at the end of the world. But I doubt it.

La muerte, he said.

Sí, I said. La muerte.

We kept on.

What happened to Cruz's leg? I asked.

Miguel shrugged:

He was working as night watchman for some militiamen. Another guard dropped a grenade in front of him. They said it had been defused, but it hadn't. I think there was a woman involved.

Miguel blew air out of his nose.

Cojito, he said. My brother.

We walked a bit more.

My other brother Pedro, Miguel said, fell from a palm tree few days ago, collecting coconuts.

Is he okay? I asked.

He broke his arm, Miguel said. Antonio's going to make a treatment for him—huasco renaco, came renaco, and renaquillo.

Miguel looked at me with the hint of a smile that he almost always wore. I could see his left eye looking out over his dark lenses, his right eye invisible behind his swollen eyelid.

A large and very loud fly began to circle around us. Miguel looked up.

Chupasangre, he said. Quiere comer carne.

Miguel taught me there are two types of ayahuasca vine—yellow and black. Several vines grow around Juliampampa, and they're all yellow. The ayahuasca that Miguel and Antonio cook is always made with yellow vine. It's good, powerful stuff, even stronger when they mix in a third plant. To make the mama coca brew we drank the other day meant at the end of the process, having cooked down a huge pot of ayahuasca and chacruna for a day already, they might toss in a handful of coca leaves. Just a few leaves was enough to add that third note.

When I drank the mama coca brew at night, the effect came on so quickly it felt I was being bombarded by images, rapidly appearing and shifting in hundreds of registers. Amidst that bombardment a magenta forcefield came and settled on me—Miguel told me it was the protective force of the tall trees I was drinking. This field approached until it was right above my face, an inch or two, where it paused as if to ask: *Are you ready? Want to try to escape?* Of course there was no escape. I laughed. And it lowered into me, mixing with my body tissue until it was indistinguishable. And the mind-bending velocity of the rapid-fire images increased: landscapes and bodies, beauty and sex, animé and organic matter, watercolors, video games from various decades, medieval miniatures, flickering half-dissolved film prints. My heart rate sped with the velocity of the changes.

At times there was a dark edge, a suggestion of crimes or abuse that was just out of view—as if you're about to accidentally catch a glimpse of what's happening in some suburban house or subterranean dungeon, but you can't quite see. It might be foreboding—if you see it you'll be changed forever. But then suddenly it's playful and lighthearted. And it's coming at you *fast*. It's unnerving, but after dozes of these sessions I'd grown used to it. I knew it would shift and clarify and that relaxed me.

I might feel paradoxes in the mind, direct contradictions that stretched and boggled the mind. Trying to balance all the relationships in the mind, all the perspectives, the historical moment, geological time. It felt like springs and objects rattling around inside my skull, pressing and poking. But I remembered to lower the bodily sensation of awareness out of my head and into my chest, where the paradoxes or whatever they were could be as lumpy and absurd and unlikely as they wanted.

I saw words but they were only *almost* legible. Not a single letter could be discerned. There was a moment when the thought arose in my mind, as if from elsewhere: *Do you want to understand the words?* And I immediately grasped that it's good for me not to understand the words. It compelled me to sense and understand in other ways—bodily sensations, intuition, some combination of inner and outer sense. As the intensity continued to rise I felt vibrations growing and pulsing—*whu-whu-whuh-whuh*. I could feel it enveloping me, and when the intensity kept rising I heard pops—*Pop! Pop! Pop!*—like plungers pulled from a tile floor. In my derangement I wondered if those sounds had a name. Perhaps they were called Carlos.

Sometimes the visions scattered traces like breadcrumbs in the forest, machete marks on tree trunks to orient you. Sometimes you find yourself having stepped into a tiger trap—the earth and leaves turn out not to be happenstance but artfully assembled, so stepping there you find yourself suddenly weightless and in slow motion feel yourself plummeting. You know you're in a vision—you'll still come to on the mat on the wood planks of the maloca—but the place you've seen, somehow traveled to, that envisioned jungle also feels real and necessary. You sense that the moment and the light it radiated is about to disappear forever into some harrowing oblivion, so you do whatever you can, toss all the breadcrumbs you have, shout so your voice echoes, hurl imaginary vines, anything so that a passerby, which may be you in the future—because what is all this but a neural tangle?—so your own roving mind might notice and recover whatever it was from total forgetting. It feels, at that moment, of utmost importance.

You might notice or be shown something the sight of which would change you forever. You might gain an insight that would guide your life or reveal the cause or existence of some hidden wound. Or it might be that the ceremony ends and one of us is gone. Oleg simply isn't there. A portal opened and he stepped through and went skipping through loops and tangles, worlds within worlds, while the rest of us settled back into our spots and selves and went on with our lives.

Transformed from beggar to thief to king, from woman to man and back again, from ant to speck to wisp to shadow of an alien inkling, the impetus is not only to understand awakening from one reality into another, the sheer accident of matter, but to see if experience gained through vision, dream, or such transformational experiences—even a plain leather shoe—can be carried across. Because once you've fallen, you might simply continue to fall, and you might gain nothing more than an acquaintance with falling, one day to manage a modicum of calm amidst such rapid changes.

In the afternoon I went to visit Eszter and found her in her hammock in her hut, up the hill from the comedor. She could see out over the valley, Tarapoto in the distance, but also looked down on the maloca, the ojé tree, the landscape that had, surprisingly, become our home.

I saw where she'd placed her candle for the night, her notebook. As much as I was at home down by the yanchama, submerged in the jungle and my internal meanderings, she was at home here, in the middle of things. I sat on a short wooden stool with my back against the wall, and we chatted about things. It was comfortable, effortless. I told her what Miguel had said about her gaining power and working here, thinking it would please her to hear that.

He said the same thing to me, she said, seeming to assess the idea—what would it mean for her to take that on?

I asked her how ajo sacha was treating her and she said very well. It was delicious.

I told her I felt like it slowed my mental circuits, as if I could sense how one thought led to the next and the next. I think that's what makes it good for addiction, I said.

She said she could feel that. But she was thinking about her father.

Several years before, Eszter's father Laszlo had been diagnosed with Parkinson's disease.

Laszlo was trained as a doctor. When Eszter was young he'd worked in a hospital in Budapest, moonlighting as an inventor. He had a brilliant, restless mind. She laughed remembering a propeller he attached to a stationary bike so they could churn the laundry while exercising, a memory associated with a happy childhood in a socialist apartment block, the bedroom where her father sang the lullaby of Jesus inside a tomato. Eventually he'd patented a device to measure joint flexibility, and Eszter remembered modeling its functionality for an informational video.

But when Eszter was ten years old her parents split up, then Communism collapsed. Laszlo watched his wife move out as red stars were removed from the Danube chain bridge. His reality disintegrated, casting all he'd believed into doubt. He quit the hospital and abandoned medicine. After a period of confusion, he got trained in a technique called Silva Mind Control, a system of autohypnosis developed in the 1950s by a radio repairman from Laredo, Texas—*What if your mind could be tuned like a radio?*—and he began teaching those techniques in Hungary.

Laszlo was not alone at that time in questioning his assumptions. History books were being rewritten, Austrians were buying up Hungarian forests, the church was reasserting itself. The way people worked and lived and studied and vacationed with their families were all being reinvented. Laszlo's version of the Silva techniques—relaxation, positive thinking, visualization, and hypnosis applied for practical ends—struck a chord. He was called onto television specials. He drove all over Hungary teaching in small towns, in big halls in the city. For some he was a beacon of hope, guiding the perplexed into new times. He was generous, kind, committed. He sang pop ballads to his students, made dumb jokes. He was unpretentious and accessible. He came to be the most prolific teacher of Silva techniques in the world, repeatedly invited to spend time with the former radio repairman's descendants in the US.

Now with the onset of the disease, though he'd still go into his office and work on new inventions, he'd stopped teaching. He was living in an apartment in the Buda hills with his new wife, a music teacher who took care of him.

Eszter, a therapist, was in the business of helping people. When her first plant medicine diet helped her go on after abandoning IVF, she felt compelled to return and study. She believed plant medicine, the connection with nature it provided, the insights and loosening of mental-emotional circuits, could be a powerful tool for therapy. And now with the world in meltdown, societies collapsing, oceans rising, the need felt urgent.

Still, her own private reveries often turned to her father. What was at the base of his illness? Was there anything she could do? When she was twenty years old, she'd had an intestinal disease doctors couldn't diagnose. At one point she'd been told she might die. She remembered her father saying he would chop off his arm to save her. Now it was her turn to feel that.

Laszlo had told me that Parkinson's only affected the highly educated, a disease of the cerebral. He believed something in his character linked him to this fate. At first he'd been determined to avoid Western medicine. He felt his illness was spiritual, related to fears he'd never faced. He resolved to face the neurological breakdown unremediated by serotonin agonists or whatever the pharmaceutical companies had derived. He believed that when the disease got bad enough he would come face to face with death, and if he could face death like that he might come out the other side. He might gain a reprieve from the disease.

Eszter had witnessed his decline with trepidation. Was this really the right way to go? She recommended nonpharmaceutical techniques that might help him, but he was determined to go straight down. It was harrowing. Soon he had trouble walking. His speech was halting. His mind, she felt, was growing brittle.

When he could no longer feed himself, out of consideration for his wife, he agreed to medicate. He went to a doctor and took alopathic medicine, and this truly did feel like a reprieve. His symptoms subsided like magic. It gave him several good years before, inevitably, the decline continued. He was going only one direction.

Eszter sat on the mat in the maloca, lay in her hammock during day ceremonies, wondering and feeling through and simply willing herself to exude beneficence to her father. The flow of pure love was supremely satisfying. It was the best she had to give.

Again I thought of how much Eszter and I had been through, what it meant to be married to someone for many years, how unlikely it was that Laszlo had become my family, too, though undoubtedly the feelings she was feeling here were private.

I told her about the surgical theater I'd sensed when I'd disintegrated into sound and emptiness under the yanchama tree, and she agreed— there might be some state like that where we could intervene and cure people, where all you were was the bare impetus to help. She found the medicine often spoke to her. Sometimes it was overwhelming and she began to speak out loud like the night before lockdown—*We're all dead!*— but now sometimes she got messages for her father, for others. She found she could ask the plants basic questions: did she need to stop eating meat? Sometimes she asked questions about her clients and received insights into the course of their therapy. She felt more deeply connected to her work than ever before. When all this circled back to the question of her father, she wondered at his fate. What could she do? Was anything she was learning here relevant to him? What space was there at the edge of the possible?

Cruz had emerged from his three-day isolation, ready to go down the hill refreshed. He and Jean-Paul and I gathered around the stone before going into the maloca, the same stone where Miguel had given me icaro lessons, asking me to follow along with his singing, where he showed me the bright stars that emerge during ceremonies, where he pointed out the stretch of dark forest where the diablitos play.

Cruz motioned up to the high peaks beyond.

When we came up here as kids, he said, as immigrants from Lamas, we used to hear people up in those mountains. We heard rhythms all through the night. They were up there drumming.

You came up with Miguel and your brothers? I asked.

And my twin sister, he said.

You have a twin sister?

Of course, he said. Cruzilda.

Miguel called us for the last ceremony. We took our places inside the maloca.

There was no mama coca tonight. Instead we'd drink cielo that Miguel bought from his friend in Pucallpa. This cielo was made with black ayahuasca that didn't grow around here, which had other qualities than the yellow vine of the sierra. People tend to say black ayahuasca is stronger, but that's not necessarily the case. We learned it could be soft and beautiful. But it has more potential to manipulate, they say. It can be dangerous in the hands of a curandero who's jealous, power-hungry, mercenary. The medicine Mashti was cooking, which spilled before he could finish it—that was black ayahuasca. I wondered if that's what gave him the power to hypnotize Herta so she'd think paying for his trips to Paraguay and Austria was her idea. No matter how much I might sympathize with his need to escape the macho milieu of Tarapoto, I'd warn a friend away from drinking black ayahuasca with Mashti. But by now I felt deeply connected to Miguel. We were bonded. In his hands cielo was safe.

Throughout the night I saw subtle abstract figurations: chemical bonds and minute threads that were the concrete blocks of existence but also purely metaphorical. I understood it as connected to drinking in the matter of the tall trees. The strength of bolaquiro and cocobolo. Remo caspi spreading out in the middle of the jungle, a good navigator because of its sweep. Deep, broad roots and crisp, spreading high branches, densely connected. Solid, unshakable, providing sustenance and shelter to others, long lived, able to tell the history of the world over many centuries, millennia. I wondered if I might drink in this longevity and hospitality, whatever it was that made the trees like huge cities. I was drinking in the communication of their sensitive root endings that chattered to each other like swarms of bees. I remembered something the biologists had told me: seeds from the same mother plant don't compete—they collaborate, identifying collectively. This collective identity was not political wishful thinking but something innate, adaptive, ancient. I thought of my friends and family, people I'd been lucky to know and grow close to all over the world. I thought of Khaled and Martina and one-year-old Walid above the funeral parlor in Harlem, Khaled keeping vigil by his dying father in Dubai and Oman, reciting *Ya sin*, the broken windows of Beirut, Aleppo in ruins while the dictator still stands, the weight we all bore of the past, what had been done to us and what had been done in our name. And I realized Miguel had asked Oleg to sing and now Oleg was singing, he'd borrowed Luis's guitar and was clumsily plucking arpeggios and singing in a low, haunting, out-of-tune baritone. Every time he sang a sour note, which was frequent, Yana laughed, but he was unperturbed, and as Oleg continued to sing and hit more and more sour notes, Yana continued to laugh until he was singing and she was laughing uncontrollably.

He's so serious! she laughed. So serious!

LIKE THIS

The mirror of life shows everything growing. It shows the excesses of the living world. It celebrates multiplicity. Its humor is joyful and generous. It laughs at hypocrisy, shows it as some scrounging and scraping by we all share. The mirror of life reflects the endless twists and turns of fate, decisions, unforeseen consequences, mistakes and corrections, blindnesses, bursts of creativity, excellence, all without judgment. There's always a new solution, a variation you never thought of. It forgives and forgives and forgives. It says God is the taste of coffee and sugar, God is Teresa's voice as she cuts melon. God is the sawblade down the block that whirs into motion with another workday. God is the touch of air on a lip.

The mirror of death has x-ray vision. It reveals meaning. Its humor is fatal but undeniable. Its truth is permanent. Looking closely, it reveals what remains when all the growing and twisting, all the bawdy joys of life evaporate and there's nothing but the approach of vacancy and extinction. In the voracious and eradicating mirror of death—poof!—everything is wiped away. The abusive ex, parents and grandparents, violent urges and morbid indulgences—poof! Resilience and poignancy, lyricism and play—poof! What we hold in our hand at the cusp of oblivion, that blank shines back on who we were and those around us. It reflects how hard it was, the inside of our confusion, all that could have been but wasn't. In its reflection our regrets burst like rising bubbles. The sting of living falls away and the sting that remains is the sting of solitude. Going over the waterfall alone, about to plummet to the rocks far below, for a moment, halfway down the fatal plummet, there's a hovering stillness. From above the roar rises a fragment of sound like the song of a diamond against a polishing scaif, figmentary and escaping description but leading somewhere.

I see my Arabic teacher, Syrian refugee in Istanbul, an anti-regime Alawite disowned by his family, unwanted in his new country, always late and sometimes drunk and unwashed, sitting beside me on the balcony of my rented apartment. We sat facing the opposite roof where baby seagulls with flightless wings paced like old men, and he tried to explain his religion. He said *Our faith is a faith in meaning.* He used the word *ma'ana* not to mean clumps of honey from the sky but something expressed in this life in this world in this way.

Mirrors of life and mirrors of death: I hold one in each palm. The mirror of life is bigger and thicker, heavy in the hand, with a rounded back and a handle covered in art nouveau reliefs. It feels good to hold. It reveals and covers and reveals and covers, shows something new and something new again. The mirror of death adheres indelibly—abstract, dimensionless, weightless, it cannot be set down. I lay in bed in the morning with a mirror in each palm. One in the right and one in the left. They keep switching. I don't know which is which. I don't know where I'm holding death and where I'm holding life. Me on this mattress, nothing but a figmentary filament, the ring after a bell has been struck, which might swell for a second but will also fade and eventually stop.

Eszter outside swats a mosquito: Off to the light you go!

———

A November morning on Prolongación Alerta, the wall of bamboo separating the garden from the river, the serpentine stretch of Shilcayo that tumbles down from the cordillera filling the air with its rush and gurgle and spray. The morning shadows against the brick wall and tile floor are crisp and optimistic. It rained earlier, and now all around La Baronesa's nook red flowers are strewn as if it rained cocktail umbrellas.

I sit at the breakfast table and scroll through feeds and news. Election returns are coming in, run-off scheduled in Georgia. Neighbors in Harlem have been dancing by the Harriet Tubman statue. Meetings of white supremacists, rumors of organized resistance. I thought of friends from the Ex-Yugoslavia describing the summer before the war, how you could sense it was coming. Was that where we were now?

Domestic travel is officially open in Peru. The province of San Martín is still in quarantine, but it's not clear what that means. In a few days, we hear, international flights will resume. We'll no longer be stuck here—to remain will be a choice. Though with winter coming in the north and still no vaccine, the president and his vile supporters bent on violence, and our friend ensconced in the Sugar Hill apartment, the choice is already made.

The *Times* ran a story about ex-Marines at an ayahuasca retreat in Costa Rica—vets from Iraq working through their traumas with Peruvian curanderos brought in to serve them.

"The American sniper likened the experience to a *final surrender* that was grueling but restorative."

I pictured the cops Khaled saw in Harlem.

Who deserves the medicine? I wondered. Us?

In Lima the impeachment of President Vizcarra finally went through. From what I gathered a corrupt congress had cried corruption and corruptly ousted an anti-corruption activist. Thousands were out on the streets to protest.

Walking back from the kitchen, I stepped onto the stone terrace and saw something sail down the path—a gliding grasshopper. Startled, it leapt away from me only to land within striking distance of La Baronesa's web-covered nook. With great speed, the tarantula emerged from her hiding place and seized the grasshopper, flipped it on its back and sank her mouth parts into its exposed belly, injecting it with venom. The grass-hopper's legs weakly kicked out its last drops of life before the spider's venom ended that struggle. Now La Baronesa dragged the motionless grasshopper into her nook to feast in privacy.

A few days ago, a tarantula corpse lay on the ground in front of La Baron-esa's spot. I assumed it was her and imagined a murder mystery playing out here in Las Coconas. *Who Killed La Baronesa?* But then I saw her back in her nook, legs gripping its edges, her preferred perch. So who was this corpse? On second look it was recognizably smaller than La Baronesa. I came to the inevitable conclusion it was a male who'd approached, looking to spawn.

Eszter read from a page on tarantulas: "Whether the encounter results in coitus or cannibalism depends on the personality of the female."

It's just us and Jean-Paul in this part of Las Coconas now. Yana went off to stay somewhere else. And Oleg decided not to come down. He preferred to prolong his saltless existence up in Juliampampa. There was enough rice and lentils on hand and plenty of plantains ripening in the orchard— he'd be fine for a couple of weeks until Miguel returned.

I wondered what would happen to Oleg, alone in the high jungle with all the creatures up there, after fifteen days drinking chiric sanango, submerged in slow-motion visions he could zoom in on and inspect at his leisure.

Before we cut the diet and descended back to Las Coconas, I was walking up from the yanchama to the comedor and passed Antonio at the shower, rinsing a bucket of chopstick-sized twigs. He said they were called cashucsha, and they went in a remedy Miguel was preparing for himself. It was called siete raíces and it was meant to bring good energy. Despite its name, it had only four ingredients: nina caspi, the cashucsha twigs, another plant called para para, all mixed in a certain kind of wild honey they came across rarely. A friend in Lamas called to say he'd found a fresh hive, so Miguel was excited to make a batch.

Do you want some? Miguel asked me. I said sure, and a week after we'd come down from Juliampampa he stopped by with a half-liter bottle of siete raíces. He said I should take it whenever I felt like it, but only after my dietary restrictions lapsed. He told me to drink a cup in the morning and a cup in the afternoon, and on those days, like now: no sex, alcohol, red meat, or spice.

Don't drink it more than five days in a row, he said.

It still sits in my fridge in Harlem.

We got in Jean-Paul's car and drove to Lamas. I'd been in Peru eight months by now, but I still hadn't been to Miguel's hometown. Mostly this was because of lockdown, but now that domestic travel was unrestricted we could make the drive forty minutes down the road to Lamas.

The founding myth, disputed by many, is that the people of Lamas descend from Tupac Yupanqui and the Chanka, great warriors whose valor provoked Incan treachery, spurring the community down the Andes into the jungle. Following waves of disease and incursions by slave raiders, a Spanish expedition in 1653 found a settled hilltop surrounded by communities along the Mayo and Huallaga rivers. The Spanish set to capturing and rounding people up, and by the seventeenth century Lamas was home to the Wayku *reduction*, a restricted area controlled by Jesuits where disparate groups who may not share a language were forced to live together.

By 1900 the indigenous population was one fifth what it once was, and over the next hundred years that decimated community survived rubber prospectors, militant Maoists, rapacious neoliberals, drug traffickers, the DEA, shifting alliances between them all, states of emergency ordered as the military tried to control the cocaine trade, leaving whoever survived to work as day laborers or be hired by wildcat miners or to guard airstrips for Peru's biggest gangster, known as El Vaticano.

The nativos of Lamas were long known as great walkers. They strapped packs of salt and sugar and cotton around their necks like Alvis and Humberto and traveled from the Napo River in the north to the Ucayali in the south. They were legendary musicians whose relentless dances lasted all night long. Their blowgun dart poison circulated like money, and they were famous for their medicinal knowledge. You could find Shipibo curanderos in far away Pucallpa who sang to plants and spirits in the Quechua of Lamas.

Miguel, Luis, Jean-Paul, and I arrived in late morning. Jean-Paul pulled off the highway from Tarapoto and we followed the winding road up the hill to the old city. We parked by a huge and bizarre structure, flags flapping atop stone turrets meant to resemble a European castle. Built by an Italian tobacco merchant as his residence in the early 2000s, I learned, its walls were hung with Amazonian scenes painted in the style of Titian.

El castillo de Lamas, Miguel laughed, before we walked downhill to Wayku.

When we got to the neighborhood we sat in the big open plaza for dances and competitions surrounded by dusty shops where Miguel knew everyone. Merchants sold textiles and ceramics, embroidered shirts and wooden whistles, coffee and cacao and tobacco. We stepped back through the alleys and came to a cluster of one-story mud houses. Eventually we came to a particular house, empty and locked up, about ten paces across, words and figures scratched into its mud facade.

This is us, Miguel said.

He and his eight brothers and sisters, now scattered through the region, had grown up in this small house. We stood looking at it. Miguel and Luis shouted at neighbors and said hi, but didn't seem overly sentimental about the situation. Miguel led us up the hill to another house.

¡Cochito! he shouted, and we stepped through to a small garden.

There was Antonio, his wife Margarita, and their daughter Judy, Miguel's longtime partner, taking care of a couple of neighborhood children. Margarita served us beans and rice and chicken. We couldn't drink the chicha because of our restrictions, but the sour scent of fermentation blew through the garden.

After lunch we drove out of Lamas to Tabalosos, an area where Miguel had bought a piece of land. We drove as far as we could, then parked and walked up the dirt path. We turned off and Luis whistled. This was his family chacra. Liborio was shelling coffee beans with a wooden mallet and Rosita was hanging clothes on the line. Chickens here and there. Soon Karen emerged from a patch of corn—Hola, amigo Brad—and poured us coffee off the fire.

We walked further through the corn and cacao, waved at neighbors in a small wooden shelter, and came to a cleared hilltop. In the middle was a large pitched roof on six supports.

Someday I'm going to get tired of walking up to Juliampampa, Miguel said, and then I'll stay here.

He showed us where he was going to build a couple of bedrooms and a bathroom. A stream for fresh water ran at the field's edge.

Come for the chocolatada, he said. Every year before Christmas we serve chocolate to everyone. This year we'll do it here.

As soon as international flights reopened a couple of New Yorkers arrived, people Eszter had been with on her first trip, anxious to diet with Miguel after months of lockdown. They would go up when Miguel rejoined Oleg, and they would stay for a month. Yana would go back up, too.

A day after the Americans arrived, Masha appeared. Not to be confused with el curandero Mashti, this was a Russian woman who'd been living in LA. She didn't know Oleg or Ivan but was put in touch with them, Oleg explained, through *Moscow esoteric circles*.

With long dark hair and thickened lips, in cotton hot pants and a sleeveless shirt, she could have been in her late thirties or early forties. She had an air of mental instability. Her movements were abrupt and hasty, as if she had no bodily awareness. Her attention was scattered and she muttered to herself in Russian, unable to speak much English or Spanish. She regularly squatted down to snort rapé, the Amazonian snuff popular among foreign visitors. Then she would sneeze profusely, blow her nose, and go back to muttering to herself.

When I saw her the first time, Yana said, I cried for two days.

She would join them for their month on the mountain.

When Oleg told me he was staying on the mountain alone, I was tempted to remain with him. Wasn't it foolish to pass up an opportunity to stay longer in Juliampampa, mostly cut off from the world, walking through the jungle every day? But now, with this new group forming, it dawned on me how unusual our circumstances had been. Usually there were new groups every month, shamanic tourists that came and went like we'd have done if it hadn't been for the state of emergency. I saw that my life was contingent on so many things beyond my control, that I couldn't attribute to myself. Still, I wasn't sure I wanted to see Las Coconas, Tarapoto, even Juliampampa once restrictions were lifted. I was relieved to be headed elsewhere.

Jean-Paul told Eszter and me about a town he liked to go on the north coast, and though the country was still under restrictions, at least we could move from one place to another. Bus service had started up again so we took a nightlong intercity across the Andes and soon were in a little rented house overlooking the Pacific. Police roamed the beach periodically kicking people off—what few of us there were—but when they were gone we could swim and lay in the sun. The verdant humidity had penetrated my bones after eight months in the jungle, and the dry desert air was clarifying. I lay in the hammock and worked on my book. Eszter talked to online clients in an empty room in back.

A man from Indiana was staying in the house in front of us. Big, blond, sixty-five years old, he had palm trunks cut to various lengths in front of his house. Sometimes in the morning he would squat and yank and heave the trunks, some ten or twelve feet long, eventually lifting them high above his head as if he were a strongman from the circus.

He told us he was in Peru looking for salt. He set up a series of glass plates in front of his little house, which he would fill with seawater, gathering the salt left by evaporation. The strongman explained this technique with pride, as if he'd invented it.

Better than salt from the mountains, he said.

Behind us was our landlord, a Peruvian from an illustrious family chased out by leftists in previous decades, so he was born in Australia. He'd moved to Peru trying to reclaim his family heritage and ended up living on this beach. He bought a bit of dune and built a couple of houses, only to have a neighbor slice off half his dune to make way for a road. Now he paced around in irritation, infuriated by Peruvians.

At the top of the hill was the house of a drug trafficker unfortunate enough to end up in prison. In his absence, his children were carving up the land around his house and selling it off bit by bit. Who knew what would be left when he got out.

The town was a series of drainage ditches carved out of the coastal desert surrounding a market and housing for a long-departed oil company. The only thing that broke up the horizon was a single oil platform rising from the ocean in the distance.

Rather than the narrow and serpentine Shilcayo with its tamarin monkeys and orange-headed gamitanas, here was the vastness of the Pacific, Sechuran foxes prowling the dunes, blue-headed parrot fish in the market and moray eels washed up on the beach. There were no toucans, but pelicans and cormorants surfed the cresting waves.

Miguel had invited us to spend the holidays with his family and New Years up in Juliampampa.

You need to learn to cook medicine, he said.

Too much to miss, we returned to Las Coconas right before the dieters were to descend from their month-long stay. We arrived to find the lodge now back in business and occupied by a few vacationing families from Cuzco and Lima. We'd never experienced the lodge open, and it felt like a violation. What were these strangers doing in our kitchen? Teodora assigned us spillover houses on the other side of the road. We went to drop off our bags and were surprised to find Oleg there, cross-legged in his draping T-shirt and harem pants.

I was happy to see him, who I'd once cursed as the fancy hippy with his hand in our honey jar.

Shouldn't you be up the mountain? I asked.

I had enough of Juliampampa, Oleg said.

He cooked us coffee and told me what had happened to him.

The weeks alone had been excellent, he said. He was happy eating plantains and rice and sitting by himself. He wasn't afraid, but he sensed spirits during the night. He heard things he couldn't explain. He was still under the effects of chiric sanango, because even though he wasn't drinking the plant any longer, he hadn't eaten salt to cut the diet. Everything was still active in him.

Then this large group came up, he said. The Americans, Yana, Masha, a couple of Peruvians from Cuzco.

Miguel asked Oleg to help him translate for the foreigners—a challenge, given Oleg's still basic Spanish. He said he felt Miguel was trying to teach him more about administering plants. During ceremonies, Oleg said, he could feel and understand more about how Miguel guides energies with his voice.

But I could see something deeper, he said, something driving the Tapullimas, some source of energy beneath them—inhuman, subterranean, dark.

He was staying in one of the huts down the hill. After a ceremony where he'd felt these looming presences, Oleg left for his hut. He opened the door and entered without a light, and when he stepped inside he felt something crunch underfoot. He drew his foot back and stepped somewhere else but there was the same crunch. As his vision adjusted he saw everything was moving—the floors, the walls—his hut was swarmed with black ants. They were everywhere. He grabbed a broom and tried to sweep them away but there was nowhere to sweep them—wherever he looked there were more.

He told me he was afraid if he went up to tell Miguel he'd spray insecticide everywhere. Oleg was determined to get rid of the ants himself. He was up all night, sweeping and sweeping. But there were too many ants. They turned his poncho to ribbons, devoured his flip flops and everything else. In the morning they disappeared and he slept for a while, but the next night they were back. He swept and swept and though they weren't as bad as the night before it was still impossible to sleep.

After that second sleepless night there was another ceremony. Jonathan was back in Juliampampa this time—Oleg didn't know Jonathan and this was the first time they'd be in a ceremony together. Miguel served the medicine and when he started to sing, Oleg felt Miguel was singing at him specifically, trying to show him something about the power of the medicine. He felt the presence of that dark, inhuman force, and he understood its connection to Miguel and Jonathan. When he heard Jonathan sing in his high and mischievous voice he understood clearly that he was in the presence of an heir to the specific medicinal power connected to Juliampampa. He understood that the strength and depth of connection, the lineage, comes with a cost. It might demand sacrifice.

Oleg got up to go outside and walked toward the toilets. Miguel followed and asked how he was doing. They both went into the toilets, but Oleg came out first. Before Miguel came back outside, Oleg left. He went back down to his hut and hid. He put his shoes out of view, locked the door from inside, didn't turn on his lamp or light a candle. He didn't want anyone to search for him and ask him come back to the maloca. He needed to be alone; he couldn't be too near Miguel, and definitely not Jonathan. He could see the dark, subterranean, inhuman force with perfect clarity, could see its shape and feel its pulse. He felt it was something that might not always materialize but sometimes sure enough it was there.

It needs to be fed, Oleg said, and its food might be you.

Oleg thought about teachers, what a teacher is supposed to be like—someone you admire and seek to emulate. They might be older than you, but you're pleased to see the way they are. Their health and wisdom and love are radiant.

And here look at Miguel, he said, his swollen eye and his shattered knee. His father and grandfather both fell from the mountain and died. It's like the universe was trying to get rid of them. There's some force that doesn't want them to prosper and be radiant and healthy.

He remembered Zina, who'd stepped one foot into the Hilton maloca at Serpentina and thought: No, this is not for me. She said she couldn't go on a diet with Miguel because there were too many dark forces around.

At the time Oleg thought: No, this woman was sent to distract him from his path, and after the diet with us staying alone in Juliampampa he felt sure. He was on his way. He was going to break through to the world of light. He would learn magic and how to guide people and Miguel would be his teacher. But now, hiding on the floor of his hut, still crawling with ants, disturbed by the dark inhuman force he'd seen, how it manifested through Jonathan, he felt that Zina had been right. There may be much to learn here, and he was grateful for all that had happened, but this place was not for him. No. This was the wrong place for him. He saw it now. He'd been naive and now he could see.

Enough, he thought. I'm leaving.

And as soon as he said that to himself he felt the floorboards around him and realized the ants were gone. They'd finally left him alone. He said he felt like he'd been compressed, locked out of himself. But now after struggle came relief. Everything was suddenly light and beautiful. He would go down to Las Coconas and then go somewhere else, to the beach or the mountains—out of the jungle.

But the next day it stormed and the rain lasted all day. He told Miguel he was going to leave and Miguel wanted to know why. Oleg tried to explain but it was difficult. He talked to Yana privately and tried to explain to her, but she didn't understand either. He asked her to promise not to enter a ceremony with Jonathan.

Okay, she said. I won't.

Everyone else was happy, Oleg said. Especially Masha. She was peaceful and enjoyed everything.

The rain passed and Oleg came down here to Las Coconas and felt relieved. He stayed alone in his room and tried to think through all that had happened, what he'd seen.

I feel very strange, he said.

I thought of all that had passed through here. I thought of disease and slave traders and Jesuits and drug traffickers, the arrival of electricity and rifles, Maoist guerrillas and French shamans with their exorcisms, poachers with their shotgun traps, seasons of hunger, encounters with animals and snakes and the limits of a person's control over their own life, European and American and Russian tourists. I thought of Jonathan and Luis, the weight of the legacy, their heritage, the injustices of the past and the drives of youth. All of that must comprise the inhuman force Oleg sensed. Its force was not only here but it was specifically here, historically here. We were part of it, too, the ants that eat everything. We were lucky to witness and savor for a while before the whole jungle was consumed by our inner ants and left shredded to ribbons like Oleg's poncho.

I told Oleg there was one thing I could say: what Miguel would have told him if he'd let him know about the ants.

He wouldn't have shown up with insecticide, I said. He'd have told you to piss on them.

Eszter and I showed up to the chocolatada with armfuls of panetón from the supermarket in Tarapoto. We found a whole crowd of people under Miguel's pitched roof in Tabalosos. Rosita and Judy ladled out chocolate from soup pots. Children ran everywhere. Eszter had brought a bag of seashells she'd spent hours collecting on the beach. I'd teased her about it, but now she offered them to the kids who grabbed them gleefully before speeding off, and she winked at me in victory.

The crowd swelled until even the mayor of Tabalosos showed up, accompanied by a priest. The father had been kind enough to conduct a service, the mayor said, in observance of a year and a half since his departed wife's passing. He'd remembered Miguel's invitation on the way back from the cemetery and thought why not bring the priest with him. The mayor gave a speech in appreciation of the Tapullima family and the community of Tabalosos. The priest gave a speech, too, thanking his guests and wishing them well for the upcoming holidays. The mayor passed out rubber balls to the kids, who immediately began kicking and throwing them and running around, the boys stopping to complain that the balls were pink and girlie and covered in princesses. Margarita passed around grapes soaked in cane brandy and Liborio poured sweet red wine from a local farm. Karen cut up the panettone we brought and it soon disappeared like the seashells. The mayor said goodbye and turned to head back to his car, but the priest had wandered off into the corn field and was lost.

Jean-Paul and Luis stood at the back talking about Tarapoto.

Did you ever go to the movie theater? Luis asked.

¡Cómo no! Jean-Paul said, and he told me about the Tarapoto cinema:

It used to be you bought a ticket and went in and bought some wildly overpriced nuts or seeds or popcorn, he said. But the mark-up was so great people protested to the point the town passed a law that movie-goers were allowed to bring their own food into the theater. Soon families were carrying in their own bags of nuts and seeds. And to go with the salty stuff they started to bring fruit. People passed around chirimoyas and granadillas. Soon families were showing up with entire watermelons to cut up and pass around during the movie. The owner of the cinema was losing money—ticket prices didn't cover building upkeep, film licensing, wages for workers, especially the cleaning crew now working harder than ever. To make extra money he set up a rotisserie chicken stand in the theater so people would buy whole chickens during the screening, but people brought their own chicken instead. The cinema was a cloud of smoke from roasting chicken, everything sticky with mango pits and watermelon seeds, and the operation was teetering on the edge of collapse. Then the pandemic came and that put an end to that.

Luis mentioned a place they used to go dancing before lockdown, and Jean-Paul turned to me.

You have no idea, he said. Tarapoto nightlife was famous—*bien sórdido.*

I'd only ever experienced Tarapoto in lockdown, under curfew. Although I'd been here for most of a year, they were describing a place I'd never visited.

On the night of December 24 we went to Miguel's brother Pedro's house around the corner from Las Coconas by the dusty soccer pitch, not far from the bench and the tree where—free of post-dietary restrictions and not drinking my siete raíces—I sat sometimes with my afternoon beer. Pedro's house consisted of a bare concrete salon with a couple of bedrooms and a kitchen in back. His arm was healing well after some trips to the hospital and treatments from Miguel. Their cousin Miki pulled out an electric guitar and played old Tarapoto cumbias by Tulio Trigoso:

Esta serpiente para despierta
le gusta todo tipo de carnes
le gusta carnes blancas y negras
y las flaquitas también

Cruz showed up at midnight with a bottle of sweet wine. He took a swig, set the bottle down, and grabbed Eszter. They sashayed back and forth into the night.

Where was Cruz's twin sister Cruzilda? I wanted to know.

I asked Miguel, who said there was no such person.

You heard him, too, I turned to Jean-Paul.

It's true, he said, but that was when Cruz was sleeping with toé flowers under his pillow.

Jean-Paul had continued his explorations, looking for a jungle village to start a new life. He showed up in the evenings in rubber boots to report what he'd seen. Eventually he thought he found something and asked if we wanted to go with him to take a look.

The next day we drove with Jean-Paul out of Tarapoto and up the valley of the Cumbaza River. The Cumbaza was broader than the Shilcayo, and its descent was gentler. Right at the edge of Tarapoto was a curve of sheer rock that formed a deep pool where Tarapoteños could dive in and cool off. Further upriver were a series of sleepy and peaceful villages. We came to one, burlap spread out on the road where coffee beans dried in the sun. Few people on the street but those we met were laughing and friendly.

I think this is my place, Jean-Paul said.

We drove just out of the center and up a dirt road. Jean-Paul stopped to chat with a family in a wooden house on the outskirts, then drove further and parked where there were no more houses. We got out and he led us down the hill. We passed through a cacao orchard and eventually entered deep jungle. Jean-Paul—inexperienced at this as he was—swung a machete to clear a path for us. There were a couple of ojé trees and two springs. At the bottom was a curve of the river, not as a broad and steep as the place outside Tarapoto, but beautiful, the perfect place for an afternoon swim, the Andean foothills rising around us.

I think this is my place, Jean-Paul repeated.

We congratulated him and enjoyed the afternoon by the river, so refreshing.

We were set to head back up to Juliampampa a few days after Christmas. Oleg was planning to head to the Sacred Valley. Yana and the Americans were gone. Las Coconas was quiet again. Though we still heard Masha sneezing in the morning after her first snuff of the day. We ran into her in the kitchen trying to cook. She'd never made rice before, she said. She tried to soften an unripe avocado by burning it on the fire. She showed us an oven rack set with five fishes charred completely black.

You want to try? she asked.

A month in Juliampampa had not calmed her. She walked with the same haste and static, full of hunger and impatience. She begged Miguel to give her more ayahuasca each day, and when he said no, that she needed to rest, she asked Oleg, who still had some bottles he'd brought from the Aguaruna and El Cristal. We told him he shouldn't give her any—that girl didn't need more ayahuasca!

She muttered to herself as she hustled around the garden, bumping into walls. I wondered if she had addiction issues. Those cocaine orgies in Moscow. Who knows what she'd got up to in LA.

She went into Tarapoto and showed up with ceremonial clothes she'd bought from the artesanía market. She put them on and stepped out to model for us, pleased as Herta had been when we'd first arrived.

She told me that coming down from Juliampampa they'd stopped at a waterfall.

Beautiful, she said, but we didn't have *this*—she clutched roughly at her breasts—or *this*—she smacked her hand against her crotch—so— she imitated looking around, stripping off her clothes, and jumping into the river.

She grinned to show her delight but I was jarred by the abrupt way she touched herself. I wondered if she were from the oligarch class like Ivan, but Teodora said no. She'd heard Masha complaining that she couldn't work because of post-dietary restrictions.

I think she meant sex, Teodora said. She mentioned giving massages.

Seems like she might be a sex worker, Eszter said.

None of us had a problem with sex workers, but we wondered if that explained something about her. It seemed like she wanted medicine every day not to learn and explore but because its intensities quieted something in her. I was annoyed when I saw Oleg grabbing a bottle from the fridge to serve her.

I thought I understood something about the medicine, about the necessity for restraint and respect.

Don't give her more medicine! I lectured Oleg.

I was alarmed when Miguel told us she was going to come up with us to Juliampampa while we were cooking medicine over New Years.

What? I said.

She wants more, Miguel said. And at least up there I can keep an eye on her. Otherwise who knows where she'll go.

I couldn't believe it. She was coming up the mountain with us?

Relax, Miguel said. Don't judge.

We'd been in Peru ten months by now, and I was starting to miss people terribly. I made regular phone calls to New York, other places in the US, to Europe. I cursed my itinerant life for resulting in such scattered friendships. I wondered what was happening with my friend in Mexico, how the pandemic had affected the city. But when I called her, her anger from the year before hadn't subsided. I told her I'd often thought of her here but she didn't want to hear about that. She mocked me for my time in the jungle—*on those drugs*, as she called it. I tried to explain it was not like that, but she seemed to take pleasure in her anger, so rather than reminisce about the chapel of the dead or the cumbia dancers by the old cantina, I only wanted to get off the phone. Don't judge, I wanted to say. When I hung up I wondered if we'd ever speak again.

Six of us hiked up to Juliampampa—Eszter and I, Masha, Miguel, Antonio, and Alvis. I set myself up in the hut by the yanchama and Eszter was back in her spot above the comedor with its sweeping view of the valley.

We'd brought up twenty kilos of yellow ayahuasca, sourced from the same part of the mountain where Sacha Wasi got their vines. It would make good medicine, Miguel said, trustworthy and powerful. He and Antonio took us down to gather chacruna leaves, teaching us to distinguish the ripe leaves that would paint our visions. We layered vines and leaves into two huge stainless-steel pots and filled each with eighty liters of water. Alvis chopped wood and Antonio lit the fire. Slowly the pots came to a boil.

It will cook all day, Miguel said. We'll strain it and cook it again tomorrow until there's a liter left in each pot.

Periodically Miguel or one of us would light a mapacho and blow smoke over the boiling pots and Miguel would sing. I at one point was stirring the pot, blowing tobacco over it, and a drop of saliva fell from my mouth into the pot. I'd drooled into the ayahuasca. I looked up sheepishly to see if anyone had noticed, and Antonio and Eszter were looking right at me. They both burst into laughter, and the three of us shared a moment like that, laughing at my drool in the medicine. What effect might it have?

People always return to the question: how did they know to cook ayahuasca vine with chacruna leaf? Because the vine grows down in the rainforest and the leaf grows up in the mountain. They grow days', even weeks' travel apart. And yet someone at some point put them in the same pot and cooked them for a long stretch and discovered the rare power of the mixture, which brought visions and insights, allowed certain people to see into the past and future with great clarity, granted power to influence events, to heal people or make them sick or barren or cause them to get lost in the forest, to lead them out into the jungle following a guacamaya or even a lowly umpalito, to focus on their hunting until they realize they're far from the path.

When people thought back on it and wondered how they'd first understood to cook the plants together like that, they thought: the plants told us. The plants spoke to us. It was like we were walking in a dream. We saw the ancient tangle of the ayahuasca vine and it spoke to us and said: cut me and macerate me and cook me together with the green and waxy leaf of the chacruna. They did so and discovered the rare power of that mixture. And then they began to cook other plants together. They added ayahuma and piri piri and nina caspi and many other plants and discovered the unique power each plant had. They came to rely on the plants to help them and guide them and heal them and favor them among others. Certain people used the plants to gain power and others used the plants to gain wisdom. The wise would rather be killed by the powerful than use the plants against others. Though they also learned that they needed to cultivate power, otherwise their wisdom was useless. They were naked with no dignity, unable to defend themselves against a lowly pigeon sent to spy on them by a rival.

They believed not that they were the source of vision but it was the plants seeing through them. They had the good fortune to be visited by the plants, so they would see what the plants saw and feel what the plants felt. It was on a timescale and in a language beyond them, but it left a residue. By cutting and cooking and drinking the plants they served the plants. They offered themselves up to the plants. They sacrificed to the jungle and the sacrifice was themselves. And they were fortunate to be sacrificed. It was like they were chosen. The plants would guide their arms as they swept their machete through the hanging vines, as they pruned the chacruna bushes so they grew robust and leafy. They knew when to stop their thrashing so as not to disturb the chaotic equilibrium of the jungle. They cultivated and hunted but always with restraint. They were absorbed into the jungle as they had always been. And when they drank the macerated pulp of the vine and the leaf they paced like the jaguar and felt the sweet taste of the quinilla fruits eaten by the nocturnal monkeys and they glowed with the colors of the guacamaya and they could see with the eyes of the eagle or condor and they hopped through the brush and pecked and chirped like the lowly umpalito and like that they were joyful. Life and death were less melodramatic as all pleasures and pains appeared to them at once.

Some say this is all bullshit. It was only a small group under the watchful eye of the Jesuits who cooked the vine and the leaf together. And it was the missionaries who popularized it. It was only in the nineteenth century that the brew spread around the region, and its spread was commercial. Beatniks seeking insights, anthropologists seeking traditional beliefs—ha! From the beginning it was about two things: spiritual warfare and cash money. Don Quique was right—it was a newfangled trick to mystify. It was *the drugs*.

The next morning while the medicine was still cooking Miguel came to see me at the yanchama, served me a cup of piri piri, and left me alone.

I noticed a mandala image on the door of my hut and realized it was a plastic sticker someone had stuck there, perhaps one of the last dieters. I remembered seeing an offering someone had placed inside the yanchama tree and went to fish it out. I found a kind of rosary made of styrofoam beads.

They think they're paying tribute, I thought, but they're just bringing their trash to the jungle. It's poison.

I was overcome with despair and derision. I saw us here, foreign seekers who bought plane tickets to come here, who allow local guys to drag our stuff up the mountain because we can't be expected to carry it ourselves, yogic fakers who've never known the underworld, Marines trying to wash away their atrocities, sheltered Americans who flit from interest to interest, spoiled Russians so removed from the depth and poetry of their traditions, so demented by influxes of money that they find themselves here, as if all this belongs to them, to us. I thought of Nurse Rosita in the Tarapoto hospital treating patients all day, taking the medicine to cry out her stress and exhaustion, all she'd absorbed of poverty and fear and mis-communication and disorganization and bad luck, so she could protect her still flickering hope. And I wanted to cry from shame. I felt done in by my choices, my confusion, my indulgence, by my inability to see the truth of things, to act on it, to stay close to some truth that must have been available at some point, until I ruined it.

I felt like the anonymous narrator of *Los pasos perdidos*, returning to the village only to find it had never been what he thought it was. I didn't think Oleg was right. I didn't sense any dark inhuman force wanting to eat us all here. No. I felt that Oleg was running from the gold miners dying in the mine that paid for his months on the beach of Vietnam, his trips to ashrams and retreat centers. His search for transcendent insight—alone with the hundred-year-old Aguaruna maestro, alone on the mountain stuffed with Miguel's chiric sanango—all of that motored by trudging miners rife with cancer and cirrhosis, dropping dead so English bankers could get rich and he could travel.

Wayward oligarchs in hippy hell.

Don't judge, I thought.

But I realized that along with the mirror of death and the mirror of life there was another mirror. Because in the afternoon when I'd gone down to visit the plants I'd dieted on, to offer mapachos to yacushimbillo and bobinsana and ajo sacha, I'd come back up past the comedor and spotted Masha sitting cross-legged on a boulder in the sun, palms upward on her knees, fingers touching in some kind of yogic hand position, a beatific smile on her face. And I realized yes, beyond the mirror of death and the mirror of life there is the mirror of Masha, and the light reflected by the mirror of Masha is brutal fluorescence. It shows the weakness of spiritual technologies, renders all magic empty, vapid, absurd, powerless. Beauty turns saccharine. Tenderness melts into pathetic bullshit. All you thought was sacred and meaningful is revealed to be laughable. The teacher is shown with all his warts and farts, weaknesses and limitations. You're back on your own, having understood nothing at all. The mirror of Masha shows us our own idiocies: she's damaged because she's a sex worker or an addict. She must be pursued by an abuser, there must be panic in her sneeze. What do I know about her? Or Rosita's tears for that matter? It's my own baby bird I feel, not theirs. Like Oleg's monster, it's all mirrors. Every judgment we ever have is small-minded, from lack of generosity. Better stay silent, see in the blue light of connection that melts our stupidities. Better set the mirror of Masha down.

What now? I wonder.

I remembered an afternoon many years ago wandering around Rome, when I'd sat in a little restaurant in Trastevere and struck up a conversation with two women eating next to me. One was a researcher at the Vatican. She said she was cataloging references to the doctrine of universal salvation.

Buried in the Vatican library, she said, were transcriptions of clerical conversations from the Middle Ages. They concluded that as Christ's compassion is universal, every last one of us, no matter what we did, how much we might have sinned, is destined for heaven.

All of us headed for the big tomato, I thought.

Naturally this conclusion was not made public, the researcher said.

I imagined stories of Catholic and Protestant shamans, sci-fi and futurist shamans, cottage core shamans, heraldic shamans, gentleman shamans, shamans of the nonbinary, of the fluid and new, frozen shamans with their medicines for nosebleed, wine-drunk shamans with their recipes for mint jam and pot roast.

When Miguel came to check on me I told him it had been a serious, tormented ceremony, that I'd been thinking over the rotten parts of myself.

Ayahuasca shows everything, he said.

I felt Miguel to be an old friend. I sensed his genuine-ness, his good and solid humanity. I thought of someone—Oleg or anyone else—who might judge him or hold him in suspicion and I felt protective.

What do you think was bothering Oleg? I asked.

And Miguel shrugged: Something inside of him.

Indeed, I thought. Mirrors all the way down.

He told me the night before he'd dreamt of his father.

My father was very joyful, he said. Sometimes I see him.

He tossed away his mapacho, then went on:

We don't know where people go when they die. Some people say there's another world, and that we'll find them there. Not like this—he batted his palm against his chest—not like flesh and blood, but in some other way. But I think . . . I think there's nothing.

I listened, and he said more.

You just missed him.

What?

He died just a few months before Eszter came the first time.

I had no idea it was so recent.

I'm sorry, I said. I'd have loved to know Maestro Pedro.

Miguel left me alone and I was there with the yanchama, still with a shamed and panicky residue from all that had gone through my head that morning.

What had I learned in these ten months that might help me right now?

Thoughtlessly I began to call to ajo sacha, who had successfully, I realized, freed me of tobacco addiction. Ajo sacha who'd softened my internal spiral, offered me respite.

Tranquilízame, I sang. Tranquilízame.

We cooked down our pots of ayahuasca, one with a small bundle of piri piri reeds, one with a handful of mama coca. On New Year's Eve we sat together in the maloca—Miguel, Eszter, Masha and me, with Alvis as guard. Miguel served us from our fresh batch of mama coca.

My drop of drool must have penetrated the medicine, because it made me good and sloppy. It came on so strong, the rapidity of the visions so mind-boggling, I thought my head would burst open and I'd drop dead. When the rush subsided I was punch drunk. Miguel asked me to sing but

277

I could only slur out a few words before I gave up and dropped into a heap on my mat. Eszter was more collected than I was, and I sensed Masha vibrating across the maloca. I was knocked out, my visions a deranged haze. Eventually it was midnight and we all went outside. By that time hours had passed and the impact had calmed. We saw fireworks explode over Tarapoto in the distance, filamental strands echoing through the chacruna scrim. Despite the usual prohibition against contact, we all hugged each other. Even Alvis, sober as he was. How did all this look to Alvis? Such a good natured, powerful man, patient and brave. It was a boon to be embraced by Alvis, at least I thought it was.

Miguel said the medicine we'd cooked was good.

Not too strong, he said.

I had to laugh.

I remembered the previous New Years. We'd been on Khaled and Martina's rooftop on St. Nicholas Ave in Central Harlem. I'd brought a bottle of champagne and after filling everyone's glasses the bottle was still half full. It was cold and we didn't stay up there long. To get back downstairs we needed to descend a steep ladder from the roof to the fifth floor landing. I was champagne drunk enough to step down the ladder with my back to it, as if it were a staircase, without even setting down the bottle and my glass. On the second or third rung I slipped and went sliding down the ladder like a cartoon—*ba-ba-ba-ba-bap*—my tailbone smacking against the metal as I slid.

When I hit the floor, however, I landed on my feet. And I saw that I'd landed without spilling a drop of champagne. Not from my glass and not from the bottle, either. I knew I'd wake up in pain, but I concluded this was a sign of excellent luck for the coming year. And now, with Eszter and Miguel and Alvis and even Masha—Antonio already asleep but Antonio, too—looking down on the fireworks above Tarapoto from Juliampampa, I thought somehow, as strange as it was, that I'd been luckier than I could have ever imagined. To have ended up here in the year of the pandemic was far beyond falling down a ladder without spilling your champagne.

Cheers, I thought. And I raised an imaginary glass to everyone. Cheers!

We came down the mountain and bussed back to the beach, moved back into the little house above the strongman. Footage of the January 6 riots rang in our mind—how lost was America? News of the vaccine roll-out reached us but still seemed far away. Oleg, before he left, had warned us against the vaccine. He said Don Quique had told him *Whatever you do, don't get the vaccine.* But on the north coast of Peru there were no vaccines to be had. I went back to writing in the hammock, gazing out at the surfing pelicans and the horizon with its oil platform, and Eszter went back to seeing clients in the empty room. The days were peaceful and the nights were cool. We bought a blender to make salsa and brought kilos of fresh fish from the market and learned to smash plantains so we cold fry up *patacones.* We were in our separate worlds during the day but sat over our meals at night and talked over everything we'd been through, all that had happened to us in Peru. Sometimes a Sechuran fox would stop by and we took to leaving out leftovers because we were happy to see those odd foxes that were half wolves.

I had spent the year submerged in writing, researching, and translating, walking and daydreaming and trying to formulate something in the notebooks I filled week by week, but Eszter had been working as a therapist, seeing clients the whole time. Whatever she'd learned, whatever the plants had imbued her with, she was putting into practice.

I'd always felt there was something beneficent about Eszter's presence. She was patient and grounded but also optimistic and open to the weirdest ideas. She was generous and thought the best of people, took them on their own terms. She had the capacity to see into the core of situations. I was confident she'd been a talented therapist right from the beginning, when she started out at a methadone clinic downtown, then working with Spanish-speaking families in Queens, finally when she'd been able to open her own practice. She was always studying some new technique or modality. She was passionate and experimental—obsessed. I wondered what it had done to her, all this plant medicine. Had it changed the way she worked?

She pushed her empty plate back and thought it over.

I mean of course it's changed me, she said. Everything is turned upside down. The world is completely transformed. Everyone is seeing their lives in new ways, and I'm here—she motioned to the broad expanse of the Pacific—after this year full of plants.

She paused for a moment, then went on.

The first time I came to Juliampampa, she said, after the hundredth miscarriage, trying everything, losing my fucking mind. I said to myself: *I need some other-level perspective on this.*

I remembered. It had been hard times for both of us. So confusing.

One of the first ceremonies that year, Eszter said. Some presence appeared to me and said: *I could do THIS*—she snapped her fingers—*and everything disappears.*

That was my introduction, she laughed.

You know I wasn't raised religious, she said, but in another ceremony something like *God* appeared and started to show me how things work.

I heard how Miguel's singing was strong and anchored. His voice had power but was also gentle and listening. It was like heat rising or a wave passing through the atmosphere. I could hear the phrase *así se hace*, and I understood: that's where you work from. Something masculine-feminine, where fierceness and love meet. I found myself thinking—you can imagine how surprised I was to be talking like this, I was raised Communist!—but I found myself thinking: *This is the mercy of God.*

At the beginning of this year, she said, the night before the ranger appeared to tell us about lockdown and curfew and closed borders, a bunch of weird heads appeared in my vision, part-plant part-extraterrestrial. They started speaking to me but not in language, in some other way that melted my mind. My mind had to contort into unknown shapes in order to understand. And once I could understand, they said: *The world has ended.* I saw a flood wash away New York City. The avenues of the Upper West Side submerged. Citibanks collapsing. It was all gone. Everything was swept away and I was in absolute darkness. I was small, and death was right behind me. And I was shouting into nothingness, shouting to God. I'm this tiny little person and I have to speak for everyone: *We'll start again, we'll do it again. And we'll learn this time.* But the whole world ended just like that being said, with a snap of the fingers. Then I begin pleading and bargaining with God—*Why does it have to be over? Let us start again!*

In one of the next ceremonies, she said, I began to hear my inner monologue as if from the outside. It was me thinking my own thoughts, then suddenly it switched. It was still my inner monologue but it wasn't me anymore. It was something plural, beyond gender, addressing me: *WE* are talking to *YOU.* I could hear their communication, and it was very loving and benevolent. They called me *my dear* and *my love.*

That's how they speak to me, she laughed, which is not how I talk. Sometimes they call me *beloved* in some strange nineteenth-century Hungarian.

She performed an absurd imitation of the plants' mannered, theatrical tone: *Szerelemetes Domján Eszter!*

If my rational analytical mind tried to understand, Eszter said—*Could this be the plants I've dieted on?*—I was missing the point. What was important was the relationship I felt. It was the plants, some elements of nature, whatever that means, starting to talk to me, and I was their apprentice. It was like I could suddenly feel the ocean as an entity, not an idea—from the bottom up. The apprenticeship began like that.

Sometimes they teach me about specific things, she said. They give me practical advice. I should avoid milk or beer. I shouldn't drink alcohol at all, except sometimes with Martina. They'd say *You can have a glass of wine with Martina.* Once they were like: *Fold your clothes, my dear, just fold your clothes and put them away in their place.*

They know! she laughed.

Now when I'm with clients, she said, something happens. I have moments of distinct clarity. I'm listening and thoughts become visible, with their own geography. A spatial map appears that I can navigate. It's helpful.

I asked her about the ceremony with Jonathan and she said it was another moment when she heard voices saying *así se hace*, telling her how to work.

It was so simple, she said, just lay your hand on him like I lay my hand on anything, and that contact, patience, attention, causes something to melt. It took a long time, you remember, but eventually his shouting stopped and he was peaceful.

I remembered.

It's as natural as a leaf falling, she said.

We sat and watched the ocean, knowing the cold Antarctic currents and the warm central Pacific were coming together there down the dunes in front of us. Behind us rose the high mountains and beyond the mountains the jungle, and here we were in this baked desert. Our Sechuran fox looked up at us, masticating a fishbone—*nyam, nyam, nyam, nyam.*

When I surveyed the marine horizon in the morning, I imagined the lone oil platform like an air traffic control station or the bridge of a spaceship. Something futuristic, interacting with inaccessible parts of the planet, performing actions that were somehow *unnatural*—extracting a flammable liquor from beneath the ocean floor.

Taking a break from writing and strolling down the beach, I came across a dive shop and stuck my head in. The next morning I joined them for a dive. The divemaster's name was Gerónimo, and he told me the platform was where they were headed. It had been abandoned for fifty years, since the military kicked out the petrochemical company that had built the town.

Since then, he said, it's become an artificial reef.

We stepped into wetsuits, walked to the beach, and swam out past the surf. Two guys on a small launch waited for us, and we climbed on board. Sea turtles watched skeptically as we set up our vests and tanks and regulators. Pelicans scooped up an occasional fish, which they guarded jealously from threatening frigate birds. The dunes receded behind us as we sped into the open ocean.

When we got close I was surprised to find that this structure was not alien or futuristic but looked like the rusted grain silos of my heartland hometown. It had the nostalgic, noir appearance of old freight trains and steel mills, other detritus of the twentieth century.

Our launch came to a stop and we pulled on gear and dropped backward into the sea. Beneath the water's surface, the platform's iron beams weaved together and disappeared into the depths. In its permanent bath of salt water, the metal had become thickly encrusted with sea flora and bivalves and it was swarmed with fish. Gerónimo pointed out a hiding octopus, and in a crevice of green fronds and black shells, I came face to face with a long-faced fish Gerónimo identified later as a borracho, with two tall white horns rising above its eyes. It seemed to meet my gaze, unperturbed and safely at home.

At a depth of thirty meters, we moved away from the structure into the open sea. From there I could take in the iron tower rising from the invisible deep to the rippling reflections above. A cloud of fish formed around us, and a banded morwong nibbled at my fingers.

With my back to the tower, gazing down, the blue depths faded quickly to black. A chill penetrated my wetsuit as we submerged into the deep ocean water flowing up from the Antarctic. The tides, I knew, changed at evolutionary speed, shifting and reconfiguring over billions of years.

When we surfaced, through the squawk of gulls and wingbeats of pelicans, I heard guttural sounds and registered a pair of walrusy beasts: large, hairy South American sea lions. They'd climbed the platform's iron webbing with their flippers, and now, with a shake of the mane, plopped into the sea and swam gracefully out of sight.

We bobbed in their absence on the upswell. The ocean, like the jungle, had the power to disguise and reveal and transform. We remained for a moment beneath the pelican-infested tower before heading back to land.

Ebbs and flows, lunar currents. There must be something new coming across that horizon, too.

THE VINES

It had been four years since the last rain in our seaside village and when the rains came now water gushed out of parched dunes, burst drainage ditches and swamped houses. The seashore filled with garbage. Dirt roads became unpassable, mud pits strewn with thorns and plastic and waste. The fetid air stank. Mosquitos bloomed from rank pools. But we were already heading back for one more stint in the jungle.

Our bus got a flat in the middle of the night, high in the Andes. Eszter sat flipping through her phone, looking at Facebook, where she paused at Abuelita's account. There was a picture of a man—a black and white photo from some previous decade. A second image showed a body on the floor of a house wrapped in a sheet, only the feet visible. The status read: *Feeling sad.* A comment appeared: *Así es mamá, ahora está con papá.* And another comment offered condolences. Eszter scrolled through, wondering who died. A brother or uncle? She sat contemplating Abuelita, that complicated person, until we lurched back into motion and descended to Tarapoto.

It was March, the end of rainy season. A year had passed since our arrival, almost to the day. Now Szilvia and Akos were meant to rejoin us for another diet.

Having made it back for her lab's reopening, Szilvia remained on the job long enough to finish the necessary experiments and gather sufficient data to publish her results. Now for several months she just had to write, which she could do anywhere. And Akos found that his job had permanently changed. Having proved he could run advertising campaigns from a hammock in the jungle on a hundred-and-fifty-dollar computer, he was never going back to his office on Canal St. They moved their stuff into storage, let their lease lapse, and flew back to Tarapoto. A month or so after the diet they intended to travel further, eventually to the glacier at the continent's southern tip.

Nafis was not coming, but he had news. He was going to be a father. He'd gone back to New York to sign his resignation and begin collecting his pension, then he'd reconnected with his girlfriend in New Mexico. Their reunion had been glorious and she was soon expecting. He arranged to rent a house in Atlanta and was moving with her home to the south.

We want to have a big family, Nafis said.

I could feel the strength of his generous heart. One could do worse than have Nafis as a father.

Jean-Paul had signed on a piece of land, a slope down to the riverbank just next to where we'd gone for a swim that lucky afternoon. He'd join the diet, too. We reconvened in Las Coconas along with Miguel, Luis, and Jonathan. Alvis and Humberto were at the gate of the reserve. Antonio and his wife Margarita were already up the mountain.

Cheeks full of mama coca, fourteen river crossings, we arrived at Juliampampa's clover-covered clearing to find peaks shrouded in mist, bobinsana trees rampant with pink and white explosions. I installed myself by the yanchama and felt very much at home.

We gathered the next morning to drink our rosa sisa and tobacco and puke off the rock wall below the maloca, feeding the bad spirits with whatever we'd gathered from the coast, what Akos and Szilvia had brought back from New York, whatever Jean-Paul had metabolized from his months away from Lima.

The constant impeachments in Peru, the blood and broken glass and rank absurdity of the capital riot on January 6, the QAnon Shaman, the murder of George Floyd, the continuing shock of the Beirut explosion. After a year of lockdown, so many ways of life interrupted, everyone questioning what they'd done up to now—what even constituted our lives now? Were we supposed to go back to work? To take any of that seriously?

Perhaps the lockdown year had been an enormous global vomit of everyone's dissatisfaction with their lives, the tedium of overdevelopment, what we'd been asked to take as meaningful activities, connections, relationships, cities and countries and communities. Really, it seemed, we'd rather flail and cry and puke our guts out, which is what we did that morning in Juliampampa.

I returned to the hammock by the yanchama spent and saddened, mournful, feeling self-pity and stupidity stirred by my pumping endocrine system. That night we had a ceremony. My negativity was still circulating and the mirror of Masha was not far from my hand. I wondered what Miguel really thought of Eszter and me, of our relationship. What had he seen? What did he know? I felt private and self-protective. Perhaps I was just externalizing my own doubts and confusion. I had no reason to think Miguel was thinking about us at all. I knew by now that the negativity accompanying the purge would pass, and I was quiet and listened as it began to rain. It wasn't violent or stormy but constant and I listened to the steady echo off the maloca's iron roof. By the end of the night the rain slowed, my anxiety faded, and we listened to the alien hoot of the spectacled owls calling to each other outside.

It was good to be with these old friends, I thought, this group of us who'd ended up here. How strange.

The next morning I began drinking the mix of vines Miguel had begun singing about in October. I sat with Antonio as he cooked all the vines together. I took a cutting from each to my hut. I set them out on the floor and picked them up one by one, touching them and smelling them and looking at each one closely. I knew these vines would become part of me, that after the next two weeks I would carry something of them in my organism. An aspect of the jungle pharmacopeia was that you rarely dieted on a plant more than once. The change, in a way I didn't understand, was permanent. It was as if the experience of the vine would somehow enter me and alter me. My cells and tissues were being shown something unforgettable. Who were these creatures I was inviting into my being?

First was murkuhuasca. The eight-inch cutting I had with me was dense and heavy, its bark grained like sandpaper, with pores like tiny volcanic mouths. If I held it to my nose, I smelled the morning, the surrounding jungle. Its name meant the swelling vine, and it was meant to be powerful but dangerous.

If you have it in you and you punch someone, Miguel said, they swell up. But if you don't respect the diet it's you who swells up.

Clavohuasca, as its name suggests, smelled like cloves, like the wild medicinal cinnamon they sell in Tarapoto. Its cross-section was trapezoidal, its coffee-colored bark brushed with white dust, mold or fungus that didn't wipe off.

Tamborhuasca was dense, its white bark splotched with moss and lichens and shallow pools of pale green. Its interior was composed of densely packed threads the color of burnt sugar. I detected a scent of crisped fat. I'd seen tamborhuasca grow wild in Juliampampa when Antonio led us around last October—a long straight white line hanging from a tall tree.

Purgahuasca was buff-colored, gray-green. There was a joint in the cutting where a narrow branch jutted out, softer and more brittle, as if midway through its growth it could transform into a different substance entirely.

I'd seen acerohuasca entwined around a ojé tree not far from the plantain orchard where it grew in great swoops and tangles. The cutting was narrow as my ring finger, very straight and handsome, with no knots. It smelled vaguely of autumn leaves. Inside, it was sand- and caramel-colored, spongy but very hard.

It's a protector, Miguel said, like a metal shield that surrounds you. You take it after you turn twenty-three years old.

Kashahuasca—the spiny vine—was narrower than a pinky, bright green and lined with tiny thorns. It was five-sided, with spongy material inside, and a layer of sticky white sap. Miguel told me it was good for the prostate.

Para que orines clarito, he said.

Finally huascarenaco, the red one. A curious plant, half-vine half-tree like renaquillo. Its interior ranged from red to rust to orange. It felt extremely hard and heavy in my hand. There was a fibrous, woody outer layer and a spongy inner layer. It smelled medicinal, vaguely sweet. A huascarenaco vine grew around the yanchama tree's vaginal opening. Miguel said it strengthens your skeleton.

Para pegar los huesos, he said.

I drank the mix of seven vines and it knocked me out for an hour, then left me feeling excellent. I walked through the jungle looking at vines, touching them, wondering about their sensitivities and movements, how they created such elaborate forms. They appeared to me like the jungle's nervous system or circulatory system. They extended fresh and delicate tendrils across the forest floor, then climbed the tall trees, swirling and spiraling along the way. The vines embraced other plants, depended on them, supported them. More than any other form of plant-life, I thought, the jungle was defined and held together by vines.

It rained again the second night and I lay listening to the drops clatter on the iron roof of my hut. Wind whipped the canopy and branches blew onto the terrace floorboards. Raindrops entered the screen and misted me where I lay trying to sleep, pulling the alpaca wool blanket over my head. The cocoon of the rainy night sent me back through the months, the unexpected year I'd spent here, and off into earlier memories, revisiting scenes from my itinerant twenties in the Balkans, those wartime scenes that had taught me so much about my own ignorance.

I remembered standing with a Bosnian friend in Dobrinja, an area at the edge of Sarajevo that had seen the worst of the war. It was apocalyptic, just rubble off to the horizon. As we stood there a boy appeared, maybe ten years old, walking through the neighborhood as if he were heading home after a day at school. He was heading toward an area marked with yellow tape that read *Danger! Mines!* I seized up with fear watching him. We needed to shout to warn him! But he ducked under the tape and kept walking, crossed the field and went on his way.

A miracle, I thought. He just walked through a minefield unharmed.

Then I realized: of course, he does that every day.

It was some thirst for experience, an urge to discover something, that had led me there. I was twenty-two, a kid from Kansas in the Balkans. I was still trying to shake free of something I couldn't see or name that was baked into the sheltered homogeneity of my native environment. I couldn't see how the same mechanisms that underwrote it had also delivered me to the edge of Dobrinja. Thinking I was acting freely, my behavior was in so many ways determined by larger forces. Like us here in the jungle, thinking we'd made a decision.

How perverse, I thought.

But as I lay in bed under the yanchama tree, I was happy I'd set off, that I'd managed to leave the US at that age. I dwelled on confused moments in Berlin and Cairo and New York, streets I'd lived on, people who'd come in and out of my life. I remembered the impatience of my early twenties, the urgency. Now two decades later I could see chapters and arcs, remember depression and loneliness and frustration but also sense a growing joy. I saw that despite all the horror and despair and disappointment that there was heft and pleasure in life that did feel like meaning, which only came into view with the accrual of years and decades, when personal upheavals and historical shocks had swept through and swept through again. On one hand we never learn anything, but something changes, our witnessing changes.

I thought of my father again, how much trouble we'd had communicating when I was young. I blamed him for everything I hated about my heartland suburb. Then as he aged, rather than calcify into his beliefs he began to read thick history books, to challenge himself. Disgust at the Iraq war shook him free of Reagan-Bush Republicanism. How few older men changed their politics? Despite the opinions of his friends, his milieu. I was proud of him for that.

May I be like Jack Fox, I thought, and keep my mind flexible.

I knew because of who I was or my choices that it was hard for me to hang onto people. I was grateful for those who'd stuck with me despite me being at times intolerable or just gone. I hoped I'd learned something, and I wondered what was next. Where would I be a year from now?

A line from Flaubert came to me and I laughed, mouthing it to the walls of my jungle hut: *She longed to die, and yet, she longed to live in Paris.*

Rain clattered on the roof all night.

In the afternoon, drinking water in the comedor, Luis tapped me on the shoulder: Do you know about congompes?

He led me into the kitchen area, showed me two snails the size of small rabbits attached by twine to a nail. Slime trails glistened on the wall behind them.

Congompes, Luis said. We found them in the waterfall. We'll wait for three days and then cook them.

How do they taste? I asked.

Delicious, Luis said.

But we weren't allowed to taste the congompes. Miguel said if we ate them we would turn into witches.

The congompe will enter your phlegm, he said, and if you spit on the ground and someone steps in it, they'll be hexed. Then you'll be hated by the community.

In the next ceremony, as the rain and thunder continued, Miguel had a vision. He said the storm announced a wave of movement through the earth that would be accompanied by the smell of copal. Around 3:00 a.m., he said, large ants that burrow beneath the ojé tree—not the leaf-cutter ants turning the world inside out, but other ants called mamacos—would stream out of the ground.

This was good news.

They're large and ferocious, Miguel said, with pinchers for jaws that can lacerate our boots, but they're edible, a delicacy.

He said he'd have to tell Antonio and Margarita so they could go together with a bucket and gather ants. Then they would tear their heads off and fry them in a pan.

Delicious as congompes, Miguel said. But different.

After the ceremony I went back to the yanchama, but I thought of the ants and imagined Antonio and Margarita gathering ants by starlight and I wanted to join them, so I put on my boots and walked back up to the ojé tree, where Miguel said they'd emerge, but the ground was sodden and there was nobody there.

When Miguel arrived in the morning to serve me my cup of vines, he showed me a couple of mamacos. A few had come out last night but not as many as his vision foretold.

Sometimes it's like that, he shrugged.

I followed him up to Szilvia's hut, and along the way he stopped—there were a few more mamacos. They were an inch long and as thick as my pinky. Their body segments were bulbous and meaty.

He showed them to Szilvia and had us both smell them—they had a rich, woodsy smell.

Mmmm, Szilvia said. Pheromone.

Miguel let one of the mamacos crawl on his hand, then crushed its head and put it in his breast pocket.

If you don't remove the heads, he said, their jaws tear your anus.

But we weren't allowed to eat the mamacos anyway.

With the rains, Miguel said, the *zancudos gringos* would appear. These were large, straw-colored mosquitos.

They're called gringos because they're big and pale, Miguel said.

When the rain relented I lay in my hut listening to the frogs. It was not quinilla season, so no monkeys stopped to peg my roof with rinds. The thrumming and pulsing and chirping of the jungle was peaceful, but my mind was restless, astir with thoughts and questions. The reunion with Akos and Szilvia, the fact they'd gone to New York and come back, made me realize this jungle seclusion could not go on forever. That thought sharpened my homesickness, my longing for other places. During the day I watched Eszter; I saw her so at home in the jungle, so complete. Her sense of vocation was transforming, a new sense of meaning opening. Whereas I could still feel the simmer of disquiet within me.

As I lay at night, I felt a rising awareness, and eventually, thinking of nothing else I could do, I remembered what Nafis had taught me, performed ablutions and prayed. I put my forehead to the floorboards and said *God is greater.* Afterward I sat and thought. This fifteen- or seventeen-year relationship, depending on how you counted—how were we supposed to go on?

The response was clear and unarguable.

Miguel came in the morning and served me a cup of ayahuasca-chacruna and left me alone with my visions. The rain was soft and the morning was humid and cool. I drifted in thoughts of the past and future, watched streaks of connectivity weave through reality like oil on glass. When Luis blew the conch hours later I went up to the comedor for saltless soup.

Eszter at the table turned to me right away and spoke under her breath:

We need to talk, she said.

Yes, I said.

We ate our soup and went back down to the yanchama. She sat on the wool blanket folded up on the floor. I sat next to her in the hammock, listening.

She said she'd heard voices again, whatever they were. The plural entities had spoken to her. They told her we're going to separate. She didn't want to hear it. She said *No! Not that!* But the plants said *It might be hard to hear but it's the truth.* And when she heard the word *truth* she felt its undeniability.

She spoke for a while, about what we were to each other, what we could still be. She asked me what I thought.

I got the same message, I said.

We cried, we talked, we knew it was true. We'd been so many things to each other, but more than anything we'd been good to each other, and that's what we were now. Over the next several days we talked and we sat in silence. Sometimes I visited her in her hut overlooking the maloca and the ojé. Sometimes we sat on the bench by the comedor and smoked mapachos and looked at the valley.

Pushed to our limits by all this, this unforeseen year, these sessions of derangement and beauty and insight and confusion, the isolation and newness and increasing familiarity of the jungle.

Soon, I realized, I'm going to go home.

And you, I said to Eszter. Somehow I have a feeling you're staying.

I think you're right, she said. I think I'm done with all that.

Yes, I thought. I could see it.

Fortune had washed her up on this mountaintop and she was happy here. It was good for her to be here. It was good for me to be here, too, but not in the same way.

We sat for a night ceremony once again, and when the visions came on I saw a splatter of blood. Tissue jabbed and sliced and blood soaked everything, an organ contracting and squeezing out bile or phlegm or lymph. Eventually the organ stopped squeezing and the liquid drained and pooled.

I went outside to sit alone by the stone wall where we puked and I thought about the bad spirits. What had we fed them this time? I thought of Oleg somewhere with his brushed cotton and his diet of raw vegetables, the impetus for cleanliness and purity. I thought of *two chips*—Don Quique's promise of moral purity. Was that what Oleg's gold miners were worth? What about the racist real estate developer my great grandfather had worked for? So much damage, irreversible damage that built up over generations. The human past, histories of ruthlessness and desperation, murder and vengeance. How many ceremonies to wash all that away? All of us magnets for toxicity, bad decisions and rotten heritage, coming here to puke it all out so it ran down the hill in the rain. We were nothing but filtration systems, vacuuming up pain and ignorance and puking it onto the mud, hoping a meaningful insight might effervesce in the moonlight. I saw Oleg on the floor with the ants, the inhuman force that lies in wait for us. I felt the presence of the bad spirits of the jungle, of the empty chullachaquis and hungry diablitos on the hunt for vulnerable, poor, and unstable souls. Like Szilvia with her witchy ancestors, I thought, better we learn to coexist. Luis had told me not to give the bad spirits a chance, but right now I didn't fear them. I felt close to them. I understood their need and incompleteness. I thought of my anxiety, the redness I'd puked out when I arrived a year ago, something striving and prideful and discontent, clinging and addictive. I wondered what I'd left behind here and what I'd carry with me further.

Miguel had told me about a plant called *shillinto*.

It's risky to drink, he said, but powerful. It can cure leprosy. You drink and start to shake. If you drink it three times you lose your skin like a snake.

He said his father took it, but Miguel never did:

My father said *oooh, I want to change my skin.*

Maybe if I'd taken shillinto I could leave my old self behind, but I knew that as much as had happened and was still happening, as much as I was anything at all I was still who I'd been when I came here. I might be changed but I haven't rewritten the rules of mathematics. The leper still lived. I thought back to when the forest floor had opened up and revealed the world to me, the reflection that was the world I live in, the here and now in all its multiplicity.

Miguel called me inside and I crept silently to my spot, then knocked over my water bottle with a clang.

Will I ever learn!

Miguel brought the ceremony to a close. Alvis lit a single candle.

We sat for a while in silence, broken by Miguel's question, addressed tonight to Jean-Paul.

Hermano, Miguel said. How do you make someone fall in love with you?

Jean-Paul was still deep in his reverie. He'd been hacking up bitter phlegm all night long. When he spoke, his voice was a thin croak.

I think, he said, you tell them the truth.

I overheard Szilvia talking to Eszter and I was surprised how easily I could understand their Hungarian.

Szilvia said she'd seen herself having a baby.

You'll be the godmother, she told Eszter. You'll be part of our family.

Many things were coming into focus.

Akos came and sat next to me. He said he'd had an encounter with some shadowy creatures that looked like huge octopuses. They'd come to see him, he said, to tell him something.

To us, the creatures told him, *surprising ruptures in scale are the funniest thing in the world, and all night long we've been laughing about the congompes.*

I've missed Akos, I thought.

The rains continued and I walked through the jungle in the rain. Down the path from the yanchama, near where I often heard the stuck-pig cries of the orange-headed ispuitinos, I found myself faced with a spectacular vine, thick as my thigh in places, faceted like cut stone. The vine wrapped around a tall and buttressed tree but extended through the whole area of jungle. It rose and fell, sometimes disappearing underground to appear elsewhere. I could see the thick vine twisting, looping, spiraling, entwining, encircling, squeezing, hanging free, dropping strands on a quick-growing tree that lifted them until they grasp another stronger, longer-lived tree and let the earlier grasping tendrils fall away. And like that the vine moved and explored and grew. The vine might extend and rest on a dead branch that's caught mid-fall by other living trees.

But when that dead branch decays and drops the vine is left in mid-air, in some position that would have been impossible to get into if not for the now decayed branch that supported it for a while. The vine looked ancient, rising and twisting for centuries, but at its ends delicate, sensitive tendrils still extended, unfurling and feeling for a new place to hold and rise and entangle.

It was a constant improvisation, I realized, relating everything to everything else. Through that ceaseless feeling around, connecting and letting go, you get these tangled forms that contain histories of the jungle, which are also pure spasms of vitality spiraling around empty space. Finally the old vines fall and drop down to be caught by other rising vines, becoming part of the brush and tangle we hack with our machetes to open a way forward.

Whatever I was drinking must communicate that improvisatory mode: to connect, balance, hover, drop, rise, and twist, where something new is formed not by a single vision but as a momentary expression of the collective, letters written by unforeseen conflagrations of forces, hoopoe birds that are tricks of light, contingent on a chance point of view, comments on comments on comments, drawn the way my life had been drawn, from within and without. The writing of the vine was like initials scratched on trunks of tall trees that grow and stretch until the letters say something we could never have thought to write, letters we can hardly read and which keep extending further, becoming more and more unrecognizable. In the hut at night in the rain with the pulse of the frogs those letters continued to stretch and bend, rise and drop, wiped away only to reform like beads of water wiped by windshield wipers, forms beaten by wind on a car barreling down a two-lane across the Kansas prairie, some childhood twisting in the breeze between nonexistence and memory, the faintly sketched dragonflies of conjecture and the unseen apes of night.

Eszter got word from a friend of ours in Budapest that her husband was sick with COVID. These were among our oldest friends. In fact it was them who'd introduced us seventeen years ago. Now my old friend was in the hospital, on a respirator, had been diagnosed with pneumonia in both lungs. We asked Luis what to do and he said in the next ceremony we should repeat our friend's full name.

Did he have a middle name? Luis asked. Repeat that, too.

So the next time we gathered in the maloca at night Eszter and I both repeated the full name of our friend. Had we learned anything that year? Was there some action-at-a-distance we could summon?

Later I talked to him and he said he was getting better.

The problem was not the virus, he said. It was the contagious hospital. He'd caught a stomach bug from another patient. Now they wanted to keep him longer and what did that mean but some other infection?

When I heard he was better I thought back on our attitude the night we'd called out his full name. Did we think we were curing him? Had we lost our minds? In the moment all such questions had evaporated.

My left ear had been blocked for years, and the morning after that ceremony it felt worse. Antonio's wife Margarita offered to help me. She drove a thin stick through a plantain and placed it on the grill. When the plantain was hot, she held one end in my ear and blew into it, sending hot air out the other side into my ear. She did it for a while, stopping from time to time to dissolve into laughter.

After that I called her Maestra Margarita and I loved her, but my ear was still clogged.

The storm returned and battered my hut through the night. Thunder shook the air so I thought the hut would slide off the mountain. Miguel was supposed to come by in the morning to bring me medicine, but the storm didn't abate and he didn't appear. I wondered if everything was okay, if he was going to come at all. Should I go check on everyone? Eventually the rain softened and I heard Miguel's whistle. He told me the shelter where they cook medicine had collapsed. Antonio had been next to the fire when he heard the beam start to give. Maestra Margarita was nearby so he grabbed her and—crash!—they jumped out of the way just as the roof collapsed. It didn't knock over the medicine but ruined a big steel pot. No one was hurt.

Miguel served me a cup of ayahuasca–piri piri and left me alone. The rain picked up again and I stayed inside the hut, cocooned in my wool blanket. My mind traveled inside my body, checked my organ systems and sinew and tissue. I existed for a while in a world composed of fibrous textures, grained, elastic, prehensile. The immediate world of the hut fell away and my senses were full of glistening substances. I passed between walls of muscle and pulsing organs. When my awareness returned to the hut, where I'd spent so much time over the year, the wooden boards that surrounded me were newly vivid, their rough texture and knots. The trees the wood came from, which had grown up here in Juliampampa, the memory and experience of those trees, which now enclosed me in this small space I'd shared with gerbil-rats and scorpions, visitors real and unreal. The rain clattered on the iron roof and my subjectivity fused with the space in the hut.

All the plants I'd dieted on, or some composite of them, came to visit me. I saw vine-like beings, florestations made of bobinsana, yacushimbillo, ajo sacha, chuchuwasha, bachuja, nina caspi, remo caspi, bolaquiro, okshaquiro, cocobolo, murkuhuasca, clavohuasca, tamborhuasca, purgahuasca, kashahuasca, acerohuasca, huascarenaco, not to mention ayahuasca, chacruna, piri piri, ayahuma, mama coca, and all the tobacco smoke. When the rain abated again I took my hammock down from the hut and hung it between two trees right next to the yanchama, healer of internal wounds, and I lay in the hammock gazing up at the majestic civilization that had arisen since the last end of the world. I heard a sound like a helicopter and turned to see a runrun hummingbird checking me out. Then I heard a familiar voice.

¡Brak! Miguel called. ¿Cómo estás?

And he sat me down on the floorboards and began to sing and beat me with the shakapa, its impact both sharp and gentle. He summoned all the plants that had just visited me, his father and grandfather and uncles, the animals and spirits good and bad, and I luxuriated in that field with the dry leaves of the shakapa beating against my shoulders and head, with Miguel's voice, searching but not pleading, with the edge of a laugh, calling the way he'd been taught to call. He smacked my head a final time and let the dry leaves of the shakapa stroke my face down to my chin.

Listo, he said.

And I thanked him.

He asked how I was doing and I mentioned what was going on with Eszter. I told him I was well.

You don't have to listen to the plants, he said. You decide for yourself.

I know, I said.

Chucha, he said.

I stood facing the ocean back on the beach. We'd taken the bus back over the mountains. At the top of the Andes we came to a stop surrounded by impenetrable fog. A familiar voice came on the radio, as Jerry Rivas sang "Yo Soy La Muerte." By the next day we were back in our little seaside town. The strongman had gone searching for salt elsewhere, so Akos and Szilvia rented his now empty house and the four of us waited out the period of post-dietary restrictions together. I walked down to the water and stared at the sea, the oil platform that looked so different now. I imagined sea lions harrumphing and splashing only to disappear into the graceful deep.

Eszter finished work and we sat chatting, looking for the visiting fox. A fine layer of mud had settled on everything after the rain, but it was steadily chipping away and the stink had dissipated. Though there were upsurges of emotions we were peaceful and reconciled to our situation. It was undeniable—the truth.

One morning when I wasn't working on my book I drank a small glassful of the medicine we'd cooked at New Year's and walked to a solitary place on the beach. I blew tobacco smoke on the sand and lay down. Very quietly the chacruna visions came, the DMT patterns, the orange of the sun through my eyelids forming into geometric and organic forms, its pace increasing. Huge vistas and secret rooms, loops in time, still with the pace increasing. And then waves of intensity swept through me, a kind of contact that required calm and patience: eyes half-closed, gaze averted, unfocused, but mind alert to changes and momentums and narrative unfoldings, meanings like odor, permeating the vision. I saw this year as a segment of growth, a notch in purgahuasca where the vine takes on an entirely different substance.

All our lives had snapped in two, I thought, and we were weightless for a moment. Anything could happen. But hovering in the air the scent of death arose, too, a reminder.

In the afternoon Akos and I walked into town to buy food from the market. We stepped along the beach past where a dead pufferfish lay on the sand.

One thing that fascinates me about the ocean, Akos said, is that we think of it as one thing, a single environment. But that's because we see it from the outside. Whereas all this—he motioned to the town, dunes rising behind a row of low buildings—we don't think of as one thing. We think of it as this building and this beach and that dune. But for the puff-erfish, this is heaven. I mean, the afterlife. When it was alive the fish could never conceive that all this existed, when all the time it's right here. I think wherever we go when we die must be just like that, as close to us as the sea to dry land. We just can't conceive of it.

It was Ramadan again and I was observing the fast. Reading the Qur'an in the morning was like listening to Akos:

Look at the earth, how I've unfolded it and filled it with plants, and they grow and that's like the resurrection.

It's not like playing dominoes or trading shells or stock certificates or giving gifts. My bones for your bones. My bones will leave my body until I am a spent flesh-sac and so will yours and then your bones will become mine and mine will become yours. We'll exchange experience only in the manner that can be understood through that kind of hard bodily matter.

Or perhaps we'll both switch out our old bones for new ones. New bones will start to grow from the mush of our marrow and spread out and harden while devouring the matter of our old bones. Then we'll have new bones without even shedding a tear or a single drop of blood. Or perhaps we'll scream bloody murder like I did on the horizon of extinction, a scream that opens some tunnel of harrowing intensity and allows something, God knows what, to happen. Bone swapping—it doesn't mean we get better. You take your chances.

I bought a ticket back to New York, flying May 2, 2021. Eszter and Akos and Szilvia stayed in the little oceanside town. They'd decided they were going to go back to the jungle. Between the three of them they would buy the little piece of land next to Jean-Paul's riverside slope, the exact place we'd gone for a swim. It wasn't huge but it was big enough to build a couple of houses.

I landed in New York with a few days left of my post-dietary restrictions. It was also the last days of Ramadan. I observed the fast and was full of spiritual emotions but had never felt so atheist. What were we but swirls of cloud-chaos that arise and dissipate, a momentary sheen on nothingness? When I read passages from the Qur'an after dawn prayers, I found it impossible to connect to.

Still, I observed the fast.

For the first few days I kept to myself. I didn't want to have to explain to anyone why I wasn't eating. But I did tell Khaled and Martina. I couldn't wait to see them and found them at their table above the funeral parlor. Martina brilliant and beautiful as ever, the articulated syllables of her Florentine accent. And Khaled with a mask hanging from his ear or around his chin, as if that would help anything.

You're fasting? Martina said as if concerned.

A big smile spread across Khaled's face and he began to say he was going to get into heaven because of me. Martina was happy to see me but any whiff of religiosity made her recoil. The whole thing, the jungle, it was anathema. But we hugged each other and I was overjoyed to see them and their son Walid with his grin full of mischief. Khaled and I walked down Lenox Avenue and sat by the park.

The fast came to an end and my restrictions lapsed and I was home now after fourteen months in the jungle. I was newly separated, alone, and the first time I went downtown happened to be the day the president first appeared on TV without a mask, indicating the pandemic was supposed to be over.

I came out of the subway at West Fourth Street to find sidewalks overflowing with revelers. A brass band marched down Seventh Ave.

My cousin waited for me at a little place in the West Village, and we split a bottle of Lebanese wine—my first drink in months. The wine tasted delicious and the swoon in my brain was immediate.

In the swirl and sun, tuba blasts down the block, I remembered my last dive into the ocean before I'd left the beach. I jumped into the waves and swam toward the oil platform knowing those soft creatures were out there, at home on the iron frame. Now after fourteen months, the city revived by the May afternoon was like the Tarapoto cinema, its lights on and its seats hungry, floors gummed with mango pits and the air rich with smoke.

Sources

The Li Shangyin poems in "We're All Dead" are from Chloe Garcia Roberts, ed., *Li Shangyin* (New York: New York Review Books, 2018).

"The Virus Is You" refers to Róger Rumrrill's *El viborero: Cuentos Amazónicos* (Morales: Trazos, 2018: 7–17). The Ibn Battuta story is from Raymond Roussel's *Locus Solus* (Paris: Jean-Jacques Pauvert, 1965: 11–15). The text, commentary, and an earlier translation of *The Song of the Banu Sasan* can be found in Clifford Edmond Bosworth's *The Medieval Islamic Underworld: The Banu Sasan in Society and Literature* (Leiden: Brill, 1976). My version can be found in *ArabLit Quarterly*'s summer 2020 "Crime Issue." The dictionary I refer to is Edward William Lane's *An Arabic-English Lexicon* (London: Williams and Norgate, 1874).

"Earthquake Season" contains lines from "Las Poblanas" as sung by Joel Cruz Castellanos during the filming of *Beyond La Bamba*, directed by Marco Villalobos (2017). The Istanbul taxi-driver story is from Sophie Calle's *La Dernière Image* (Paris: Adagp and Galerie Perrotin, 2012). The goat story refers to Haytham El Wardany's "Ana Sultan Qanun Al-Wujud," from *Ma la yumkin islahuh* (Cairo: Al-Karma, 2020) as adapted by Maha Maamoun in *Dear Animal* (2016). The lullaby Eszter sings is an old Csangó Christmas song called "Paradicsom közepibe"—a quick search will find an unaccompanied version sung by Svorák Katalin.

"The Minute You Lose Your Head," refers to missionaries arriving in the 1950s as described by Wade Davis in *One River: Explorations and Discoveries in the Amazon Rainforest* (New York: Simon & Schuster, 1996: 257–264). The account of Sachawasi draws on Beatriz Labate and Clancy Cavnar's *Amazonian Shamanism in the Amazon and Beyond* (New York: Oxford University Press, 2014) and David Dupuis's "L'ayahuasca et son ombre: L'apprentissage de la possession dans un centre chamanique d'Amazonie péruvienne" (*Journal de la Société des américanistes* 104 [2], 2018: 33–64). On the exorcism prayer, see Kevin Symonds, *Pope Leo XIII and the Prayer to St. Michael* (Boonville, NY: Preserving Christian Publications, 2015). Lenin's line ("истина всегда конкретна") is from *One Step Forward, Two Steps Back* (*Шаг вперёд, два шага назад*. Geneva: отдельной книгой, 1904). The story of David Livingstone Pent is told in Eduardo Fernández and Michael Brown's *War of Shadows: The Struggle for Utopia in the Peruvian Amazon* (Berkeley: University of California Press, 1991). Rummrill's odes to Axpikondiá are in *Magias y canciones* (Iquitos: Ediciones Grupo Cultural "Bubinzana," 1972). I first learned about the chullachaqui and yakuruna figures from Miuler Vásquez González's *Yakuruna* (Morales: Trazos, 2019). *Wizard of the Upper Amazon: The Story of Manuel Córdova Rios* (New York: Atheneum, 1971) was ghostwritten by Bruce Lamb, and César Calvo describes his meeting with the old curandero in *Las tres mitades de Ino Moxo y otros brujos de la Amazonía* (Lima: Peisa, 2015). The biologists' findings were published in Marilena Marconi et al's "An Updated Molecular Phylogeny of the Stingless Bees of the Genus *Trigona* (Hymenoptera, Meliponini) of the Northern Peruvian Forests" (*Journal of Hymenoptera Research* 96, 2023: 751–760.).

"This Could All Be Yours" quotes Adrian Nathan West's version of Alejo Carpentier's *Los pasos perdidos* (*The Lost Steps*. New York:

Penguin, 2023). The Mae West line is altered; the original line, quoted by Emily Wortis Leider in *Becoming Mae West* (London: Thorndike Press, 2001: 409) is: "I knew in some marvelous way I had touched the hem of the unknown. And being me, I wanted to lift that hemline a little bit more."

The book Jean-Paul carries in "Tiger Trap" is Arantzazu Saratxaga Arregi's translation of Byung-Chul Han's *Die Müdigkeitsgesellschaft* (Barcelona: Herder Editorial, 2010). On the self-help technique Eszter's father taught, see José Silva and Philip Miele's *The Silva Mind Control Method* (New York: Simon and Schuster, 1977).

The article about an ayahuasca retreat for Marines mentioned in "Like This" is Ernesto Londoño's "'A Hail Mary': Psychedelic Therapy Draws Veterans to Jungle Retreats" (*The New York Times*, August 30, 2020, A-10). The brief history of Lamas is drawn from Christina Maria Callicott's *Music, Plants, and Medicine: Lamista Shamanism in the Age of Internationalization* (Dissertation. University of Florida, 2020: 77–137) as well as from Anahí Chaparro's "Territorio habitado y territorio como derecho: reflexiones desde el caminar Kichwa Lamista" (*Virajes* 23[1], 2021: 118–147) and "Los Kichwa de San Martín: impactos de las dinámicas territoriales en las cuencas de los ríos Mayo y Huallaga" (in *La situación de tierras, territorios y recursos naturales de los pueblos indígenas en la Amazonía Peruana*, Ministerio de Desarrollo Agrario y Riego, 2021: 107–112). The Tulio Trigoso song is the title track from Sonido 2000's *El baile de la serpiente* (2018). On ayahuasca-chacruna as a recent phenomena, once again see Labate and Cavnar, *Amazonian Shamanism*, especially Anne-Marie Losonczy and Silvia Mesturini Cappo's "Ritualized Misunderstanding Between Uncertainty, Agreement, and Rupture: Communication Patterns in Euro-American Ayahuasca Ritual Interactions" (pp. 105–129) and Bernd Brabec de Mori's "From the Native's Point of View: How Shipibo-Konibo Experience and Interpret Ayahuasca Drinking with 'Gringos'" (pp. 206–230).

The line from Flaubert quoted in "The Vines" is from *Madame Bovary*. The original is "Elle souhaitait à la fois mourir et habiter Paris" (Libre de France, 1921: 64). I'm quoting a version I remember from Eric Henry's *Wood Technology and the Design of Structures* (1997). The supposed line from the Qur'an is a paraphrase of *Surat al-Qaf* (7–11).

Translations are mine unless otherwise noted. Names of plants and animals have been checked against *Catálogo de plantes útiles de la Amazonia peruana* (Lima: Instituto lingüístico del verano, 3rd edition, 2008) and *Vocabulario Quechua del Pastaza* (Lima: Instituto lingüístico del verano, 2nd edition, 2008). Sometimes I've used less common spellings— chuchuwasha instead of chuchuhasi, for example, because that's what I encountered while living with the Tapullimas. A few names used by the Tapullimas—ispuitino, sapoina, umpalito, urfa—are not widespread even within the Quechua-speaking community. Likewise, Szilvia is my authority for the spelling of terms such as *vracskaz,* used by her family.

Acknowledgments

I am most grateful for the care and friendship of Miguel Tapullima Cachique and the whole Tapullima family. Luis was a brother and companion through many difficult and wonderful moments, and witnessing the harrowing of Jonathan was unforgettable. I reunited with the family in April 2024, when I told them I intended to write this book, and I'm grateful for their permission to use their names and do my best to describe what happened to us. I'm equally grateful for the willing participation of Eszter Domjan, who was family for so long and remains close, to Szilvia Galgoczi and Akos Papp and Nafis Sabir and Jean-Paul Du Bois, and to Martina Rugiadi and Khaled Malas in New York, all of whom reviewed drafts and helped me finalize the book, who were generous with their stories and their friendship (with a wink to Levi who was foreseen). All other names have been changed and I thank those unnamed as well. Madhu Kaza was an important reader and advisor through the whole process: *It's a minefield. That's why you should do it.* Sofia Velázquez Núñez offered astute and laughing counsel from Lima. It was a luxury to know I could turn to Yasmine Seale and Edward Charlton-Jones when I needed them. Claire Messud, Wayne Koestenbaum, Joan Richardson, and Ammiel Alcalay were key mentors and supporters. The National Book Foundation's Science and Literature program stunned me with their support.

And I had the good fortune to be resident at MacDowell and Chateau La Napoule and at Still Art Residency in Johannesburg. Thanks to Ayana V. Jackson for the opportunity to work in South Africa, and for her close collaboration and inspiration. Lucy Alford, Kristin Zahra Sands, Rafi Zabor, Raphael Aladdin Cohen, Andrew Hefler, Lili Török, Aron Köszeg, Graham Burnett, Marco Villalobos, Monique Long, Leonard Burg, Yasmin El-Rifae, Omar Hamilton, Mert Erogul, Antonio Burr, Alexandra Marin, German Zea, Héctor Guzmán, Rabia Williams, Justin Ruiu-Smith, Eugene Lim, and Jem Cohen helped in important ways. It was a true blessing to be represented by Akin Akinwumi. And it's been a privilege to work with Ben Schrank, Alexis Nowicki, Tara Sharma, Tiffany Gonzalez, Frankie DiGiovanni and everyone at Astra. To Erin LeAnn Mitchell for commitment and vision. And to my family in Brooklyn and Kansas City. The book was written at a time of horror and genocide, with friends under bombs in Beirut, that culminated in the reelection of a hateful US president and the delirious fall of the Assad regime. I dedicate this book to everyone persevering humanely through this madness. Finally let me pour one out for Serge Ungaro and Carlos Cons. Salud, maestros. Sempre arriba. Much love to all.

Lindokuhle Ndlovu

About the Author

Brad Fox's first book of nonfiction, *The Bathysphere Book: Effects of the Luminous Ocean Depths* won the National Book Foundation's Science and Literature Award. His novel *To Remain Nameless* was a finalist for the Big Other fiction award. His stories, articles, and translations have appeared in in *The New Yorker*, *Guernica*, *The Paris Review*, and *The Public Domain Review*.